Lecture Notes in Artificial Intelligence 1571

Subseries of Lecture Notes in Computer Science
Edited by J. G. Carbonell and J. Siekmann

Lecture Notes in Computer Science

Edited by G. Goos, J. Hartmanis and J. van Leeuwen

T0223225

Springer
Berlin
Heidelberg
New York
Barcelona
Hong Kong
London
Milan
Paris
Singapore
Tokyo

Pablo Noriega   Carles Sierra (Eds.)

Agent Mediated Electronic Commerce

First International Workshop
on Agent Mediated Electronic Trading
AMET-98
Minneapolis, MN, USA, May 10th, 1998
Selected Papers

Springer

Series Editors

Jaime G. Carbonell, Carnegie Mellon University, Pittsburgh, PA, USA
Jörg Siekmann, University of Saarland, Saarbrücken, Germany

Volume Editors

Pablo Noriega
INEGI
San Juan Mixcoac, Mexico DF 03720, Mexico
E-mail: 2x3@compuserve.com

Carles Sierra
IIIA, CSIC - Spanish Scientific Research Council
E-08193 Bellaterra, Catalonia, Spain
E-mail: sierra@iiia.csic.es

Cataloging-in-Publication data applied for

Die Deutsche Bibliothek - CIP-Einheitsaufnahme

Agent mediated electronic commerce : selected papers / First International
Workshop on Agent Mediated Electronic Trading, AMET-98, Minneapolis, MN, USA,
May 10th, 1998. Pablo Noriega ; Carles Sierra (ed.). - Berlin ; Heidelberg ;
New York ; Barcelona ; Hong Kong ; London ; Milan ; Paris ; Singapore ; Tokyo :
Springer, 1999
  (Lecture notes in computer science ; Vol. 1571 : Lecture notes in artificial
  intelligence)
  ISBN 3-540-65955-2

CR Subject Classification (1998): I.2.11, K.4.4, C.2, H.3.4-5, H.4.3, H.5.3,
I.2, J.1, K.5

ISBN 3-540-65955-2 Springer-Verlag Berlin Heidelberg New York

Typesetting: Camera-ready by author
SPIN 10703024   06/3142 – 5 4 3 2 1 0   Printed on acid-free paper

Preface

Electronic Commerce —a gamut of activities involving economic transactions performed through software that may be more or less autonomous over a network (mostly an open network like the Internet)— is an emerging reality. It is, undoubtedly, a reality that has been coming into being for some time, perhaps since the old teleprocessing days of the late sixties, and certainly inherits many traits from soundly established practices in banking and business. However, what we currently identify as Electronic Commerce (EC) is a brand new phenomenon mainly because of the sociological impact of personal computing and the Internet. For example, we might have glimpsed at new forms of "immediacy" or at a different notion of "proximity" thanks to teleprocessing, but the size and diversity of a truly world–wide *digital village* is only recently becoming apparent. Consequently, notions that were fundamental in traditional commercial activity, such as territoriality (e.g. national borders) and timing (e.g. opening hours), are undergoing a profound revision because of this form of globalization, with the result that new business practices (and liabilities) are quickly becoming available. However, even if "accessibility" is at the core of the Electronic Commerce eclosion, it is not the only relevant innovative feature in Electronic Commerce. EC is also spawning new technologies and innovative uses of older technologies which in turn question in radical ways many traditional concepts and practices. Notably, as may be grasped in this volume, agent-based technologies and their potential effect on the standard views of "presence", "accountability" or "trust".

A number of strategic studies claim that Electronic Commerce is a major growing business, and it is not surprising that both governments and business have shown serious concern about its potential opportunities and risks. It is, likewise, because of its inherent complexity and value, a wonderfully rich environment for theoretical and practical innovation; and, also quite naturally, a field for testing old technologies as well. Such a burgeoning reality could hardly be free of opportunism, but serious technical literature has obviously also been published. Although a sound and thorough classification of this technology may be premature, there seems to be a clear preference for what may be seen as "enabling" concerns, such as:

- The role of EDI and similar standards.
- Identity of participants and transaction security.
- Taxation.

We thought it was time to look into other aspects of Electronic Commerce. As its name indicates, the AMET–98 workshop aimed at a more focused approach: Firstly, we were interested in those challenges and opportunities that Electronic Commerce opens for a particular technology: software agents. And secondly, we were interested in exploring interactions among agents, thus the choice of "trading" over a more generic "commerce". Agent-based technologies thrive on the metaphor of an "autonomous" software agent: a program that shows some sort of purposeful behaviour, reacting to a changing environment and persisting over time or locations. The metaphor is suggestive and has seen its share of incarnations and associated developments, and the Internet offers a digital reality where these incarnations can accomplish useful tasks, taking advantage of many Artificial Intelligence tools and techniques. Electronic Commerce, in particular, has strongly attracted the attention of agent–makers; and agent technologies in turn seem quite likely to contribute decisively to this field. As one of the workshop participants (N.R. Jennings) put it, "EC is the most important application for Agent Technologies, because it is reality–based and constitutes a massive market". It may also be worth mentioning that we are now witnessing a second generation of agent technologies where agents are not limited to simple information gathering tasks, but are increasingly becoming involved in the more complex (and consequential) process of actual trading: making purchases and negotiating deals.

A quick list of current theoretical challenges and practical concerns associated with the use of agent technologies in electronic trading is not difficult to produce:

- ideal and actual agent behavior such as rationality, autonomy, situatedness, optimality and trust–building features;
- roles of agents and their inherent qualities: identity, delegability, liability, and reliability of participants (be they software representatives or mediators);
- ontologies, interaction standards and social conventions: market institutions; insurance, financial and certification instruments; acceptable interactions; trading conventions;
- new products, services and practices: market–specific agent shells vs. more generic trading tools; payment and contracting methods; risk–assessment and coverage; quality, prestige and performance certification, ...

These were the type of topics mentioned in the workshop invitation and we are happy to report that these topics and many more were raised and debated at AMET–98. They are now here made available to the reader through a revised version of the accepted workshop papers.

The AMET–98 workshop took place on the 10th of May, as one of the workshops that preceded the Agents–98 Conference in Minneapolis (USA). After a thorough evaluation process, 11 papers were accepted for publication, 10 out of these were presented at the workshop, which included also two round tables where theoretical and practical issues of agent-mediated trading were debated. This volume contains the 11 accepted papers that have been revised to incorporate the workshop discussions and the comments of the reviewers. These contributions reflect the variety of interests present in that part of the agents community working in Electronic Commerce, and as such, the collection can be seen as a guide to the state of the art in agent–mediated electronic trading from the agents community perspective.

Maes and Gutman's paper serves as good introductory reading for the basic concepts and areas of activity in the field, in addition to giving a detailed account of one type of agent–mediated trading that the MIT group has been developing for the past few years. The reader will find that there is a well–defined interest on foundational issues in some of the AMET–98 papers; it is most apparent in, for example, Andersson and Sandholm's work in which a Game Theoretic approach provides a formal framework to model agents as optimal decision makers; Matos and Sierra study the benefits of using evolutionary computing in the process of finding good negotiation strategies; other theoretical approaches are also present, that is the case of the paper by Garcia *et al.* which uses possibility theory to model individual decision-making; based on the same Fishmarket auction example as Garcia's *et al.*, the paper by Padget and Bradford discusses the advantages and limitations of a Π–calculus formalism to produce a formal specification of a trading convention. The workshop also attracted presentations that dealt with more empirical concerns. For example the paper by Parkes *et al.* looks into auctioning conventions and examines some classical protocols (and their inherent issues such as trust, cost and fairness) under the new light of an agent–biased perspective. In a similar pragmatic vein, a group of papers look into the problem of establishing and sharing ontological or deontological standards, the paper by Collis and Lee, for instance, presents an agent toolkit prototype that can produce "utility agents" to be tailored by users to trade according to standardized trading conventions; similarly, Steinmetz' *et al.* paper advocates the establishment of standard trading practices that allow software trading agents and agent–based arbitration, and discusses one potentially attractive example. Eriksson *et al.* complement these papers advocating for a uniform communication framework for agent–based markets. In this same line of thought, Ghidini and Serafini discuss the problem of information integration and its central importance for Electronic Commerce. A large–scale application is discussed in the paper by Goldsmith *et al.*; here, an agent–based system is used to deal with the intricate process of in–bond manufacturing, and constitutes an excellent example of how agent–based technologies may profit from EDI standards and Object Oriented methodologies when deploying real–world systems.

We would like to take this opportunity to acknowledge the participation of round–table speakers. Katia Sycara, Yao-Hua Tan, Hans Voss, Robert Guttman and Nick Jennings debated on practical issues related to agent–mediated electronic trading. Likewise, Frank Dignum, Michael Wellman, Thuomas Sandholm, Chiara Guidini, Julian Padget and Cristiano Castelfranchi did the same on theoretical issues.

We would also like to thank all the members of the program committee and the reviewers of submitted papers for their guidance and their valuable suggestions to authors and organizers. Finally, we would like to mention the encouragement and support we received from the Agents–98 conference organizers and staff, and from Alfred Hoffman of Springer–Verlag for the publication of this volume.

January 1999   Pablo Noriega and Carles Sierra
                                                Program Chairs AMET'98

Organization

This workshop took place on the 10th of May 1998, as one of the workshops of the Second International Conference on Autonomous Agents held in Minneapolis, USA.

Program Committee

Ken Binmore	University College London, UK
Frank Dignum	University of Eindhoven, The Netherlands
Fausto Giunchiglia	IRST, Italy
Nick R. Jennings	Queen Mary and Westfield College, UK
Sarit Kraus	Bar-Ilan University, Israel
Jack Lang	ESI, UK
Pattie Maes	MIT, USA
Joerg Muller	Zuno, UK
Pablo Noriega	LANIA, México
Julian Padget	University of Bath, UK
Jeff Rosenschein	Hebrew University, Israel
Tuomas W. Sandholm	Washington University, USA
Carles Sierra	IIIA-CSIC, Spain
Katia Sycara	Carnegie Mellon University, USA
Walter van de Velde	Riverland, Belgium
Hans Voss	GMD, Germany
Mike Wellman	University of Michigan, USA
Mike Wooldridge	Queen Mary and Westfield College, UK

Extra reviewers

Loris Gaio	University of Trento, Italy
Chiara Ghidini	University of Trento, Italy
Mike Gibney	Queen Mary and Westfield College, UK
Enric Plaza	IIIA-CSIC, Spain
Fernando Tohme	Washington University, USA

Acknowledgements

The workshop chairs want to thank the European project COMRIS (ESPRIT LTR 25500) for the support received in the organization of the workshop.

Table of Contents

Building Electronic Marketplaces with the ZEUS Agent Tool-Kit

Jaron C. Collis and Lyndon C. Lee

Intelligent Systems Research Group,
MLB1, PP12, BT Laboratories,
Martlesham Heath, Suffolk,
United Kingdom, IP5 3RE

Email: {jaron, lyndon}@info.bt.co.uk
WWW: http://www.labs.bt.com/projects/agents/

Abstract. The increasing popularity of the Internet provides personal computer users with direct access to a wealth of information sources and services, and potentially a massive global marketplace. Unfortunately current home shopping systems are primitive; what the consumer wants is a personal shopping agent – an intelligent, reliable proxy who is aware of personal preferences, and who can take over the tedious task of searching the Internet for the best possible deal. Likewise retailers would like to use the Internet to attract a much larger volume of potential customers, who could be serviced quickly and efficiently at a much lower cost. This vision is seductive, so why has it not yet been realised? This paper considers why agent-based commerce is inherently difficult, and advocates collaborative agent technology as a means of more easily building distributed marketplaces. To illustrate this principle we have built a prototype multi-agent virtual marketplace with ZEUS, a generic collaborative agent tool-kit.

1. Introduction

Although shopping through the Internet is in its infancy, it is conservatively estimated that online retailing will be worth $7 billion by the year 2000, [1]. It is a boom driven by the lower cost of doing business through the Internet, and the increased choice and convenience offered to the customer. However, current online shopping systems are relatively primitive, having evolved from existing tele-sales and mail order systems.

Agent technology has the potential to make online shopping more than just a set of web-based front-ends to mail order catalogues. The goal is smarter shopping, whereby the best deal for the customer can be quickly located at minimal cost, and with minimal user effort. Likewise, agent based commerce should also benefit vendors by lowering their costs and increasing their customer base. Many companies are already taking advantage of the lower costs of doing business online, as they have no expensive shops to maintain, and can sell goods direct to their customers.

There is, however, considerable room for improvement; for instance, consider the following scenario. A user is thinking about buying a car, but has not yet decided on a particular manufacturer and model. With so many confusing options to choose from, the user seeks the help of their Personal Shopping Agent, (PSA). The PSA possesses the expertise needed to find and buy a car, and starts by eliciting the user's preferences. After supplying answers to as many of the questions as possible the PSA will begin contacting the Sales Agents of different car manufacturers.

Upon receiving a preliminary enquiry, the Sales Agent will use the initial preferences sent by the PSA to tailor its response, supplying appropriate information on models that might interest the consumer. This is a subtler form of targeted advertising, intended to help match the customer's own preferences to the features offered by various models in the manufacturer's range. This may include multimedia, like video clips of individual cars, or "don't take our word for it" links to car reviews on other web-sites. This information can be used by the consumer to refine their requirements, which their PSA will use to create more specific enquires.

Eventually, the user will have narrowed down the options to one particular model or a few alternatives. The next stage will be to find a vendor who is able to provide the best deal, taking into account not just the retail price, but also factors like optional extras, payment options, delivery time, etc. This involves the PSA and Sales agents negotiating on behalf of their respective owners to arrive at a mutually agreeable deal, whereupon the transaction can take place. Thus to implement such hypothetical Shopping and Sales agents three significant issues must be considered:

- **Personalisation**. As the consumer's representative during the shopping process, the PSA needs to learn about its user's preferences in order to communicate their requirements to other agents. Obtaining user information can be done overtly by asking pertinent questions, or covertly using a technique like adaptive profiling [2], whereby machine learning is used to learn users' preferences by observing their interactions with different online information sources. Information from a user's profile will influence how the PSA ranks equivalent products and vendors without needing the user to arbitrate.

- **Product/Vendor Identification**. Once equipped with its owner's profile, the PSA will automatically locate other agents capable of satisfying its owner's requirements. To be effective the PSA must search the marketplace thoroughly, communicate its requirements to the agents found, and filter responses so that its owner is not overwhelmed with too much information.

- **Negotiation**. The ability to negotiate enables agents to set the terms of the transaction dynamically, allowing the retail price to vary according to global supply, demand and the quality of service desired. Negotiation may occur as potential products or vendors are being identified, with the outcome used to rate the suitability of each party. Negotiation may also be used to determine the final criteria of a transaction, allowing both parties to agree on the price and quality of service involved.

These three issues seem realisable given present software technology, so why do such undoubtedly useful personalised shopping agent not yet exist? In this paper we consider some of the primary obstacles to agent-based commerce, and how a virtual marketplace of collaborative software agents could provide a more efficient environment for both consumers and vendors to do business.

In Section 2 we present what we believe are the major obstacles to deploying agent-based e-commerce applications. In Section 3 we introduce *collaborative agent technology*, a potential solution that involves a society of distributed co-operating software entities. Section 4 describes the features of the ZEUS agent building tool-kit, which has been used to construct the agent-based virtual marketplace demonstrator described in Section 5. In Section 6 we situate our work in relation to some other agent-based virtual marketplace systems, and in Section 7 we briefly describe the crucial features that all these marketplace systems currently lack. Section 8 concludes the paper by summarising its main points.

2. Challenges facing Agent-based Commerce

Currently there are several significant technical problems preventing the deployment of personal shopping agent software of the kind described in the Introduction. Most of these problems are rooted in the poor or non-existent interoperability between the many heterogeneous and distributed computing systems that would be involved during the various stages of the purchasing process. Some of the main problems include:

The Information Discovery Problem

Finding the right information in a massive decentralised network like the Internet has always been a problem. At present information about particular products tends to be distributed across the Internet on the web sites of individual companies and special interest groups. As the quantity of information online continues to grow, so will the problem of finding and integrating the available information to determine which products or vendors best satisfy a consumer's particular requirements and constraints.

Unfortunately today's most popular solution - keyword searching - suffers from limited coverage and an inability to cope with synonyms, making it unsuitable for agents that need to scour the network for particular concepts. What is required is a directory similar to the 'Yahoo!' index, (www.yahoo.com), which agents can consult to discover what relevant information sources exist for particular concepts.

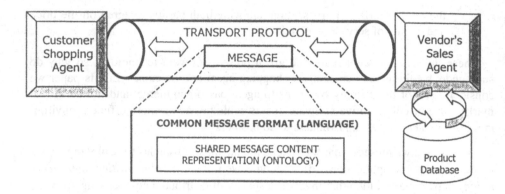

Fig. 1. The three prerequisites for effective inter-agent communication. For the Shopping Agent to obtain product information from the product catalogue it requires some means of transmitting its request to the Sales Agent. For both parties to understand one another, their messages must be in a common language that is grounded in a shared ontology. Once a message is received, the Sales Agent will use its knowledge of the ontology to translate the request and extract the relevant information from the Product Database.

The Communication Problem

Suppose a solution to the information discovery problem exists, and the PSA is able to locate a vendor's Sales agent who has access to a product catalogue. In order for the PSA to obtain product specific information it must communicate its requirements to the Sales agent; this raises three challenges. Firstly, both parties must adopt a common transport protocol that enables the request and results to be transmitted, as shown by the pipe in Fig. 1. Fortunately, this problem is easily solved, for instance we could employ the TCP/IP protocol (Transmission Control Protocol/Internet Protocol), which already facilitates information transfer through the Internet.

The next challenge is to devise a common communication language that both parties understand. Currently, the lingua franca of the Internet is the Hypertext Mark-up Language (HTML), whose standard format enables browser software to interpret pages on the World Wide Web. However, HTML web pages were designed for presentation of information for human perusal, and so valuable information is typically intermingled with formatting instructions — necessitating 'wrapper induction' software programs [3], to parse the pages and extract the information from the formatting instructions. Clearly, given our desire for automated commerce, a language geared towards direct machine-to-machine communication is preferable.

With the transport and structure of messages agreed, the final challenge is for the Shopping and Vendor agents to agree on the list of terms to be used in the content of messages, and the meanings of these terms. This obstacle is known as the ontology problem, and is perhaps the main problem preventing widespread interoperability of heterogeneous, distributed co-operating systems. In electronic commerce this is evidenced by the lack of inter-operable product catalogues, [4]; we shall expand on this problem next.

The Ontology Problem

The ontology problem can be illustrated by returning to the scenario depicted in Fig. 1. For the Shopping and Sales agents to interact, both must agree on and then share a common definition of product-related concepts. The ontology (or concept definitions) specifies the terms each party must understand and use during communication, e.g. vehicle categories, engine attributes, lease definitions etc. Creating an ontology involves explicitly defining every concept to be represented; consider the term "sports utility vehicle", what are its characteristic attributes, and what does each attribute mean pragmatically? The creators of ontologies must also ask what are the constraints on valid attribute values, and how are the attributes of one concept related to those of another?

The Legacy Software Integration Problem

Legacy systems are large pieces of software, based on older technologies, and generally not designed for interoperability with other systems; the product database shown in Fig. 1 is an example of a legacy system. Although inter-operability is a prerequisite for agent-based commerce, too much has already been invested in legacy systems for their owners to replace them with an agent-oriented alternative.

Consequently the legacy system problem involves devising some mechanism that enables legacy systems to communicate with external systems like the PSA. As Fig. 1 suggests, the solution is likely to involve a proxy, like the vendor's Sales agent. The Sales agent will be responsible for translating requests made using the shared ontology into queries in the internal language of the legacy system, and then translating the results received from the legacy system back into the shared ontology for the benefit of the requesting agent.

The Reasoning Problem

Now suppose that solutions to the aforementioned problems exist, and the PSA is able to communicate with vendors' agents. Now the PSA must attempt to reconcile its owner's requirements with what the vendors' agents offer, using a technique like constraint satisfaction to rank the available options. An agent will need customised reasoning strategies for different buying processes, since the important criteria for choosing a domestic mortgage will differ from those used to select a car.

An agent may also benefit from having the ability to plan, as this will enable it to make intelligent decisions when confronted by inter-dependent requirements; for instance, when it needs to evaluate the true cost of a car, it must first calculate the car's annual group insurance cost. Planning is also essential for vendor-side agents who produce or obtain products through a supply chain.

The Negotiation Problem

Successful negotiation requires all parties involved to behave in a predictable and coherent manner. For instance, if the price of a product is to be decided by auction the selling agent will have the opportunity to set the 'house rules': parameters that describe when bids are expected, when negotiation will occur and the conditions for closing a deal. These rules must then be communicated to the other agents participating in the auction so that they know when and how to bid. Consequently for a collection of agents to act coherently each participant requires some means of customising its behaviour.

Negotiation is applicable to more than just auctions though. For instance, a prospective client will investigate the market with the intention of creating a short-list of vendors and products, which may be ranked by price or some set of criteria. This raises issues like multi-party negotiation, multi-attribute negotiation and preference induction.

This section has introduced the problems that must be solved before agents can begin autonomously buying and selling on behalf of their owners. Interestingly, these problems are very similar to those faced by the developers of collaborative software agents. So in the next section we shall explore how the techniques used within collaborative agent systems may facilitate progress towards agent-based electronic commerce.

3. Using Collaborative Agents for Electronic Commerce

In order to explain what distinguishes a collaborative agent from the numerous other software entities that are called agents, we must consider the characteristics exhibited by agents. Jennings & Wooldridge [5] specify four main attributes that determine agent-hood:

- *autonomy* - able to function largely independent of human intervention,
- *social ability* - able to interact 'intelligently' and constructively with other agents or humans,
- *responsiveness* - able to perceive the environment and respond in a timely fashion to events occurring in it, and
- *pro-activity* - able to take the initiative whenever the situation demands

Using these four attributes and a fifth: learning, Nwana [6] has proposed a typology of agents. Of particular interest in this paper is the sub-type that Nwana calls 'Collaborative Agents'. The two distinguishing characteristics of agents of this type are that they are autonomous, (i.e. possess their own goals and are in control of their own resources), and they are socially communicative, (i.e. capable of interacting with other agents in order to achieve their objectives). Collaboration is not necessarily motivated by a desire to co-operate, it may have become necessary because expertise and/or resources are distributed across the community of agents such that no one agent is, on its own, capable of performing a particular task.

In order to ensure coherent execution of their joint endeavour, the agents need to plan and/or negotiate the terms and conditions of each individual's contribution. Such negotiation typically involves the exchange of high-level messages concerning, for example, requests for information or specification of contractual obligations. Collaborative agent technology has been applied to a number of problem domains requiring co-operation between disparate autonomous systems, e.g. in applications such as telecommunications network management [7], air traffic control [8] and 3-D scientific data visualisation [9].

In our hypothetical scenario, the personal shopping agent displays the characteristic collaborative agent attributes of autonomy, (by functioning largely independent of user assistance), and social ability, (by communicating and negotiating with remote autonomous systems such as retail agents). Hence it would seem worth investigating how the collaborative agent system creators have developed (or adapted from classical AI and software engineering) solutions to the issues outlined in Section 2.

Tackling the Information Discovery Problem

We would expect our future online marketplaces to be dynamic in nature, with new potential purchasers continually entering the market, and potential retailers periodically revising what they offer. Thus it is wise to avoid hard coding into our agents the addresses of their peers and the descriptions of what they offer. This principle can be seen in many current agent-based commerce systems that create centralised virtual marketplaces (Kasbah, [10] and Fishmarket [11] provide good examples).

To enter the virtual market each buyer and seller must register their interest with a specialised agent, usually called a *Broker* or *Facilitator*. This agent maintains a record of those currently present in the market; and this index will be used by agents to find others who might be buying or selling something of interest. In effect the *Facilitator* is providing a 'yellow pages' directory service, alleviating the need for the other agents to maintain their own model of the marketplace.

Tackling the Communication Problem

The almost universal adoption of the TCP/IP transport protocol means that, in effect, the communication problem chiefly concerns what languages are used to express the structure and content of messages. A working solution will require every communicating party to agree on what instructions, assertions, requests etc. will be supported, and what syntax is used. Recently some inter-agent communication languages have been proposed based on speech act theory performatives, wherein the speaker's intent of the effects of a message on the hearer is communicated by specifying the type of the message, e.g. *ask*, *tell*, or *achieve* message types.

The most notable examples are KQML (Knowledge Query and Manipulation Language) [12], the FIPA ACL (Agent Communication Language) [13], and MIL (Market Interaction Language), [14]. Of these, MIL is the only inter-agent language to have been specifically designed with electronic commerce in mind, and so it seems a simpler and more efficient language as a result. However, the success of any communication language will ultimately be determined by how widely it is adopted.

Most agent communication languages do not specify a syntax or semantics for the contents of their messages; the rationale being that different application domains may require different content languages. Nonetheless, a number of general-purpose content languages have been developed, e.g. KIF (Knowledge Interchange Format) [15], typically used with KQML, the FIPA SL [13] the preferred content language for FIPA ACL, and MIF (Market Interest Format) [14] that is used in conjunction with MIL.

Tackling the Ontology Problem

The most obvious solution to this problem is for every participating agent to share a common trading ontology listing the items that can be exchanged, and the attributes they are expected to possess. Central to the success of this approach is the widespread adoption of particular ontology, this can occur when a powerful outside body enforces a standard, like for instance the U.S Department of Defence, which was able to dictate the product catalogue that contractors should adopt[1]. Bodies such as the Library of Congress and the various construction materials standards organisations are also in a good position to derive and enforce their own ontologies.

An alternative approach is to create a new ontology, and encourage users to adopt it on the grounds that it will make electronic trading more efficient. This is the approach taken by, for example, the PersonaLogic[2] company, which provides ontologies to vendors that serve as product guides for potential customers. Such ontologies tend to be narrow in scope, focusing on a particular product type, e.g. Cars or Computers - in sufficient detail to allow consumers to differentiate products.

The above approaches rely on every interested party adopting the same ontology. However this may not be realistic, and there are some that argue in favour of creating smaller-scale specific ontologies and converters for translating between them, [16]. The Jango[3] 'ShopBot' illustrates this principle; it maintains a list of potential vendors, and a set of wrappers that can extract product information from the vendor's web pages. Once product information is extracted it is translated into a common representation that can be compared. Whilst this approach complements the decentralised nature of the Internet, it is difficult to achieve and only a few product attributes are returned, (like price, shipping costs and delivery times). This makes product differen-

---

[1] This product catalogue is maintained by PartNET Inc., and is accessible through
http://search.part.net/partnet/
[2] More information is available from http://www.personalogic.com
[3] Jango is available at http://www.excite.com/channel/shopping/

tiation inherently difficult, and means this approach is best suited to commodity-like goods, like books and CDs.

Tackling the Legacy System Problem

Genesereth & Ketchpel [17] discuss the problem of integrating legacy software with agent systems, and suggest three possible solutions to the problem. The first option, rewriting the software, is a costly approach and probably impractical for vendors who would like to enter online marketplaces with minimal costs. The second option is to use a separate piece of software called a *transducer* that acts as an interpreter between the agent communication language and the native protocol of the legacy system. This provides a relatively inexpensive way of making legacy system data available to other agents. The final option is the *wrapper* approach, whereby the legacy program is augmented with an agent proxy that both provides the functionality of a transducer, and augments the legacy system with additional intelligence, allowing the hybrid system to interact more efficiently and appropriately with other agents in its society.

Tackling the Reasoning and Negotiation Problems

The major differences between agents and ordinary software processes is that the environment an agent acts within, and the problems it is likely to encounter are complex, dynamic, unstructured and sometimes fuzzy. However, users are demanding, and expect their agents to find the best possible solution even though the information available is noisy or incomplete. Thus to improve the performance of agents they are usually augmented with AI techniques developed for these types of problems. For example, classical planning enables agents to (re) schedule their actions by means of high-level reasoning and execution monitoring; various optimisation techniques and search mechanisms allow optimal to sub-optimal solutions to be found efficiently; and constraint technologies are concerned with finding solutions satisfying constraints to different degrees.

In a distributed system like an agent society, where many agents must interact with one another to pursue their goals, an additional problem concerns resolving the agents' conflicts and co-ordinating their actions. Typical approaches to handling co-ordination include the formation of organisations, (e.g. hierarchical structures, markets, adaptive organisations); reasoning approaches, (e.g. multi-agent planning, game-theoretic techniques), rules of interactions, (e.g. social laws) and negotiation (prescriptive, pseudo-human, search-based, and algorithmic models), [18].

The advantages of co-ordinating agents by means of organisations stem from the *organisational co-ordination knowledge* the agents inherit about their interaction processes from the nature of the organisations. Accordingly, uncertainties can be reduced and the behaviour of the agents is more predictable. Different forms of organisations trade off complete autonomy in order to reduce communication costs and information overloading, and so balance the decision making process.

For instance, communication can be very expensive in markets, whilst processing can be intensive in hierarchies because of the volume of information exchanged and the centralisation of decision making. To reduce the communication and processing overheads, agents can employ reasoning techniques to attempt to predict others' possible actions. This facilitates co-ordinated behaviour by enabling agents to model abstract interactions, and to create explicit models of the agents with whom they communicate.

Negotiation can also be made easier by imposing some structures, rules or conventions on agent interactions. This enables agents to know what is expected of them, and to anticipate the behaviour of their peers. A good example of a typical co-ordination mechanism is the classic contract net protocol [19]. In this protocol, a manager agent that is looking for another agent to perform a task will announce a contract, receive bids from other interested contractor agents, evaluate the bids and award the contract to a winning contractor. The simplicity of this scheme makes it one of the most widely used co-ordination mechanisms.

Negotiation combines reasoning and the structured rules of interaction to provide communication processes that further co-ordination. When negotiating, the agents engage in dialogue exchanging proposals, evaluating other agents' proposals and then modifying their own proposals until a state is reached when all agents are satisfied with the set of proposals.

There are many approaches to modelling negotiations, for instance pseudo-human models of negotiation in distributed AI are based on theories and principles discovered in human negotiation strategies. These are usually coupled with various AI techniques to model opponents' strategies in order to improve the efficiency of the negotiation. Search-based negotiations see co-ordination as a distributed search, and attempt to develop novel AI techniques based on the characteristics of human negotiations. The Prescriptive approach involves attempting to discover the properties of a negotiation under certain formal theoretical frameworks and assumptions. Typically this is through the use of game-theoretical or decision-theoretical tools, which are used to study how agents should react during a specific interaction. The algorithmic approach concentrates on investigating the impact of different negotiation processes on outcomes of negotiations. An introduction to these approaches to multi-agent co-ordination can be found in [20].

In summary, we believe to make good decisions in potentially open and unstructured marketplaces agents will need to be equipped with sufficient reasoning capabilities. Indeed given the diversity of behaviour to be expected from future electronic commerce applications, it could be advantageous for the agents to possess many reasoning and co-ordination strategies, which could then be used in different scenarios.

This section has described the similiarity between the challenges faced by electronic commerce application developers and the obstacles confronting collaborative agent system developers. Therefore, it would be ideal if e-commerce applications could be built by reusing solutions originally devised for the creation of generic collaborative agents.

Fortunately, the current trend is towards tool-kits of reusable agent components, [21], enabling developers to spend less time worrying about the intricacies of a particular technology, and more time implementing solutions to their problems. With the provision of well-engineered and relatively standardised class libraries, we would expect the time and cost involved in developing agent-based commerce systems to fall considerably. This goal of reducing the high development overhead normally associated with multi-agent applications motivated the creation of the ZEUS Agent Building Tool-kit; which is described in the remainder of this paper.

4. Introducing the ZEUS Tool-Kit

The ZEUS tool-kit was motivated by the need to provide a *generic*, *customisable*, and *scaleable* industrial-strength collaborative agent building tool-kit. The tool-kit itself is a package of classes implemented in the Java programming language, allowing it to run on a variety of hardware platforms. Java is an ideal language for developing multi-agent applications because it is object-oriented and multi-threaded, and each agent consists of many objects and several threads. Java also has the advantage of being portable across operating systems, as well as providing a rich set of class libraries that include excellent network communication facilities.

The classes of the ZEUS tool-kit can be categorised into three functional groups: an agent component library, an agent building tool and an agent visualisation tool, (the main components of which are shown in Fig. 2). Each of these three groups will be described during the course of this section.

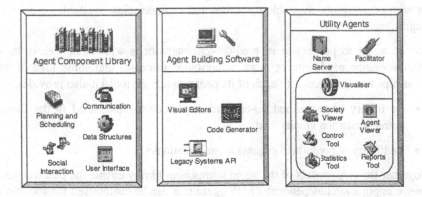

Fig. 2. The Components of the ZEUS Agent Building Tool-Kit

4.1 The Agent Component Library

The Agent Component Library is a package of Java classes that form the 'building blocks' of individual agents. Together these classes implement the 'agent-level' functionality required for a collaborative agent. Thus for communication the tool-kit provides:

- a performative-based inter-agent communication language,

- knowledge representation and storage using ontologies, and

- an asynchronous socket-based message passing system

In order to maximise future compatibility, the components of the ZEUS tool-kit utilise 'standardised' technology whenever possible; for instance, communication currently takes place through TCP/IP sockets using KQML messages, (we plan to add support for the FIPA ACL [13] in the near future). These components provide the necessary functionality to implement two important 'utility' agents - the *Agent Name Server*, which is responsible for resolving agent names to network locations; and the *Facilitator*, which maintains a directory of currently available agent services.

Next, to provide the agents with reasoning facilities, the tool-kit provides:

- a generic planning and scheduling system, and

- an event model along with an application programmers' interface (API) that allows application programmers to monitor changes in the internal state of an agent, and externally control its behaviour

To enable inter-agent co-operation, the tool-kit provides a 'co-ordination engine' – a finite state machine that controls the behaviour of an agent. The functioning of the engine is influenced by the agent's knowledge context, e.g. its organisational relationships with other agents, available resources and competencies, available co-operation strategies, etc.

For an agent to participate in goal-driven interactions with other agents its co-ordination engine needs one or more behavioural strategies and some idea of what relationships the agent has with each of its peers; hence the tool-kit also provides:

- a library of predefined co-ordination protocols, represented in the form of state-transition graphs, and

- a library of predefined organisational relationships

Together the components of the agent component library enable the construction of a generic application independent ZEUS agent that can be customised for specific applications by imbuing it with problem-specific resources, competencies, information, organisational relationships and co-ordination protocols. How the tool-kit supports the construction of agents is considered next.

4.2 The Agent Building Software

The design philosophy of the ZEUS tool-kit was to delineate the sort of *agent-level* functionality that is implemented within the Agent Component Library from *domain-level* problem-specific issues. In other words, our intention has been to provide classes that implement communication, reasoning and co-operation, leaving developers to concentrate on defining the agents necessary for their application, and to provide the code that implements their agents' particular domain-specific abilities.

Because so many aspects of conventional agent system development are handled by the ZEUS tool-kit, developers need a means of understanding what is expected of them. Consequently the ZEUS tool-kit was developed in parallel with an agent development methodology, (a description of which can be found in [22]). This methodology is supported by the ZEUS Agent Generator tool: a suite of integrated editors that facilitate the agent development process by enabling users to interactively create agents by visually specifying their most significant attributes.

In order to generate the agent program code for a specific application system, the Generator tool *inherits* code from the Agent Component library, and *integrates* it with the data from the various visual editors. The resulting Java source code can then be compiled and executed normally. Existing (legacy) systems can then be linked to the agents using the Application Programmers' Interface (API) of the (generic ZEUS-defined) wrapper class that wraps up the inherited code and the user-supplied data.

The intention is that when used together, the Agent Component Library and the Agent Building Software will facilitate the engineering of collaborative agent systems. The developer describes the intended agents with the agent creation tools, which generates the source code using classes from the component library. Once their tasks have been implemented the agents can be executed, and observed using the visualisation tools that are provided as part of the ZEUS tool-kit.

4.3 The Visualisation Tools

An inherent problem of a distributed system like an agent society is attempting to visualise its behaviour. This is because the data, control and active processes are all distributed across the society. Consequently analysing and debugging of multi-agents systems is difficult, as each agent has only a local view of the whole. This arrangement places the onus on the user to integrate the large amounts of limited information generated by each agent into a coherent whole.

The ZEUS tool-kit provides a solution to this problem through the provision of a third utility agent, called the Visualiser, which can be used to view, analyse or debug societies of ZEUS agents; (as described in [23]). The Visualiser agent is a prime example of our reuse philosophy, having been built from the same fundamental components as the agents it will observe and visualise. It works by periodically querying each agent about its states and processes, and then collating and interpreting the replies to create an up-to-date model of the agents' collective behaviour. This model can be viewed from various perspectives through different visualisation tools, with each presenting a different aspect of the agent society. For instance, the Society Viewer shows every agent known to the Visualiser and the messages they exchange, which the Reports Tool displays the state of an agent's tasks and sub-tasks

The multi-perspective visualisation approach provided by the different visualisation tools gives users the flexibility to choose what is visualised, how it is visualised and when it is visualised. The visualisation tools are generally used *online*, to visualise the interactions in a multi-agent society live, as they happen. However, the society, report and statistics tools can also operate *off-line* by recording agents' interaction sessions to a database. Once stored, recorded sessions can be replayed, video-recorder style, using the forward, rewind, fast-rewind and fast-forward buttons.

At this point it is worth emphasising that the ZEUS tool-kit was designed to create general-purpose collaborative agents; it was never intended as an electronic commerce application tool-kit. So in the next section we shall consider the suitability of ZEUS agents for a virtual marketplace application.

5. The ZEUS Virtual Marketplace Demonstrator

The intention of this demonstrator was to investigate the difficulty of applying generic collaborative agents to a distributed marketplace application. The marketplace assumed was a virtual commodity auction, consisting of a variable number of agents, each of which should be capable of buying and selling items from their shared trading ontology. These assumptions avoided potential ontology problems, and enabled agent behaviour to be limited to a set of well-understood auction protocols.

Another assumption was that the virtual marketplace would be open, with an indeterminate number of participating agents spread across a local area network as processes on different machines. The intention being that each agent would be able to join or leave the market at will, by registering its presence or intentions with its peers. As there was no distinction between vendors and purchasers in our marketplace, each agent needed to be capable of both buying and selling.

The agents that participated in the marketplace were implemented using the ZEUS tool-kit, and then augmented with the additional functionality required for their new role. Each agent was created with the inherent ability to communicate, plan and negotiate, and these generic agents were then supplied with the market's trading ontology, and a set of negotiation protocols enabling them to participate in auctions. By supplying both bidding and selling strategies the agents can adopt either role.

The terms of each commodity transaction are negotiated through an auction process. The particular auction convention used can be set dynamically, taking advantage of the fact that new behaviour can be added to ZEUS agents by providing new state-transition graphs. This enables vendors to choose the auction convention that best suits their requirements. For instance, the 'Vickrey' auction tends to conclude quickly, ensuring a quick sale. Likewise both buyers and vendors could specify the deadline for a transaction and their preferred price.

Another intention was for agent behaviour within our marketplace to be semi-autonomous; i.e. all agents would be under the ultimate control of a human user, although the user could choose to delegate decision making to their agent. This necessitated the construction of custom user interfaces that would enable each user to issue instructions to their agents. This requirement has been realised by creating several windows through which the user can enter their intentions, and linking the resulting windows to the underlying agent through the API the tool-kit provides. The information supplied to the agent will determine its objectives, and how it behaves in response to market conditions. One of our design decisions was to try to hide as much of the underlying complexity of the marketplace from the people who would be participating in it. The features of this marketplace will now be discussed with reference to the windows that enable its participant to observe and interact with it.

The Marketplace Window

This window, shown as Fig. 3, provides the user with their agent's view of the current state of the market. Items offered for sale are listed, together with details of the vendor, the current market price, and the time remaining for bids. All offer information is colour-coded to represent its current state, e.g. on offer, changed, expired, deal struck etc. State information provides a means of filtering so, for instance, only offers that have changed recently can be displayed.

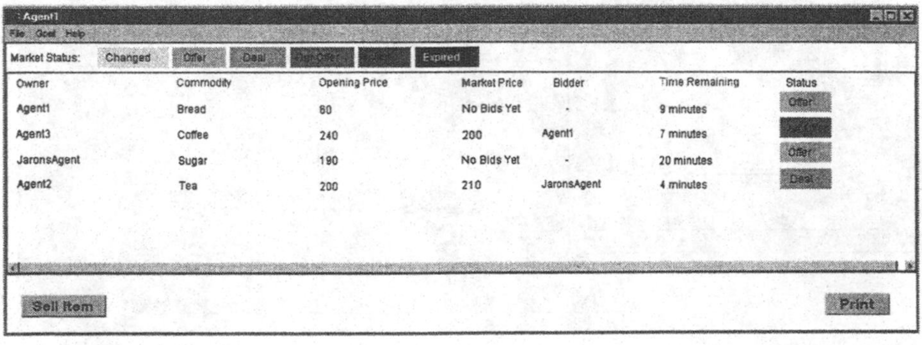

Owner	Commodity	Opening Price	Market Price	Bidder	Time Remaining	Status
Agent1	Bread	80	No Bids Yet	-	9 minutes	Offer
Agent3	Coffee	240	200	Agent1	7 minutes	
JaronsAgent	Sugar	190	No Bids Yet	-	20 minutes	Offer
Agent2	Tea	200	210	JaronsAgent	4 minutes	Deal

Fig. 3. A ZEUS Agent Marketplace Window, showing the state of all current bids

Other transaction options are accessed through the Marketplace window; for instance to offer a new item for sale the user would choose the 'Sell Item' button, which brings up the Selling Window. Whereas if an existing offer is double-clicked the Buying Window appears, unless the item in question is owned by the user, in which case the Selling Window re-appears allowing them to change the offer parameters.

The Selling Window

To offer an item for sale a user needs to tell their agent the opening price, the length of time available to complete the transaction, and how many times over this period the price will be recalculated. The agent must also be instructed how the asking price will change in response to offers, or the lack of them. To describe the change of a price we have adopted the approach described in [10] - as a graph with three distinct portions, (shown in the left-hand window in Fig. 4), namely:

- an initial static period, this represents an 'ideal price' where the agent will not alter its selling price
- a dynamic period, when the agent will progressively increase or decrease its price according to demand
- a final static period, this 'plateau' corresponds to the floor price, this prevents the price free-falling below a pre-set reserve price

The vendor's graph depicts the change in price (downwards) that occurs over time if the asking price is not met. For convenience users can choose the shape of this graph from a library of predetermined graphs. One such example is 'cool-headed' - this graph remains static for a short period, and then gradually falls. Alternatively, the user can change the graph parameters using the slider bars provided, giving the user the flexibility to customise their own transaction policy.

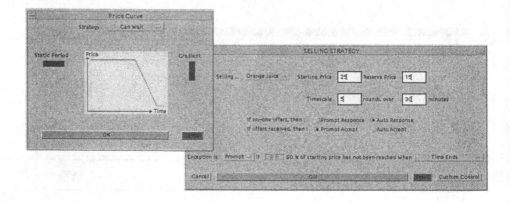

Fig. 4. The Selling Strategy Window, with pop-up Price Function Window (left)

The window through which the current selling strategy is displayed and configured is shown on the left in Figure 4. The two other parameters necessary to form the selling strategy are the initial asking price and the auction duration; these values are entered through the main Selling window, shown on the right in Figure 4. Once the strategy and its parameters have been specified the agent's asking price can be automatically recalculated in response to market conditions. Of course, this is a rather simplistic approach to implementing a bidding strategy. More sophisticated approaches exist, like those described in [27], which include learning strategies created from knowledge-based systems and game-theory models.

The Selling Window shown in Figure 4 also shows the other parameters the vendor can specify, such as the *exception policy*. This parameter compels the agent to perform some action if the highest bid received by some point in time is below a certain threshold. This allows the user to be alerted or withdraw the offer if no sufficient bids are received. The user can also set an *authorisation* policy - if the 'prompt me to accept' option is chosen, the agent will ask its user before agreeing to any transactions. Alternatively, choosing the 'auto accept' option endows authority to the agent to perform transactions when a reasonable offer is received. (Each agent also possesses a Buying window, whose fields are the converse of the Selling window).

5.1 Using ZEUS for Electronic Marketplaces

One of the motivations for our virtual marketplace demonstrator was to investigate the potential of collaborative agents for distributed electronic commerce applications. Implementing a working agent-based marketplace took 2 developers approximately 2 months, with the majority of the work involving the user interfaces. The brief evaluation presented here will consider how the collaborative agent solutions provided by the ZEUS tool-kit have addressed the problem issues identified in Section 2.

The Impact of ZEUS on the Information Discovery Problem

In a marketplace agents need some means of discovering what is on offer, and where on the network the vendor can be found. Given the dynamic nature of the market it is not sensible to hard-code this information into the agents, but rather to provide an index of agents and current offers that can be updated frequently. As the ZEUS Agent Name Server and Facilitator agents already provide these services to the market participants, we did not need to re-solve the problem of information discovery during the development of our marketplace.

The ZEUS Facilitator agents can provide an important brokering service, enabling agents wishing to buy or sell particular items to identify an appropriate trading partner. In other words, these agents provide a 'notice board' or 'classified ads' service, freeing agents from having to poll every other agent in the society in order to determine what items are available to trade.

The marketplace may possess more than one broker, which would be desirable for several reasons. Firstly, there is the issue of redundancy, as a market dependent on a single broker will collapse if it ceases. Then there is the desire for competition, to ensure that if brokers charge other agents for their information then the broker's costs should remain competitive. Finally there is the issue of scalability - because of their centralised nature, brokers are the potential bottlenecks of the marketplace, and there is a danger that as the number of trading agents increases the load on the broker will become too great for it to manage.

To avoid scalability problems local brokers could be created to service their 'own' local portion of the marketplace, as is the case with global commodity markets. We hope to use our virtual marketplace to perform scalability experiments in order to determine how many agents a single broker can comfortably support under various conditions. Once this point is reached additional brokers may be required to reduce the computational load experienced by the individual broker agents.

The Impact of ZEUS on the Communication Problem

The absence of a universal inter-agent communication language is a potential problem for any potential open agent marketplace. As all our agents originate from the same source, each uses the same communication mechanism, making them inherently compatible. The real challenge, however, will be to inter-operate with 'foreign' agents, which we have not yet attempted. This is where our usage of non-proprietary languages like KQML and FIPA ACL may well prove worthwhile.

In the absence of a 'standard' trading ontology we have created our own small trading ontology of the concepts the market supports; this is supplied to each agent when it joins the market. Thus another future challenge will be the adoption of a universal ontology, or a means of translating between different ones.

The Impact of ZEUS on the Negotiation Problem

Negotiation strategies define the behaviour of an agent during negotiation. It can involve numerous aspects: learning other agents' strategies; evaluating the effectiveness of his current strategy; finding out the best response strategy; and so on. As the potential complexity is considerable, no tool-kit could be expected to accommodate the requirements of every agent designer. Hence ZEUS has been designed to allow individual agent designers to include their own strategies into their agents. To create a new strategy, three aspects of an interaction need to be modelled:

> - the response when no message is received;
> - the response when messages are received; and
> - the conditions whereby interactions are accepted

These three parameters seem sufficient to support a wide range of behaviour. For instance, if a selling agent receives no bids it can opt to reduce its asking price and re-broadcast it. Acceptance occurs when a message is received which accepts the seller's asking price. (What we have just defined here is an agent performing Dutch auction).

These custom strategies run on the generic Co-ordination Engine inside each agent. This declarative approach avoids the need to re-implement the Co-ordination Engine when new behaviour is desired. We have already created strategies that implement the 'house rules' of several types of auction; the best known being the English, Vickrey and Dutch auctions. With these new protocols we have been able to convert our generic collaborative agents into marketplace participants.

In summary, we attribute the rapid development of our agent-based marketplace to the reuse of solutions that were already implemented as part of the ZEUS tool-kit. This has only been useful because the components provided by the tool-kit were generic enough to be used in our prototype electronic marketplace application with little modification.

6. Related Systems

A comparison with other agent building tool-kits is difficult since at time of writing no other tool-kits seem to have been used to implement a marketplace. There are however several agent-based virtual marketplaces that use auction protocols for negotiation. Of these, it is felt that the most similar systems to our experimental marketplace are Fishmarket[1], [11], AuctionBot[2], [24], and Kasbah[3], [10]. A brief comparison of the features of each is shown in Table 1.

The criteria used for comparison in Table 1 are as follows: the "Distribution of Agents" category describes the organisational architecture of the marketplace, and whether the users' agents are autonomous processes with their own embedded features or 'thin' clients that call services on the server side. "User defined price functions" relates to how the user exerts control over their agent's behaviour, and "Two-way bargaining" refers to the ability to make offers and counter-offers.

Of the other categories, "Multiple auction types" refers to the support for different co-ordination protocols. "Seller:Buyer cardinality" refers to the number of potential sellers who will be in competition for an individual transaction; whilst "Merchant Brokering" refers to the process whereby users identify who has a desired item for sale, and at what price.

---

1 http://www.iiia.csic.es/Projects/fishmarket/newindex.html
2 http://auction.eecs.umich.edu
3 http://kasbah.media.mit.edu

Feature	AuctionBot	Fishmarket	Kasbah	ZEUS Virtual Market
Distribution of Agents	Web-based client, server side agents	Network based with centralised seller and distributed buyers	Web based client, server based virtual market	Buyer and Seller agents distributed across a LAN
User defined price functions	Configurable via HTML form or programs using API	Function parameters configurable via GUI	Limited to choice from a list	Strategies and function parameters configurable via GUI
Two-way bargaining	Yes	Not relevant to auction scenario	Yes	Yes
Multiple auction types possible	Yes	Yes	No	Yes
Seller : Buyer cardinality	1 Seller : n Buyers	1 Seller : n Buyers	n Sellers : n Buyers	n Sellers : n Buyers
Merchant Brokering	Users choose vendors from category index	'Auctioneer' chooses goods to offer from available lots	Facilitated by dedicated broker agents	Users choose vendors from publicised offers

Table 1 - A comparison of the features of some agent-based Marketplaces

In summary, AuctionBot implements a server-side auction whose participants can configure their strategies through an API that is accessible through a web interface. Kasbah is also web-based, consisting of server-side agents that enable users to buy and sell; whilst it is less configurable, it provides a better support infrastructure, providing brokers to match buyers to sellers.

The Fishmarket system also differentiates buyers from sellers, although the auction is not conducted through the web. A significant feature of Fishmarket is that its conventions can be readily customised, this has been used to simulate a real-world fishmarket where the auctioneer chooses what to offer and invites bids from interested parties. In ZEUS, like Fishmarket, reconfiguring the finite state machine implementing the auction rules can change the conventions of the market. A unique feature of the ZEUS market is its participants are distributed client-side agents that have the ability to both buy and sell. Significantly, all these systems allow users to differentiate their agents from their rivals by configuring the buying and selling parameters, and all provide a means to react to market conditions.

7. Future Work: the Differentiation Issue

The problem with the marketplaces described in the previous section is that they lack sufficient means of differentiation. Traditionally traders attempt to attract customers using the "5 P's": product, price, place, position and promotion. These attributes allow traders to differentiate themselves from their competition through factors like physical proximity to the customers, transport costs, value-added services (like warranties), and lures such as loss leaders and loyalty schemes. These differentiation factors can be represented in an electronic marketplace, but only if the trading ontology is rich enough. The problem is that detailed trading ontologies are time-consuming and difficult to build.

Nevertheless, the provision of differentiation is vital because it allows vendors to avoid 'commoditisation', a situation where *identical items* from *different retailers* become perfectly substitutable, (i.e. equally as good as each other). Ultimately the danger is that without differentiation the market can become "friction-less". In economics the term 'friction' refers to the factors that keep markets from working according to the textbook model of perfect competition, [25]. In a theoretically frictionless market the only differentiation possible between vendors is *price*.

Friction-less markets are rare in conventional retail because of the inherent cost of shopping for the shopper, as finding a product costs time and effort. With an index of vendors and the ability to query vendors electronically, shopping agents could minimise the cost of shopping and find the lowest possible value. As a result vendors may be drawn into a price-cutting war to attract customers; however they risk being caught in a discounting feedback loop, which will ultimately lead to a 'price crash'. Consequently some means of differentiation is vital to maintain market stability, without it, potential vendors will be reluctant to compete against 'discount' retailers, whose low overheads make them the current beneficiaries of price-only comparisons. Without a diverse choice of retailers, products and purchasing options consumer choice will be limited, and interest in online commerce will be stifled.

Therefore, attracting consumers and vendors online will necessitate means of product and merchant differentiation. This need is well advocated in [26], which also argues against auction-based selling and in favour of a more sophisticated mutually beneficial means of negotiation. We agree with this analysis, and expect future electronic commerce research to move towards issues like how to maximise differentiation through comprehensive multi-attribute trading ontologies.

As the underlying ontology becomes more expressive, the scope for more sophisticated negotiation increases accordingly. For instance, buying agents will be able to take into account the additional costs of any goods they consider, like delivery costs or extended warranties. This additional information, coupled with the user's personal preferences and profile, will enable their agent to be equipped with much more sophisticated reasoning facilities. Such intelligence is a prerequisite for personal shopping agents that will add value by independently locating and selecting the most appropriate products and retailers.

8. Conclusions

Online shopping is effectively a 3-phase process that can be summarised as find - bid - exchange. Whilst it is already possible to find and buy goods online, the agent solution aims to integrate these existing partial solutions into a process that is much easier to use, and potentially more efficient for buyer and vendor alike. Agents also enrich the shopping process with the ability to negotiate, enabling comparison shopping, individual discounting and the setting of an agreed quality of service.

One potential disadvantage of complex software entities like agents is their high development overhead, but with our prototype market we hope to have shown that a collaborative agent building tool-kit can expedite development and supply the necessary functionality for a marketplace.

Although online shopping is currently a cumbersome process that accounts for a fraction of all transactions, the potential for growth is enormous. A recent authoritative U.S. Department of Commerce report [1] has predicted that online retailing between businesses and customers will be worth at least $7 billion by the year 2000, and could be as high as $115 billion by 2006. The figure for electronic transactions between businesses is even higher, and could be worth up to $300 billion by 2002.

For agent technology to make an impact on these figures several problems must first be solved. These are not the headline issues like credit card security and privacy protection, but technical challenges like finding the most appropriate product and vendor for one's own requirements. Likewise, vendors will want a means of distinguishing themselves from their competitors, and a means of efficiently targeting their products to potential customers. These do not seem insurmountable technical challenges; in fact they should be solvable by aggregating existing technologies. In which case, practical agent-based marketplaces should be within our reach.

Acknowledgements

Thanks to Divine Ndumu, Hyacinth Nwana, Haydn Haynes and Barry Crabtree for their contributions to the project and their feedback regarding this document. This work was funded by BT Laboratories.

References

[1] **The Emerging Digital Economy**. U.S. Department of Commerce, April 1998. Available online from: http://www.ecommerce.gov/emerging.htm

[2] **Automatic learning of user profiles: towards the personalisation of agent services**. S. Soltysiak, & B. Crabtree, *BT Technology Journal*, 16(3), July 1998. Available online from: http://www.labs.bt.com/projects/agents/

[3]   **Wrapper induction for information extraction**. N. Kushmerick, PhD Thesis. Technical Report No. UW-CSE-97-11-04, Department of Computer Science and Engineering, University of Washington, 1997.

[4]   **Catalogs for the Digital Marketplace**. Research Report No. 97-03, CommerceNet, 1997. Available from: http://www.commerce.net/research/research.html

[5]   **Software Agents**. N.R. Jennings & M. Wooldridge, IEE Review, p17–20, January 1996.

[6]   **Software Agents: An Overview**. H.S. Nwana, The Knowledge Engineering Review, Volume 11(3), p205–244, 1996.
        Available from: http://www.labs.bt.com/projects/agents/

[7]   **Applying the Agent Paradigm to Network Management**. R. Davison, J. Hardwicke, & M. Cox, *BT Technology Journal*, 16(3), July 1998.

[8]   **BDI agents: from theory to practice**. A.S. Rao, & M.P. Georgeff. In *Proc. 1ˢᵗ International Conference on Multi Agent Systems*, San Francisco, California, 1995, p312–319.

[9]   **3D-scientific data interpretation using cooperating agents**. R.J. Gallimore, N.R. Jennings, H.S. Lamba, C.L. Mason & B.J. Orenstein. In Proc. of PAAM'98, March 1998, p47–56.

[10]   **A Real Life Experiment in Creating an Agent Marketplace**. A. Chavez, D. Dreilinger, R. Guttman & P. Maes. In Proceedings of PAAM '97, p159-178, April 1997. Available online from: http://ecommerce.media.mit.edu/

[11]   **FM96.5 A Java-based Electronic Auction House**. J.A. Rodríguez, P. Noriega, C. Sierra & J. Padget. In Proceedings of PAAM '97, p207-224, April 1997.

[12]   **KQML as an Agent Communication Language**. T. Finin & Y. Labrou. In *Software Agents*, J.M. Bradshaw (Ed), MIT Press, Cambridge, Mass., p291–316, 1997.

[13]   **Towards a standard for software agents**. P.D. O'Brien & R. Nicol. *BT Technology Journal*, 16(3), July 1998.

[14]   **SICS MarketSpace – An Agent Based Market Infrastructure**. J. Eriksson, N. Finne & S. Janson. In Proceedings of AMET'98, p33-48, May 1998.

[15]   **Knowledge Interchange Format, Reference Manual, v3.0**. M.R. Genesereth & R.E. Fikes, (eds). Computer Science Department, Stanford University. Available from: http://www-ksl.stanford.edu/knowledge-sharing/papers/README.html#kif

[16]   **A translation approach to portable ontology specifications**. T. Gruber, *Knowledge Acquisition*, **5**(2), p199–220, 1993.

[17]   **Software Agents**. M.R. Genesereth & S.P. Ketchpel, *Communications of the ACM* **37**(7), p48–53, 1994.

[18]   **Progressive Multi-Agent Negotiation**. L.C. Lee. Proceedings of the 2ⁿᵈ International Conference on Multi-Agent Systems, Kyoto, Japan, p173-180, December 1996. Available online from: http://www.labs.bt.com/projects/agents/

[19] Negotiation as a metaphor for distributed problem solving. R. Davis & R.G. Smith. Artificial Intelligence 20, p63–109, 1983.

[20] Co-ordination in software agent systems. H.S. Nwana, L.C. Lee & N.R. Jennings. BT Technology Journal, 14(4) (1996) p79–88. Available online from: http://www.labs.bt.com/projects/agents/

[21] Research and Development Challenges for agent-based systems. D.T. Ndumu & H.S. Nwana. IEE Proceedings on Software Engineering, Volume 144(1), p2-10, 1997. Available online from: http://www.labs.bt.com/projects/agents/

[22] ZEUS: A Toolkit for Building Distributed Multi-Agent Systems. H.S. Nwana, D.T. Ndumu, L.C. Lee & J.C. Collis. *Applied Artificial Intelligence Journal, Vol. 13, No. 1,* 1999. Available online from: http://www.labs.bt.com/projects/agents/

[23] Visualisation of Distributed Multi-Agent Systems. D.T. Ndumu, H.S. Nwana, L.C. Lee & H.R. Haynes. *Applied Artificial Intelligence Journal, Vol.13, No.1, 1999.* Available online from: http://www.labs.bt.com/projects/agents/

[24] The Michigan Internet AuctionBot. P. R. Wurman, M.P. Wellman & W. E. Walsh. Technical report.
Available from: http://www-personal.engin.umich.edu/~pwurman/Papers/

[25] The Friction-Free Economy. J. Case, Inc. Magazine, June 1996, p27. Available online from: http://www.inc.com/incmagazine/archives/06960271.html

[26] Agent-mediated Integrative Negotiation for Retail Electronic Commerce. R.H. Guttman & P. Maes. In Proceedings of AMET'98, p77-90, May 1998. Available online from : http://ecommerce.media.mit.edu/

[27] Behavior of Trading Automata in a Computerized Double Auction Market. J. Rust, R. Palmer & J.H. Miller. In The Double Auction Market: Institutions, Theories, and Evidence, edited by D. Friedman and J. Rust, p155-198. Addison-Wesley, 1992.

Accounting for Cognitive Costs
in On-Line Auction Design

David C. Parkes[1], Lyle H. Ungar[2], and Dean P. Foster[3]

[1] Computer and Information Science Department, University of Pennsylvania,
Philadelphia PA 19104 dparkes@unagi.cis.upenn.edu
[2] Computer and Information Science Department, University of Pennsylvania,
Philadelphia PA 19104 ungar@central.cis.upenn.edu
[3] Department of Statistics, University of Pennsylvania, Philadelphia PA 19104
foster@hellspark.wharton.upenn.edu

Abstract. Many auction mechanisms, including first and second price ascending and sealed bid auctions, have been proposed and analyzed in the economics literature. We compare the usefulness of different mechanisms for on-line auctions, focusing on the cognitive costs placed on users (e.g. the cost of determining the value of a good), the possibilities for agent mediation, and the trust properties of the auction. Different auction formats prove to be attractive for agent mediated on-line auctions than for traditional off-line auctions. For example, second price sealed bid auctions are attractive in traditional auctions because they avoid the communication cost of multiple bids in first price ascending auctions, and the "gaming" required to estimate the second highest bid in first price sealed bid auctions. However, when bidding agents are cheap, communication costs cease to be important, and a progressive auction mechanism is preferred over a closed bid auction mechanism, since users with semi-autonomous agents can avoid the cognitive cost of placing an accurate value on a good. As another example, when an on-line auction is being conducted by an untrusted auctioneer (e.g. the auctioneer is selling its own items), rational participants will build bidding agents that transform second price auctions into first price auctions.

Keywords: electronic commerce, auctions, semi-autonomous agents.

1 Introduction

Electronic commerce has made possible many market institutions that are too inefficient and expensive in traditional marketplaces [4]. Auctions have typically been reserved for special domains, such as the FCC spectrum auction [7], fine art auction houses (e.g. Sotheby's and Christie's), or selling perishable goods, such as in Spanish fish markets [10]. Auctions are preferred to posted prices in these domains because the goods are of uncertain value, and dynamic price adjustment will often maximize revenue for a seller. In traditional off-line auctions the interested parties must gather in one physical location, or be prepared to participate in a protracted auction by correspondence (e.g. the FCC auction). The infrastructure of electronic commerce significantly reduces the costs of participation, and allows auctions to reach a large and physically distributed audience. Furthermore, artificial bidding agents can represent the preferences of interested parties, bids are electronic, and auctions can be automatically cleared in electronic clearing houses. Auctions provide a useful framework for agent mediated electronic commerce [1].

The design of mechanisms for on-line auctions should be informed by the costs placed on users,[1] the possibilities for effective agent[2] mediation, and also by the trust relations between users and auctioneers. The most important cost to a user in an agent mediated electronic auction is not the communication cost of participation (an agent can cheaply and autonomously monitor auctions and place bids on behalf of a user), but the cognitive cost of deciding on the value of a good. Traditional auction theory assumes that buyers *know* the value of a good (private values assumption), or that the value of a good will follow from new information (affiliated or common value auctions). In fact, the problem of determining the value of a good can be computationally complex, and a buyer's value might still be uncertain when a bid is required [14].

We identify auction mechanisms that allow a user to avoid the cognitive cost of determining an accurate value for a good whenever possible, while enabling an agent to place the same bids in auctions that would be optimal with an accurate valuation. We argue that progressive auctions, such as the English auction, are preferable to sealed bid auctions when there is a high cost associated with determining the exact value of goods but users can determine approximate values more cheaply. Furthermore, when progressive auctions are coupled with semi-autonomous agents that are able to request more accurate valuations from users when necessary, the high monitoring and communication costs of progressive auctions can be hidden from users. We survey commercial on-line auctions from the perspective of our analysis, and suggest a new design for automatic bidding agents.

---

[1] A user refers to an interested human participant, either a buyer or a seller.

[2] An agent refers to a software agent that can participate in an auction on behalf of a user.

2 Auction-based Negotiation for Electronic Commerce

Agent mediated electronic commerce enables cheap negotiation between buyers and sellers on the details of an individual transaction – product features, value-added services, financing and price. Agents that can dynamically negotiate transaction terms with vendors are a natural extension of first-generation shopping agents that compare the posted-price of goods across static on-line vendor sites [5]. While personalized negotiation has traditionally been too expensive, except for high value and highly configurable goods, such as new cars, agent mediated negotiation absorbs many of the costs and inconveniences of negotiation.

The design of auction servers and market-aware computational agents presents a key challenge for agent technologies, artificial intelligence, and real-time systems [14, 19, 20]. We can make some challenges easier through the design of market mechanisms that enable straightforward and provably optimal agent strategies, at least for simple domains [17].

There are a number of testbeds for agent mediated electronic trading: *AuctionBot* [21] is a general purpose Internet auction server with an Application Programmable Interface (API) that allows software agents to participate in user-configured auctions; *FM 97.6* [11], another multiagent test bed, simulates complex Dutch auctions; and *Kasbah* is a prototype agent-based bilateral exchange market for buying and selling goods [3]. Kasbah illustrates a key feature of useful agent mediated electronic trading systems. It reduces the cognitive cost to users of the system by requiring that users provide only a few high-level parameters in order to specify their preferences. The bidding agents within Kasbah are given autonomy to pursue strategies consistent with the stated preferences.

Auctions provide a well-defined and simple framework for negotiation between self-interested buyers and sellers in a market. Although auctions traditionally allow negotiation over price alone, auction mechanisms can be extended to include negotiation over product features, warranties, and service policies – still within a framework that assumes self-interested, possibly insincere and strategic agents. For example, in the recent FCC spectrum auction buyers had synergies over combinations of spectrum rights over a geographically consistent area. The FCC implemented a simultaneous ascending auction that allowed bidders to place bids for multiple goods, and dynamically adjust over the course of the auction the precise combination of goods that they tried to acquire [7]. In a combinatorial auction buyers can express synergies directly by submitting bids for combinations of goods (or for one good with a specific combination of features) [13]. Wurman *et al.* [21] are developing languages that allow users to represent their preferences over bundles of interdependent goods efficiently.

Bidding agents need to make *tradeoffs* between features and price within an auction framework. The space of different product specifications is often very large, particularly when goods are nonstandard, and the problem that one must address as an auction designer is how to elicit only *necessary information* from users on their preferences between different product specifications when many feature combinations might prove to be unavailable or too expensive. We assume that this information is costly for a user to provide. We compare standard single-unit auctions over a large and diverse space of possible goods, from the perspective of reducing the cognitive costs involved in providing information to a bidding agent. We assume that a user can specify hard constraints over product features that she will consider, but does not know (or does not wish to specify) her exact value tradeoff within this space.

3 Traditional Auction Theory

Auctions are simple and robust mechanisms for selling nonstandard and short supply items with uncertain market values. Auction mechanisms discover the optimal price for a good through the bidding action of self-interested agents. We characterize price discovery mechanisms as progressive (ascending price, descending price) or sealed bid, and first price or second price. In ascending price auctions the auctioneer continuously reveals the highest bid received, and the *ask price* is a minimum increment above the price of the current highest bid. The auction terminates after a period of inactivity. In descending price auctions the auctioneer lowers the ask price until the first bid is received, when the auction is immediately terminated. In a sealed bid auction all bids are private, and the auctioneer selects the winning bid after a fixed period of time.

In all simple auction mechanisms the good is sold to the bidding agent with the highest bid. In first price auctions an agent pays the price of its bid, while in second price auctions an agent pays the highest amount that was bid by another agent [6, 9]. While there are many combinations of auction characteristics, some auction mechanisms are redundant and do not have general use. For example the second price ascending auction is strategically equivalent to the first price ascending auction for small bid increments, and will have the same revenue and efficiency properties.

Traditional auction theory emphasizes the allocation efficiency and expected revenue properties of auction mechanisms, given assumptions about how buyers assign value to goods [6]. For example, the prevalence of the first price ascending (English) auction in traditional auction environments (e.g. fine art auction houses) is best explained with a model that assumes that buyers' values are affiliated: when one buyer places a high value on a good it is more likely that other buyers will also value the good highly [8]. A progressive price auction maximizes revenue for sellers in this environment because bids reveal information, and the knowledge that one buyer values an item highly can increase the valuations of other buyers [6]. A sealed bid auction does not allow this dynamic information sharing between buyers.

Second price sealed bid (Vickrey) auctions are attractive in traditional auction domains because they avoid the communication cost of multiple bids in ascending auctions, and the "gaming" that is required to estimate the second highest bid in first price sealed bid auctions. Furthermore, privacy and information revelation considerations often favor a sealed bid auction over an (open) progressive auction (e.g. government procurement contracts). However, there are few real-world examples of second price sealed bid auctions, possibly because the Vickrey auction is vulnerable to manipulation by an untrusted auctioneer that overstates the second highest bid (unless the bid must be verified in some way), and because buyers are often reluctant to reveal their true valuations for goods [12].

In our analysis of mechanisms for on-line auctions we make standard assumptions about how buyers assign value to goods: (a) private value assumption – the value of a good only depends on a buyer's own preferences; (b) independence of bids – the values placed on a good by buyers are statistically independent. Given these assumptions the *revenue equivalence theorem* [18] states that the four most common auctions (English, first price descending, first price sealed bid and Vickrey) all yield the same expected revenue for risk-neutral agents. However good auction design can still increase expected revenue by lowering the costs of participation. Theoretical analysis of revenue equivalence assumes that a fixed set of buyers participate in the auction, irrespective of the mechanism. In reality the costs (cognitive and communication) and conditions of trust within a system will affect the number of buyers that participate. *A seller can expect to receive a higher sale price for a good if she is able to attract bids from more buyers.*

4 Auction Cost and Trust Properties

The design of an auction mechanism for on-line agent mediated auctions should be informed by the costs placed on human participants in the system, and the conditions of trust that exist between the buyers, the sellers and the auctioneer. Auctions for agent mediated on-line electronic commerce require somewhat different cost structures than more traditional off-line auctions, and conditions of trust are often more critical. In this section we introduce some key auction *properties* that influence both the cost of participation in an auction, and the trust requirements that are placed on parties. We claim that the most important barrier to user participation in an agent mediated on-line auction is the cognitive cost of deciding values for new, previously unvalued, goods.

Standard economic theory assumes that a buyer knows the value of a good when the good is for self-consumption (private value assumption), or that the value of a good is set exogenously and cannot be known by an agent without further information (common value assumption). However, in many real situations a good can only be valued by careful reasoning. This is a cognitive cost that cannot be easily transferred to an electronic bidding agent, indeed buyers often cannot even formulate the tradeoffs that determine their exact reservation price for a particular good. That there is a nontrivial cost to decide what the reservation price is: "how much am I willing to pay for this item?" may not be obvious, but note that people often take a lot of time deciding whether they want to buy a given dress, bike or house, even when the price is posted. In business settings determining the value of a given item, such as a quantity of crude oil, or a shipment of electronic components, may require solving a complex optimization problem.

We summarize the cost and trust properties over six different auction mechanisms in Table 1 and Table 2.[3] We will introduce two new auction properties: *bounded-rational compatible* and *untrusted-auctioneer compatible*. The properties listed are all beneficial, they either reduce the cost of participation, or reduce the degree of trust that is required between agents within the auction for faithful implementation.

4.1 Cost Properties Relevant to On-Line Auction Design

The costs to participation in an auction are *cognitive* (information gathering and processing) and *communicative*, and depend on the mechanism, the goods that are being auctioned, and the complexity of the local problems of buyers. The costs that are important in an on-line agent mediated auction differ from the costs in a more traditional off-line auction.

Cognitive costs can be separated into two processes. First a buyer must estimate her *reservation price* for a good, the maximum price that she will pay for a good. The reservation price is equal to the perceived value of a good to the buyer, and depends on her preferences. Although a buyer can place a bid in an auction on the basis of her reservation price alone, in some auctions counterspeculation is also useful – and a buyer might choose to reason about the preferences and strategies of other buyers in the system when placing a bid. This is the second cognitive process. We can design auction mechanisms and agents that reduce and remove this second cost, either through mechanisms that make counterspeculation redundant, or through bidding agents that implement complex bidding strategies for a user. The premise of our work is that the cost of the first cognitive process, that of determining a reservation price for a new, previously unvalued, good is nontrivial, and will often dominate any other costs to participation in an agent mediated on-line auction.

In an auction that is *buyer incentive compatible* (IC_B, Table 1) the dominant strategy for a buyer is to bid her true value for a good [9]. It is not necessary for a buyer to incur the cognitive cost of strategic counterspeculation that can be useful in some auction mechanisms. In buyer incentive compatible ascending price auctions, such as the first price ascending auction, a buyer will maximize her expected utility by placing a new bid whenever the current highest bid is below her reservation price and held by another buyer.

---

[3] The second price descending auction is not a standard auction format. The auctioneer starts with a high price, and lowers the price until two bids have been received. The agents are not informed of the first bid until the second bid has also been made. The item is then sold to the highest bidder at the price of the second highest bid. The auction is strategically equivalent to the English and Vickrey auctions. Furthermore, the auction is "bounded-rational compatible" because a good upper bound on a buyer's reservation price determines an optimal strategy when the auction terminates before the upper bound is reached.

Table 1. Cost properties of common auctions. **Key:** IC_B Buyer incentive compatible, BRC Bounded-rational compatible, $COMM_L$ Low communication cost.

	Ascending Price	Descending Price	Sealed bid
First price	IC_B, BRC	BRC	$COMM_L$
Second price	IC_B, BRC	IC_B, BRC	$IC_B, COMM_L$

A buyer in an incentive compatible sealed bid auction should simply bid her reservation price. For example, the second price sealed bid (Vickrey) auction is incentive compatible because the price that a buyer pays for a good is determined by the bids received from other buyers, and does not depend on her own bid. Instead, the price that a buyer bids defines a range of prices that she is willing to accept (any price up to and including the price of her bid). It is a dominant strategy to submit a bid equal to her reservation price [9]. When all buyers adopts this dominant strategy the good is sold to the buyer with the highest reservation price, for a price equal to the second highest reservation price.[4] In comparison, the optimal strategy for a buyer in a *first price* sealed bid auction is to place a bid that is just above the highest bid of another buyer, so long as the price is below her own reservation price. In this case a buyer can use information about the valuations and strategies of other buyers in the system to increase her expected utility.

Different auction structures require vastly different expected effort by buyers to determine a value for a good that is being auctioned. We introduce a new auction property, *bounded-rational compatible* (BRC, Table 1). A bounded-rational compatible auction, such as the English auction, will often allow a bidding agent to follow an optimal bidding strategy with only approximate information on the value of a good. We assume that it takes less effort for a buyer to place bounds on her value for a good than it does to compute her exact value for a good. For example, consider the behavior of a bidding agent in an English auction that has a lower and upper bound on the value that a buyer places on a good. The bidding agent will place a bid whenever the ask price is below the lower bound on value, and drop out of the auction when the ask price is above the upper bound on value. The buyer avoids the cognitive cost of refining its valuation when the auction terminates with an ask price that is either below its lower bound or above its upper bound. The buyer only needs to compute an accurate valuation when other buyers have similar reservation prices. Compare this with a sealed bid auction, where an agent that has an estimate of the value of a good risks

---

[4] This is the same outcome as is achieved with an English auction, but without the overhead of multiple bids.

winning the good for a price that is above the buyer's true value, or missing a price that is below the buyer's true value.

Finally, we also consider whether an auction mechanism has low communication costs ($COMM_L$, Table 1). The communication cost of an auction mechanism depends on the size of a single bid, and the expected number of auction rounds. Sealed bid auctions have low communication costs in comparison with progressive auctions because they require only one bid from each agent in each auction while progressive auctions may require several rounds of bidding.

The importance of communication cost depends on the infrastructure of the auction. For example, the amortized per-message communication cost in a traditional off-line auction is much greater than the per-message cost in an electronic on-line auction. In a traditional auction the cost includes the need to physically meet in one location for a period of time, while the per-message communication cost in an Internet-based electronic auction is minimal [1]. Furthermore, users in an on-line auction can be physically distributed and use bidding agents to automatically monitor auctions and place bids.

4.2 Trust Properties Relevant to On-Line Auction Design

Trust is another important consideration that drives auction design – will users have any reason not to trust that an auctioneer will implement a bidding mechanism truthfully? It is not unusual in on-line commerce for the seller and the auctioneer to be the same firm (e.g. www.onsale.com). There is a clear conflict of interest. The auctioneer has an incentive to inflate the price of a good. We can design auction mechanisms that are not vulnerable to this kind of direct price manipulation.[5]

We introduce a new auction property, *untrusted-auctioneer compatible* (*UAC*, Table 2), for auctions that are not vulnerable to *direct* price manipulation by a strategic auctioneer. Direct price manipulation is strategic action by the auctioneer, or parties acting on behalf of the seller, that is risk-free (while undetected) and can only increase revenue. An auction is secure to this type of price manipulation when the buyer that wins the auction pays an amount equal to the price that she bid. For example, the first price sealed bid auction is untrusted-auctioneer compatible because the auctioneer cannot inflate the price that the winning buyer pays. However, an untrusted auctioneer in a second price sealed bid auction can receive all the bids, create a false bid just below the highest outside bid received, and then charge the buyer with the highest bid a price just below her bid [12]. This is possible because the price paid by the highest bidder is different from the price that is bid, and revealed only to the auctioneer.

A rational participant in a sealed bid auction with an untrusted auctioneer will build a bidding agent that transforms second price auctions into first price auctions because buyer incentive compatibility is lost. This will occur when there

---

[5] An alternative (institutional) solution to untrusted auctioneers is to provide trusted third parties that are certified to manage auctions.

Table 2. Trust properties of common auctions. **Key:** IC_S Seller incentive compatible, UAC untrusted-auctioneer compatible.

	Ascending Price	Descending Price	Sealed bid
First price	UAC	IC_S, UAC	IC_S, UAC
Second price	UAC		

is reason to believe that the auctioneer might profit from the final sale price of the good.

An auction that is also *seller incentive compatible* (IC_S, Table 2) is secure from *indirect* price manipulation. Indirect price manipulation is strategic action by the auctioneer, or parties acting on behalf of the seller, that includes some risk of decreasing revenue, for example when information about the preferences and strategies of buyers is not fully accurate. In a seller incentive compatible auction it is optimal for a seller to bid her true valuation for a good, because her ask price does not affect the price that she receives, but defines the range of prices that she is willing to receive. Seller incentive compatibility is necessary and sufficient for preventing the type of indirect price manipulation that we consider here.

First price descending and sealed bid auctions are seller incentive compatible because the ask price does not directly determine the price that a seller receives. The optimal strategy for a seller is to set the ask price equal to her reservation price. Second price auctions are not seller incentive compatible because the seller can influence the price that she receives for a good, for example by setting the ask price just below the highest bid price. Similarly, the first price ascending auction is not seller incentive compatible because a seller can increase her expected revenue by setting her ask price just below the highest reservation price of the buyers in the system.

When an auction mechanism is not seller incentive compatible the price that the seller receives can be manipulated through a third party that places bids on behalf of the seller, called a *shill*. For example, a shill in a first price ascending auction can compete with the buyer with the highest reservation price, and try to drive the ask price to just below that buyer's reservation price. This type of price manipulation is not risk free without perfect information about the preferences and strategies of the buyers in an auction. The seller might be left with a good that she could have sold for a profit.[6]

---

[6] In traditional English auctions all participants are present in the same room, and a shill can reduce his risk with visual clues about when a bidder has been pushed close to her reservation price.

We can also compare the auction mechanisms with regard to manipulation through buyer collusion. A group of buyers can form a coalition, and elect one member to participate in the auction, bidding up to the highest reservation price of the members of the coalition. The buyers can then re-auction the good among themselves, and share the surplus that is extracted from the seller. Possible in any auction mechanism, this type of static collusion that occurs prior to an auction is hard to detect and prevent. Collusion may also occur dynamically *during* a progressive auction, if the active bidders can reach a self enforcing agreement to stop bidding and re-auction the item amongst themselves [15]. One key property that is necessary for dynamic collusion is the identification of bidders. A progressive on-line auction can offer some protection from buyer collusion by posting all bids anonymously.

5 Agent Mediated Progressive Auctions

In this section we use the earlier analysis of the cost and trust properties of auctions (Section 4) to identify an appropriate auction mechanism for agent mediated electronic commerce, paying particular attention to the need to delay and avoid the cost to a buyer of valuing a good.

Aside from cognitive costs, we can simplify the design of optimal bidding strategies for software agents through good auction design. With well-designed auctions the set of optimal strategies that might be useful to an agent is small, and we can program agents with a complete set of strategies – there is no need for agents to learn better strategies from success or failure [2]. In particular, agents in *buyer incentive compatible* auctions can maximize expected utility by bidding according to their own reservation price, and without consideration of the preferences or strategies of other agents in the system. For example, the optimal strategy of an agent in a first price ascending auction is to bid whenever the current highest bid is below its reservation price, and held by another agent.

Furthermore, because the space of interesting goods that a bidding agent might encounter is potentially very large, we would like *bounded-rational compatible* auctions that allow optimal bidding strategies with only approximate reservation prices. This allows buyers to defray, and if possible avoid, the cognitive cost of placing an accurate valuation on a good.

The auction mechanisms that we have considered that are both buyer incentive compatible and bounded-rational compatible are the first price ascending auction and the second price descending auction (see Table 1). We rule out the second price sealed bid (Vickrey) auction because it is not bounded-rational compatible and we want to avoid the high cognitive cost of computing the reservation price for every auction.[7]

We prefer the first price ascending auction to the second price descending auction for a number of reasons. Firstly, an agent in an ascending price auction can drop out of an auction before it terminates, when the ask price is greater

---

[7] Sandholm [16] has noted some other limitations of Vickrey auctions in computational multiagent systems.

than its reservation price upper bound. In a descending price auction an agent must monitor the auction as long as it is open, and accept an ask price that is below its reservation price lower bound. Secondly, in an ascending price auction bidding agents control the rate at which the price of a good is increased as they refine their valuations for goods. This is preferable to a descending price auction where the auctioneer must lower the price of a good at a rate that is appropriate to the bounded rationality of the bidding agents, in order to avoid missing a price that an agent would accept given enough time to reason about the true value of its reservation price.

Furthermore, when we consider the trust properties of auctions, we see that the descending second price auction is susceptible to manipulation by an untrusted auctioneer in the same way as the Vickrey auction, while the first price ascending auction is untrusted-auctioneer compatible because the winning agent pays the price that it bid (UAC, Table 2). Both progressive auctions are however susceptible to indirect price manipulation (IC_S, Table 2). It is interesting to note that it is impossible for an auction mechanism to be both buyer and seller incentive compatible (compare Table 1 and Table 2) [22], and that we must accept indirect price manipulation in return for simple optimal bidding strategies.

We conclude that the most suitable auction for agent mediated on-line auctions, when the space of possible goods is large and diverse, and users do not know their reservation prices for all goods, is the first price ascending auction. In on-line auctions it is worth having agents submit many bids if this enables some users to avoid computing accurate valuations in order to participate. Prices in progressive auctions provide feedback that allow users to avoid and delay the cognitive cost of determining an accurate value for a good.

5.1 Bidding Agent Design

When progressive auctions are coupled with semi-autonomous bidding agents users can achieve significant cost savings. While a fully autonomous agent requires a complete set of preferences in order to represent a user correctly in all situations that it might encounter, a semi-autonomous agent will bid on behalf of the user when it has enough knowledge to proceed, and query the user when its best action is ill-defined given its current information.

The design of bidding agents should be appropriate to the auction mechanism, and sensitive to the cost characteristics of users. An autonomous agent that places bids up to the value of a fixed reservation price, a "reservation-price agent", is appropriate for users that have precise valuations for goods that are auctioned. A reservation-price agent competes in relevant auctions while the current ask price is above its reservation price or until the agent is sold the good.

When users have approximate valuations for goods, and would prefer to avoid the cost of providing accurate valuations, then an agent that is semi-autonomous and requests a refined valuation as necessary, a "progressive-price agent", is more appropriate. A progressive-price agent is initialized with a *lower bound* and an optional *upper bound* on the true reservation prices of the user. The agent always places a bid when the current ask price is below its lower bound and the agent does not hold the highest bid, and will leave an auction when the ask price is above its upper bound. Given this strategy, the agent is sold a good whenever the auction closes at a price below its current lower bound. The agent behaves autonomously while current ask prices are below the lower bound or above the upper bound. The agent will request more information from the buyer, in the form of refined lower and upper bounds on its valuation, whenever the current ask price lies within the range of uncertain value between the two bounds. The agent will leave the auction if the new upper bound is below the current ask price, place a bid if the new lower bound is above the current ask price, and request further refinement if the ask price remains between the bounds.

For example, consider a user that is interested in purchasing an automobile. The user initializes a progressive-price agent that will make bids on any convertible VW Beetle that was made after 1975, has done less than 40000 miles, and is in mint condition. The user provides a lower bound of $3000, but no upper bound. The bidding agent will behave autonomously while no such vehicles are for sale (search), or while the current ask price in an auction is less than $3000 (bid). The agent will only request further information from the user when the price of a suitable car increases above $3000. With updated reservation price bounds the agent will continue to bid, or drop out the auction – as appropriate. This is the sense in which the bidding agent is semi-autonomous. The user provides the bidding agent with some initial information, and is ready to provide new information when necessary.

As another example, consider a user who wants to buy a notebook computer with features that satisfy a set of hard constraints, but does not know her exact price tradeoff, for example between a Pentium-166 and a Pentium-233 processor. Instead she initializes a progressive-price agent with upper and lower valuation bounds over the feature space of satisficing goods. When her agent finds an auction for a notebook with suitable features it will bid while the price is below the lower bound for that particular set of features. Should the auction end with the agent winning the notebook for a price below the reservation price, then the agent can complete the transaction. However, if the price in the auction rises above the upper bound, then the agent can stop monitoring the auction, and move to another auction. The agent only needs to request a more accurate value for the notebook (with this particular set of specifications) if the price stops within the region of uncertain value.

6 Commercial On-Line Auctions

There are many on-line auctions that are currently in use [23]. Some sites are run by discounters selling multiple goods, often from odd lots (Major Vendor auctions), while others are open to the public and anyone can sell (Person-to-Person auctions), see Table 3. It is illuminating to look at the design of real on-line auctions in the light of the above discussion.

Table 3. Commercial on-line auctions. **Key: M** – Major Vendor Auction, **P** – Person-to-Person Auction

Company	M / P	Mechanism	Bidding Agent	Automatic notification
auctionworks.com	P	English	"proxy bidding system"	yes
auctionuniverse.com	P	English	"RoboBid"	yes
ebay.com	P	English	no	yes
haggle.com	P	English	"proxy robot"	no
onsale.com	M	English	"BidAgent"	yes ("BidWatch")
zauction.com	M	English	no	no
surplusauction.com	M	English	no	no

Most commercial on-line auction mechanisms are a variant of the English auction. The auctions often include a deadline for the auction (whether or not there is any bidding activity), and the final stage is sometimes a sealed bid auction to avoid strategic bids that seek to take advantage of Internet communication latencies. In some auctions the deadline is extended with a "going going gone" phase that continues while there is bidding activity.

Rudimentary bidding agents are provided at many Person-to-Person auction sites.[8] For example, onsale.com provides a "BidAgent" that is initialized with a reservation price, and will monitor an auction and place a bid when the current highest bid is below the agent's reservation price and held by another agent. The agent will also provide automatic e-mail notification when the ask price rises above the reservation price of the agent, the price that the agent is authorized to bid up to. This enables a user to set a new maximum bid price if appropriate. Most on-line auctions encourage a user to initialize a bidding agent with an accurate reservation price, although they do (implicitly) allow a user to refine a lower bound on her reservation price through this "e-mail and update" mechanism.

The bidding agents actually implement a second price auction, but do so in a way that allows the current second highest bid to be publicly posted so

---

[8] A user of an untrusted auction might prefer to implement and execute her own bidding agents, given that the bidding agents implemented and executing at the auction site will hold information on her reservation price – information that could be used to the advantage of an untrusted auctioneer [20].

that other potential buyers can judge whether it is worth their time to enter the bidding. The bidding agents also reveal the incentive compatibility of a second price sealed bid auction to the users [20].

In another complication of the simple auction, sellers are often permitted to start the auction at a price below their reservation price in order to generate interest. An auction is sometimes marked as a "reservation price auction" in this case. The seller does not have to sell the good if the highest bid falls below her reservation price. A better way to generate interest, that avoids the spectacle of auctions closing without the highest bidder receiving the good, is to provide a "seller agent" that will bid for the *seller* if an outside bid is received that is lower than her reservation price.

7 Conclusions

Real auctions differ from those typically analyzed by economists and computer scientists. Issues of cost and trust drive these differences. On-line electronic commerce provides a cheap and readily available communication infrastructure (the Internet), that makes differences in the communication efficiency of sealed bid and progressive auctions unimportant. The largest overhead to user participation in an on-line auction is deciding what to buy, and how much it is worth. This is a much greater problem on-line than off-line because there are many different goods available across many different auctions. In traditional off-line auctions goods are typically sold in special lots to a group of invited experts.

We have argued that first price ascending (English) auctions have many advantages over other mechanisms for on-line auctions. In particular English auctions enable semi-autonomous agents that can act on behalf of users, and follow optimal bidding strategies with only approximate valuations for goods that they encounter. A request is made to a user for more accurate valuations only when necessary – when it will affect the outcome of an auction. This frees users of the need to provide accurate valuations for every single good that the agent might encounter (or equivalently for every possible combination of features for a particular type of good).

Semi-autonomous agents may not always be desirable. For example, if it is important to a user to choose *when* to provide information to her agent, then she might prefer to decide on an accurate reservation price when she has time to do so, and request that her agent behaves completely autonomously until a later predetermined time.

Although theoretical analysis of the revenue equivalence of private-value auctions assumes risk-neutral agents, and human buyers tend to be risk-averse, we believe that our conclusions are still valid. The first price sealed bid and first price descending bid auctions have a greater expected revenue than English auctions for risk-averse agents [6]. However, we consider an *open system* with voluntary participation, where the number of buyers that choose to participate in an auction is determined by the costs (cognitive and communicative) and conditions of trust within a system. A seller can expect to receive a higher sale price for a good if she is able to attract bids from more buyers. We believe that the positive effect on increased participation from an English auction will more than outweigh any negative effect on expected revenue for the set of buyers that choose to participate.

Finally, we emphasize that when designing a mechanism for on-line commerce it is critical not only to consider the allocation efficiency and revenue maximization properties of a mechanism, but also the costs that are relevant to participants in the auction.

8 Acknowledgments

This research was funded in part by National Science Foundation Grant SBR 96-02053.

References

1. Beam, C., Segev, A., Shanthikumar, J. G.: Electronic negotiation through Internet-based auctions. CITM Working Paper 96-WP-1019 (1996) <http://haas.berkeley.edu/~citm/wp-1019-summary.html>
2. Beam, C., Segev, A.: Automated negotiations: A survey of the state of the art. CITM Working Paper 96-WP-1022 (1997) <http://haas.berkeley.edu/~citm/wp-1022-summary.html>
3. Chavez, A., Maes, P.: Kasbah: An agent marketplace for buying and selling goods. Proceedings of the First International Conference on the Practical Application of Intelligent Agents and Multi-Agent Technology (PAAM'96) (1996)
4. Guttman, R., Moukas, A., Maes, P.: Agent-mediated electronic commerce: A survey. Knowledge Engineering Review 13(3) (1998) <http://ecommerce.media.mit.edu/papers/ker98.ps>
5. Guttman, R., Maes, P.: Agent-mediated integrative negotiation for retail electronic commerce. Workshop on Agent Mediated Electronic Trading (AMET-98) (1998)
6. McAfee, R. P., McMillan, J.: Auctions and bidding. Journal of Economic Literature 25 (1987) 699–738
7. McAfee, R. P., McMillan, J.: Analyzing the airwaves auction. Journal of Economic Perspectives 10(1) (1996) 159–175
8. Milgrom, P., Weber, R. J.: A theory of auctions and competitive bidding. Econometrica 50(5) (1982) 1089–1122
9. Milgrom, P.: Auctions and bidding: A primer. Journal of Economic Perspectives 3(3) (1989) 3–32
10. Rodríguez-Aguilar, J. A., Noriega, P., Sierra, C., Padget, J.: FM96.5 A Java-based electronic auction house. Proceedings of the Second International Conference on the Practical Application of Intelligent Agents and Multi-Agent Technology (PAAM'97) (1997)
11. Rodríguez-Aguilar, J. A., Martín, F. J., Noriega, P., Garcia, P., Sierra, C.: Competitive scenarios for heterogeneous trading agents. Proceedings of the Second International Conference on Autonomous Agents (Agents'98) (1998) 293–300
12. Rothkopf, M. H., Teisberg, T. J., Kahn, E. P.: Why are Vickrey auctions rare? Journal of Political Economy 98(1) (1990) 94–109

13. Rothkopf, M H., Pekeĉ, A., Harstad, R.M.: Computationally manageable combinatorial auctions. Rutgers University, RUTCOR research report **13-95** (1995)
14. Sandholm, T. W., Lesser, V.: Issues in automated negotiation and electronic commerce: Extending the Contract Net framework. First International Conference on Multiagent Systems (ICMAS-95) (1995) 328–335 <ftp://ftp.cs.umass.edu/pub/lesser/sandholm-icmas95-issues.ps>
15. Sandholm, T. W., Lesser, V.: Coalition formation among bounded rational agents. Fourteenth International Joint Conference on Artificial Intelligence (IJCAI'95) (1995) 662–669
16. Sandholm, T. W: Limitations of the Vickrey auction in computational multiagent systems. Second International Conference on Multiagent Systems (ICMAS-96) (1996) 299–306 <http://www.cs.wustl.edu/~sandholm/vickrey.ICMAS96.ps>
17. Varian, H.: Economic mechanism design for computerized agents. First USENIX Workshop on Electronic Commerce (1995) 13–21 <ftp://alfred.sims.berkeley.edu/pub/Papers/mechanism-design.ps.Z>
18. Vickrey, W.: Counterspeculation, auctions, and competitive sealed tenders. Journal of Finance **16** (1961) 8–37
19. Wellman, M. P., Wurman, P. R.: Market-aware agents for a multiagent world. Forthcoming, Robotics and Autonomous Systems (1998) <ftp://ftp.eecs.umich.edu/people/wellman/maamaw.ps>
20. Wellman, M. P., Wurman, P. R.: Real time issues for Internet auctions. First IEEE Workshop on Dependable and Real-Time E-Commerce Systems (DARE-98) (1998) <ftp://ftp.eecs.umich.edu/people/wellman/dare98.ps>
21. Wurman, P. R., Wellman, M. P., Walsh, W. E.: The Michigan Internet AuctionBot: A configurable auction server for human and software agents. Proceedings of the Second International Conference on Autonomous Agents (Agents'98) (1998) 301–308
22. Wurman, P. R., Walsh, W. E., Wellman, M. P.: Flexible double auctions for electronic commerce: Theory and implementation. Forthcoming, Decision Support Systems (1998) <ftp://ftp.eecs.umich.edu/people/wellman/dss98.ps>
23. Yahoo! Online auction <http://www.yahoo.com/Business_and_Economy/Companies/Auctions/Online_Auctions>

SICS MarketSpace –
An Agent-Based Market Infrastructure

Joakim Eriksson, Niclas Finne, and Sverker Janson
Email: {joakime, nfi, sverker}@sics.se

Intelligent Systems Laboratory
Swedish Institute of Computer Science
Box 1263, SE-164 29 Kista, Sweden

Abstract. We present a simple and uniform communication framework for an agent-based market infrastructure, the goal of which is to enable automation of consumer goods markets distributed over the Internet. The framework consists of an information model for participant interests and an interaction model that defines a basic vocabulary for advertising, searching, negotiating and settling deals. The information model is based on structured documents representing contracts and representations of constrained sets of contracts called interests. The interaction model is asynchronous message communication in a speech act based language, similar to, but simpler than, KQML [7] and FIPA ACL [8]. We also discuss integration of an agent-based market infrastructure with the web.

1 Introduction

The Internet has evolved from an information space to a market space with thousands, potentially millions, of electronic storefronts, auctions and other commercial services. This market space is not without problems. A major problem is the difficulty of finding relevant offers. Another problem is coping with the multitude of different styles of interfaces to different marketplaces. Yet another problem is how to automate routine tasks in such an environment.

We present one possible solution to these problems. An *agent-based market infrastructure* helps customers and commercial sites find matching interests, and, when desired, negotiate and close deals. Each participant has an agent that acts in the interest of its owner. The infrastructure is entirely open and decentralized, just like the web itself, allowing anyone to enter the market. Interaction is entirely symmetrical. Any rôle on a market can be played by any participant. The benefits of automation, lowered transaction costs, are made available to all.

At the core of the infrastructure is a communication framework, consisting of an *information model*, for describing user interests, and an *interaction model*, defining a basic vocabulary for searching, negotiating and settling deals. The information model is based on structured documents representing *contracts* and representations of sets of contracts called *interests*. Interests are encoded in the *Market Interest Format* (*MIF*). The interaction model is asynchronous message communication in a simple speech act based language, the *Market Interaction Language* (*MIL*). The rôles of MIF and MIL in the agent-based market correspond loosely to those of HTML and HTTP for the web. We hope to, by these examples, encourage further study into and development of *simple* yet useful standards that will pave the way to automated Internet markets, and avoid the unwanted generality and overwhelming complexity of most agent communication frameworks.

The proposed infrastructure is intended to complement, and work in close integration with, the web, email, and other human-oriented forms of communication. We will discuss how agents are integrated with the web, smoothly combining web browsing and agent-based automation.

In the remainder of this paper, we provide background and related work in the areas of electronic commerce and agent-based systems (Section 2), introduce the information model (Section 3) and interaction model (Section 4), discuss integration with the web (Section 5) and conclude with a discussion of future directions of this work (Section 6).

2 Background and Related Work

2.1 Electronic Commerce on the Internet

The Internet offers the hope and the promise of the global perfect market. In principle, the activities can be automated. But, in practice, since all development is driven by self-interest, it is entirely focused on producing advantages local to single or small groups of participants, not on producing a uniform platform for automation of commerce between participants that benefits all and none in particular.

A commerce model typically includes activities such as advertising, searching, negotiating, ordering, delivering, paying, using, and servicing (Fig.1, next page).

Storefronts and search engines offer Internet-wide search and negotiation, although not with much precision. Future developments of metadata, e.g., based on the W3C RDF/XML (Resource Description Framework mapped onto XML) [6], will increase precision. But to facilitate automation, and offer sufficient expressiveness, the metadata framework has to be based on uniform design principles.

Progress can be made without metadata. The web-based service (shopbot) Jango [1] (now part of Excite [13]) provides a simple interface for searching and ordering from a number of storefronts, thus serving as a kind of an integrating "meta-shop". Its operators use tools that automate the creation of interfaces to the web based storefronts, to simplify this otherwise arduous task. If information and interaction were standardized, the creation of a Jango-like service would be a much simpler, almost trivial, task, and more attention could instead be placed on domain specific value-adding services.

Other services, e.g., auctions, also include negotiation mechanisms. If this trend is taken further, a single site could provide for all activities desired, a one site globally accessible marketplace, owned and controlled by a single participant. This is clearly strongly in conflict with the ideals of free markets.

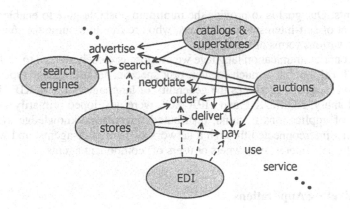

Fig. 1. Electronic commerce on the Internet

While EDI (Electronic Document Interchange [14]) offers standards for information and interaction between trading partners, current EDI standards are intended for use in static long-term relationships on the basis of detailed trading partner agreements, not for spontaneous commerce on the Internet.

A number of object-oriented platforms have been proposed for building distributed commerce applications integrated with the web. The most ambitious effort to date is perhaps the CommerceNet eCo System project [5], aiming to develop an architectural framework compatible with all major Internet commerce platforms. Interaction between agents in a Common Business Language (CBL) is suggested, but insufficient information is available to make a comparison with the framework presented here. Another similarity with the work presented here is the integration of web clients and servers with distributed objects augmenting web-based interaction, in a manner analogous to our proposal for web-aware agents.

2.2 Agent-Assisted Commerce

We propose a framework based on the notion of agents, software components owned and controlled by the participants, which provide assistance to a range of market activities by interacting with the agents of other participants. Agents share a common language, a formalized subset of commerce communication, but are otherwise unrestricted in their behavior.

Anthony Chaves, Pattie Maes, et al, at MIT Media Lab have developed an agent-based market called Kasbah [4]. Users may assign the task of buying or selling a specified good to an agent, which then performs negotiation and settlement of deals, fully automatically, according to the users' choice of predefined strategy. The system has served a useful platform for experiments with groups of users [10], but was never intended to be a general market infrastructure, and hence does not offer distribution nor general information or interaction models.

The Stanford [11] and University of Michigan [12] Digital Library projects both employ agent-based architectures. These are strongly influenced by a top-down hierarchical view of system design, a priori subdividing responsibilities into a number of components. Our goal is to provide the minimum possible glue to enable automation of a market of self-interested participants, who are free to assume the rôles of buyers, sellers, or various forms of mediators.

The agent communication language we propose is closely related to KQML [7] and FIPA ACL [8], but has a much smaller, task specific, set of message types. Similarly, our content language sacrifices the generality of languages such as KIF [15] for simplicity. Notably, KQML/KIF and FIPA ACL were developed primarily with a different class of applications in mind, distributed information/knowledge systems, with components interconnected through a network of facilitator agents, and with no concern for the self-interest of (owners or users of) component agents.

2.3 Motivating Applications

The SICS MarketSpace framework and infrastructure is being developed for and together with the following concrete applications (in close collaboration with Telia Research):

1) An agent-based marketplace for consumer goods and services, complementing, and emphasizing integration with, web-based commerce.
2) An agent-based workflow system for market-based organizations, which supports the dynamic generation of workflows from a market of available activities.

The examples in this paper pertain to the first of these domains.

3   The Information Model

3.1   Contracts and Interests

Our information model is based on the assumption that the goal of the activities of participants in a market is to close deals. As our basic information unit we choose the *contract*, for our purposes a structured document (see Fig.2). To assist the process of identifying which deals are possible, participants will, through their agents, exchange *interests*, which are (representations of) sets of contracts. Participants can use interests to advertise their true goals of buying or selling, or just reveal approximations of their true goals to enable an initial contact. Interests can be used both for communication and for the user models of user agents.

3.2   Example Interests

The following interests are easily expressed in terms of sets of contracts.

- Buy things cheaper than $1
- Buy pizza within an hour
- Sell these books
- Buy books on software agents

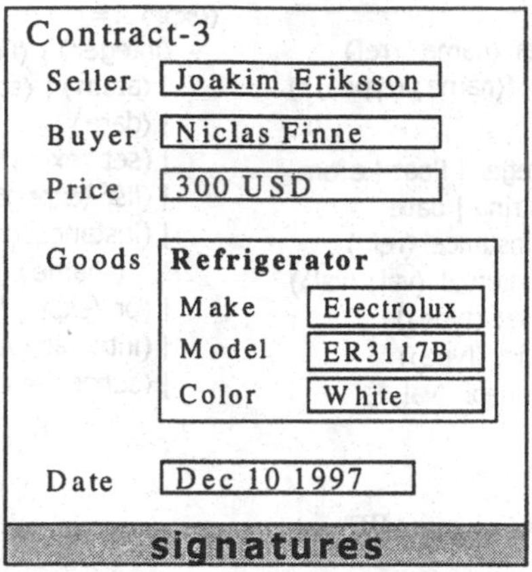

Fig. 2. A contract represented as a structured document

For example, the interest that I would like to buy something for a price of less than \$1 is the set of contracts such that I am the buyer of a good (or service) and the price is less than \$1. That I want something within an hour is a restriction on the date (a field in a contract type). And so on.

Requirements of the following more general kind

- Environmentally friendly
- What Joe (Jill) likes

may be captured as relations to other agents, which can be asked if they share a certain interest.

3.3 Concepts and Ontologies

Contracts are defined in terms of *concepts* (the record types that are the building blocks of the structured documents), which in their turn are defined in *ontologies* (collections/modules of concept definitions).

Concept identifiers are URLs, referring to concepts as local names in ontologies. Thus, a concept identifier "http://somesite.dom/basic.ont#contract-3" refers to a definition of "contract-3" in"http://somesite.dom/basic.ont". Concepts only serve as building blocks of structured documents, no semantic information is attached to a definition other than the types of its components. They play the rôle of records in programming languages.

For certain tasks, agents will need to have knowledge of some concepts built in. For example, agents will typically need to know how to contact the agent of a person who has published a certain interest. More specialized agents will have knowledge of product categories and know how to negotiate the price its user is willing to pay for a given quality. For other tasks, it is only necessary that users use the same concepts, or rely on services to bridge differences due to insufficient standardization, since they are only there to be matched against, not understood.

```
⟨def⟩ ::=                          ⟨expr⟩ ::=
    (def ⟨name⟩ ⟨ref⟩                  ⟨integer⟩ | ⟨float⟩ |
         (⟨name⟩ ⟨type⟩))*)            | ⟨atom⟩ | ⟨string⟩
⟨type⟩ ::=                             | ⟨date⟩
    integer | float | atom             | (set ⟨expr⟩*)
    | string | date                    | (list ⟨expr⟩*)
    | (instance ⟨ref⟩)                 | (instance ⟨ref⟩
    | (interval ⟨val⟩ ⟨val⟩)               (⟨name⟩ ⟨expr⟩))*)
    | (set ⟨type⟩)                     | (or ⟨expr⟩*)
    | (list ⟨type⟩)                    | (interval ⟨val⟩ ⟨val⟩)
    | (oneof ⟨val⟩*)                   | (subset ⟨expr⟩*)
```

Fig. 3. The Market Interest Format (MIF)

The semantics and pragmatics of concepts will need to evolve both through formal and informal processes of standardization. They will only be reflected in the interpretation given to contracts by humans and in the behavior built into agents.

3.4 Encoding Interests

An interest is a set of contracts. By an *expression of interest* we mean a representation of an interest, in some language. Several possible languages could be used for encoding interests. In particular, the content languages KIF [15] and SL [8] from the KQML and FIPA ACL communities could be used. However, in their most general form KIF and SL are not computationally tractable, and well-defined proposals for useful subsets do not yet exist.

We propose initially to use simpler formats for describing structured documents. It is possible that W3C RDF/XML (Resource Description Framework mapped onto XML) [6] will become general enough to serve our purpose, but this is not yet available. To avoid working against a moving target, we are using a simple custom design language, the Market Interest Format (MIF).

3.5 The Market Interest Format (MIF)

The Market Interest Format is a simple frame language in Lisp syntax (Fig.3 above). As basic types, it offers numbers, symbols (atoms), strings and dates, and as composite types concepts (frames), sets, lists, and enumerations. When expressing an interest, basic types may be given as values or intervals (ranges), sets and lists may be given with any expression as elements, instances of concepts may be given with any subset of attributes, alternatives may be given for any value, and subsets may be given for set types.

In Fig.4 (next page) are shown abbreviated examples of a MIF definition, which should be located in an appropriate ontology, and a MIF expression of interest, which could be an interest known to and stored in a user agent or the content of a message.

```
(def car "trade-object"
    (color (instance "pantone-color"))
    ...)
(instance "contract-3"
    (date (interval 1/1/98 6/30/98))
    (buyer (instance "person"
            (name "Joe Smith")
            (agent-address ...)))
    (goods (instance "car"
            (color (instance "red"))))))
```

Fig. 4. A MIF definition and expression

The expression of interest says that Joe Smith is the buyer of a red car in a contract signed between 1/1/98 and 6/30/98. This could, for example, be used by Joe to advertise such an interest, or by the agent handling it to respond to incoming queries.

Note that we will assume that agent addresses are associated with the descriptions of the participants named in the contract. This eliminates the need for separate mechanisms for advertising interests and the addresses for agents.

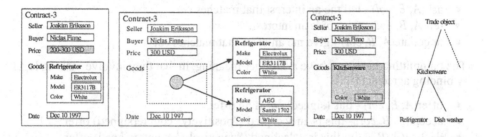

Fig. 5. Visualizations of MIF expressions. The leftmost illustrates intervals, the middle illustrates alternatives, and the rightmost illustrates generalization in a hierarchy of concepts.

MIF is designed with simple visual presentation of interests in mind (see Fig.5). Although users are not expected to enter their interests only in terms of structured documents (see Section 5.4), it is necessary that users are able to understand what they may reveal about themselves to other agents.

4 The Interaction Model

4.1 The Market Interaction Language (MIL)

The Market Interaction Language (MIL) is an agent communication language in the same family as KQML [7] and FIPA ACL [8], and shares with these its Common Lisp based serial syntax. (See Fig.6 next page for an example.)

```
(offer
    :from "map://onesite.dom/agent1"
    :to "map://othersite.dom/agent2"
    :in-reply-to i
    :reply-with j
    :language "MIF 1.0"
    :content "<MIF expression>"
)
```

Fig. 6. An example of a Market Interaction Language (MIL) message. The fields *from*, *to*, *in-reply-to*, *reply-with*, *language*, and *content* correspond to the fields with the same names in KQML. MIL expects references to ontologies to be part of the content language.

Below is an overview of message types (in an abstract syntax where A is the sender, B the receiver, and *eoi* an expression of interest which is the content of the message), The six message types fall into two groups, the noncommitting messages used for searching and advertising, and the committing messages used for negotiation.

The noncommitting messages follow with an informal description of their intended meaning.

- ask(A, B, *eoi*) - tell me an interest that matches *eoi*
- tell(A, B, *eoi*) - this *eoi* is an interest.
- negotiate(A, B, *eoi*) - give me an offer that matches *eoi*

The committing messages have a stronger meaning, in that they involve making legally binding agreements.

- offer(A, B, *eoi*) - this (signed) *eoi* is an offer
- accept(A, B, *eoi*) - this is an accepted ("positively" countersigned) offer
- decline(A, B, *eoi*) - this is a declined ("negatively" countersigned) offer

Note that these message types allow agents to forward offers, etc., made by other agents. This does not mean extending the offers to the new recipients. They serve as "for your information" messages, proving the existence of binding agreements.

4.2 Example

The following is a simple, but illustrational, conversation between A (an agent with the task to buy a refrigerator), D (a directory service), and B and C (refrigerator vendors). For simplicity, interests are written in English with a brief interpretation as part of the explanation of each message.

- ask(A, D, "sell me a refrigerator") – A asks the directory service D for interests matching an interest where A is the buyer and the good of type refrigerator
- tell(D, A, "B and C") – the directory service replies with an interest where A is the buyer of a refrigerator and B and C are possible vendors
- negotiate(A, B, "sell me a refrigerator") – A ask B for an offer matching an interest where A is the buyer of a refrigerator

- negotiate(A, C, "sell me a refrigerator") – A asks the same of C
- offer(B, A, "Electrolux 3117B for $350") – B gives A an offer (a signed interest) where B is the seller and A the buyer of a specific refrigerator at the price of $350
- offer(C, A, "Electrolux 3117B for $300") – C gives A the same offer but for the price of $300
- offer(A, B, "C sells for $300") – A prefers B as a vendor, and forwards C's offer to A to B, suggesting to B to match or improve on the offer
- offer(B, A, "Electrolux 3117B for $300") – B gives A an improved offer
- accept(A, B, "B's last offer") – A accepts B's offer
- decline(A, C, "C's offer") – A declines C's offer

By switching the rôles of buyer and seller in this example, we get an English auction style bidding procedure. The auctioneer sends negotiate messages to the participants to initiate bidding. Each bid is redistributed to the other participants. The auctioneer ends the auction by accepting the highest, and declining the rest. Similarly, and given that the parameters were known by the agents, we could emulate a simple form of Dutch auction by letting the auctioneer initiate bidding by a negotiate message, thereby starting the clock. Bids are required to be inversely proportional to the time when they are given. The auctioneer ends the auction by accepting the first valid bid. There are many other aspects to implementing auctions, but we believe that agent-agent communication in a wide range of auction types can be supported by MIL and MIF.

4.3 How to Talk to Whom?

By introducing several different interaction protocols, such as auctions, we introduce the problem of knowing and deciding how to talk to whom.

We have adopted the solution of associating the interaction protocol with the agent handling the interest. The expected protocol and its parameters is expressed in MIF and is associated with the agent address in interests. Several handler agents can be named that use different interaction protocols. This solution offers sufficient flexibility for our present purposes. The interaction protocol has to be known and the problem remains how to introduce new protocols into the agent-based market.

5 Integration with the Web

5.1 Agents and the Web

Seamless integration with the web is critical. The web is the way people access information and services on the Internet, now and in the forseeable future. Fig. 7 (next page) illustrates the basic setup for our integration of agents and the web.

The user has two browser windows, one (small) for interacting with the user agent, another for accessing the web interface of services. When the user accesses agent augmented services through the web, the user agent is informed (e.g., using JavaScript) and is given the opportunity to contact the service and assist the user.

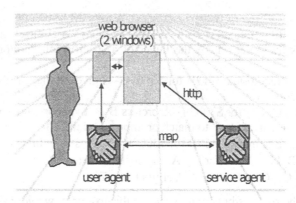

Fig. 7. Interaction between agents and the web. (MAP is the Market Agent Protocol for plain TCP/IP transmission of messages between agents.)

5.2 Personalized Services

The scheme for integration with the web also allows for personalization upon first contact. (1) The user accesses the service via the web browser. (2) The service sends a "redirect" web page containing service agent contact code whereafter it awaits a first contact from the user agent. (3) The web browser sends the contact code to the user agent, which contacts the service agent. (4) The service agent is notified about the user's current interest and generates a suitable personalized page.

5.3 The Agent Browser

The (small) agent browser window is the user interface to the user agent. It will typically reside on a contiuously running server to never be off-line, while the agent browser may run on any machine. The agent browser offers functions such as creating, editing, and viewing interests, manually sending and receiving messages, and assigning sub-agents (with unique addresses and possibly different protocols) to handle the interests. Interest handling agents have their own user interfaces for setting user preferences, supervising progress, and for reporting results upon completion of the task.

5.4 Services that Generate Interests

The interest editor in the agent browser is a general editor for structured documents, and not all that intuitive for describing specialized interests. As a complement to this we envisage a plethora of agent augmented web-based services that specialize in offering tools for describing cars, houses, etc (see Fig. 8, next page). The completed interest is delivered to the user agent by agent communication at the request of the user.

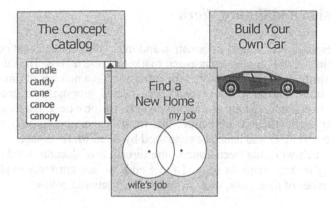

Fig. 8. Services on the web for creating interests. A simple service of the first form is available in the current prototype.

5.5 The SICS MarketSpace Prototype

The current SICS MarketSpace prototype was developed entirely in Java. (An earlier prototype was developed in Prolog [2,3,9].) It consists of:

- A personal assistant agent allowing the user to describe his/her interests in terms of structured documents, interact directly with other agents, and access agent augmented web services.
- Two agent augmented web shops, which generate personalized pages (show special offers relevant to the user's current interests).
- A directory service, which allows user and service agents to register interests and find agents with matching interests.
- An agent augmented web-based interest description service that allows users to describe their interests in terms of suitable MIF concepts. Completed interests are sent to and stored in the user agent.

The prototype is based on the SICS JavaBase library for implementing web- and internet-aware agent based systems. It consists of classes for:

- communication in MIL (and KQML)
- reading, writing, matching, typechecking MIF
- web clients and servers
- miscellaneous other Internet formats and protocols
- examples: web page objects, web file servers, cgi scripting, negotiating agents, interest directories, auctions, simple assistants

SICS JavaBase is available from the authors for non-commercial purposes, with the usual caveats for experimental research software.

6 Discussion and Future Work

We have presented very simple information and interaction models that could serve as a starting point for creating an agent based market infrastructure. The design strongly emphasizes simplicity and leaves room for extensions in a number of directions.

In this volume can be found several sophisticated proposals for market mechanisms, agent behaviour, and agent-user interaction. To the extent that these works deal with agent-agent interaction, we believe that most of them could be implemented in terms of MIF and MIL, and hence be supported by SICS MarketSpace.

But, not much work has been done in the direction of decentralized markets, and we expect higher requirements soon. To this end, we are currently exploring extensions in a number of directions, three of which are discussed below.

6.1 Interests with Preferences

MIF currently allows interests to be expressed as sets of contracts. No preferences in this set can be expressed. This is a concious design choice. Interests are not intended to reveal more information than necessary to enable participants with matching interests to find oneanother. Negotiation will locate the mutually preferred deals. A user's preferences are expressed to the agent that performs negotiation.

However, we may wish to delegate this task to a mediator, in which case we need to express our priorities. For this purpose, we are exploring representations supporting utility functions and/or uncertainty.

6.2 Openness to New Interaction Protocols

MIL provides a basic vocabulary for market interaction. Together with the convention that interaction protocols can be named and parameters given as parts of interests, considerably flexibility is achieved. But, the interaction protocols have to be known beforehand, and MIL cannot express every possible statement in market interaction.

We are exploring a new architecture that uses interaction protocol plugins, which are retrieved dynamically as needed. The problem is moved from agent-agent protocols to agent-plugin interfaces. If plugins can be trusted, these interfaces can be made very simple and generic for large classes of protocols.

6.3 Openness to New Information Formats

Once the ability to download trusted components is available, the interest format standard, MIF, can be replaced by an information interface standard, making the benefits of object-oriented programming available to agent based systems, but not in the form of distributed objects, nor in the form of mobile agents.

In this view, MIF is replaced by GOF (the Generic Object Format), the purpose of which is to provide a global namespace of record types, for which the record definition and its properties (the ontology) can be retrieved using the name as a URL, as in MIF, possibly the smallest possible foundation for agent based computing.

References

1. The Jango shopbot. See http://www.jango.com.

2. Joakim Eriksson, Niclas Finne, and Sverker Janson. Information and interaction in MarketSpace. In *2nd USENIX Workshop on Electronic Commerce*. USENIX Press, 1997.

3. Joakim Eriksson and Niclas Finne. MarketSpace: an open agent-based market infrastructure. Master's Thesis. Swedish Institute of Computer Science, 1997.

4. Anthony Chavez and Pattie Maes. Kasbah: An Agent Marketplace for Buying and Selling Goods. In *Proceedings of PAAM'96*. Practical Applications Company, 1996.

5. Jay M. Tenenbaum. eCo System: CommerceNet's Architectural Framework for Internet Commerce. White Paper. See http://www.commerce.net/eco/.

6. W3C Resource Description Framework. See http://www.w3.org/Metadata/RDF/.

7. Yannis Labrou and Tim Finin. *A proposal for a new KQML specification*. UMBC Technical Report, 1997. See http://www.csee.umbc.edu/~jklabrou/publications/tr9703.ps.

8. FIPA ACL. Foundation of Intelligent Physical Agents. Agent Communication Language. See http://drogo.cselt.stet.it/fipa/spec/fipa97.htm.

9. Joakim Eriksson, Niclas Finne, Sverker Janson, et al. An Internet software platform based on SICStus Prolog. In *WWW6 workshop "Logic Programming and the Web"*. See http://www.cs.vu.nl/~eliens/WWW6/papers/joakime/.

10. Chavez, D. Dreilinger, R. Guttman, and P. Maes. A Real-Life Experiment in Creating an Agent Marketplace. In *Proceedings of PAAM'97*. Practical Applications Company, 1997.

11. Stanford Digital Library Project. See http://www-diglib.stanford.edu/.

12. University of Michigan Digital Library (UMDL) Project. See http://http2.sils.umich.edu/UMDL/.

13. Excite – Search Engine. See http://www.excite.com.

14. Getting Started with EDI. See http://www.premenos.com/edi/edi.html.

15. Knowledge Interchange Format Specification. See http://logic.stanford.edu/kif/specification.html.

Sequencing of Contract Types for Anytime Task Reallocation

Martin R. Andersson and Tuomas W. Sandholm[1]

{mra, sandholm}@cs.wustl.edu
Department of Computer Science
Washington University
One Brookings Drive
St. Louis, MO 63130-4899
Phone: +1-314-935-6160

Abstract. Task (re)allocation is a key problem in multiagent systems. Several different contract types have been introduced to be used for task reallocation: original, cluster, swap, and multiagent contracts. Instead of only using one of these contract types, they can be interleaved in a sequence of contract types. This is a powerful way of constructing algorithms that find the best solution reachable in a bounded amount of time. The experiments in this paper study how to best sequence the different contract types.

We show that the number of contracts performed using any one contract type does not necessarily decrease over time as one might expect. The reason is that contracts often play the role of enabling further contracts. The results also show that it is clearly profitable for the agents to mix contract types in the sequence. Sequences of different contract types reach a solution significantly closer to the global optimum and in a shorter amount of time than sequences with only one contract type. However, the best sequences consist only of two interleaved contract types: original and cluster contracts. This allows us to provide a clear prescription about protocols for anytime task reallocation.

Keywords: Multiagent systems, Performance profiles, Negotiation, Contracting, Task allocation

1 Introduction

The importance of automated negotiation systems is increasing as a consequence of the development of technology as well as increased application pull, *e.g.*, vehicle routing systems [13] and electronic commerce [8, 18]. A central part of such systems is the ability for the agents to reallocate their tasks. Generally, the tasks have a dependency upon each other, as well as upon the agents. That is, some of the tasks are synergistic and preferably handled by the same agent,

---

[1] Supported by NSF CAREER award IRI-9703122 and NSF grant IRI-9610122.

whereas others interact negatively and are better handled by different agents. The agents also have different resources that lead to different costs for handling the various tasks.[2] Furthermore, all of the agents may not be capable of handling all of the various tasks. Definition 1 is a formal definition of the task allocation problem that includes the properties discussed above and on which the discussion herein is based.

Definition 1. Our *task allocation problem* [16] is defined by a set of tasks T, a set of agents A, a cost function $c_i : 2^T \to \Re \cup \{\infty\}$ (which states the cost that agent i incurs by handling a particular subset of tasks), and the initial allocation of tasks among agents $\langle T_1^{init}, ..., T_{|A|}^{init} \rangle$, where $\bigcup_{i \in A} T_i^{init} = T$, and $T_i^{init} \cap T_j^{init} = \emptyset$ for all $i \neq j$.[3]

In the case where agent i cannot handle a specific set of tasks, T_i, the cost function c_i takes the value infinity. In our example problem the agents incur different costs for handling the tasks, but all the agents have the capability to handle any task. The agents in the example problem are *self-interested* and *myopically individually rational*. This means that an agent agrees to a contract if and only if the contract increases the agent's immediate payoff which consists of the side payments received from other agents (for handling their tasks) minus the cost c_i of handling tasks. Recently, new types of contracts were introduced [13, 15, 16] to be used in contract nets [21]. Earlier research has applied each of these contracts to a task allocation problem and found the local optima they reach [1, 4, 5]. In order to improve the achievable social welfare, these contract types can be sequenced in a number of different ways. In this paper the entire negotiation is divided into five *intervals*, and in each interval only one of the contract types is used. In this manner performance profiles for all possible sequences of contract types are created.

The example problem is the same multiagent TSP that has been used in earlier work by Andersson and Sandholm [1, 3, 4, 5]. It is defined in Section 2. A summary of the contract types and how they are sequenced is found in Section 3, followed by the algorithm used to solve the problem, Section 4. In Section 5 the results are presented and Section 6 concludes the paper.

2 Example Problem

The multiagent TSP is defined as follows [1, 2, 3, 4]: Several salesmen will visit several cities in a world that consists of a unit square (square with sides of length one), see Figure 1. Each city must be visited by exactly one salesman, and each

---

[2] The dependencies between tasks in human negotiations are discussed in [11]. The concepts of linkage and log-rolling are also presented, which are similar to swapping tasks and clustering tasks.

[3] This definition generalizes the "Task Oriented Domain" presented by Rosenschein and Zlotkin [12] by allowing different cost functions among agents, and the possibility of some agent not being able to handle some task sets (corresponds to infinite costs).

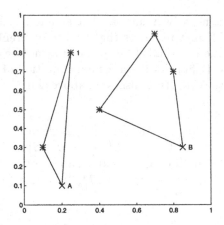

Fig. 1. *An example problem instance of a multiagent TSP consisting of five cities (*) and two salesmen (X). If salesman A contracts out city 1 to salesman B, the social welfare will increase due to less travel, i.e., lower costs.*

salesman must return to his starting location after visiting the cities assigned to him. A salesman can visit the cities assigned to him in any order.

The outcome of the system is the social welfare, *i.e.*, the negative of the sum of all the salesmen's costs (distances traveled). Initially the location of the cities and starting points of the salesmen are randomly chosen as is each salesman's initial assignment of cities to visit. After this initial assignment, the salesmen can exchange cities with each other. The payoff of a salesman consists of the side payments received from other salesmen (as compensation for handling their tasks) minus the side payments paid to other salesmen (to compensate them for handling some of this agent's tasks) minus the cost of travel, c_i. As discussed above, the salesmen are individually rational and myopic, which means that they agree to a contract if and only if the contract increases the salesman's immediate payoff. Therefore, in the case of full commitment protocols, the sum of all salesmen's total distance traveled decreases monotonically, *i.e.* social welfare increases monotonically.

2.1 Objectives of the Agents

The cost c_{qr} of traveling between locations q and r (either city or location of salesman) equals the Euclidean distance between the locations. The total cost each salesman incurs, c_i, when visiting his cities, is the sum of the costs along his tour:

$$c_i = \sum_{\substack{q \text{ and } r \text{ that} \\ \text{are consecutive} \\ \text{cities on the tour} \\ \text{of salesman } i}} c_{qr} \qquad (1)$$

The objective of agent i is to maximize payments received from others (for handling their tasks or from incurred decommitment penalties) minus the agent's own total cost of traveling, c_i, and the decommitment penalties paid. The social welfare is given by the negative of the sum of all agents' total costs, $-\sum_i c_i$. Neither side payments nor decommitment penalties affect the social welfare as they merely redistribute wealth among agents. In the following discussion the general multiagent task allocation terms, "agent" and "task" will be used instead of the TSP specific terms "salesman" and "city".

3 Contracts and Sequencing of Contracts

The contract most commonly used in multiagent contracting systems only allows for one task to move from one agent to another at a time [20, 21]. We will refer to this type as an *original* (O) contract. In order to allow for more efficient contracting, four new types of contracts have been introduced [13, 15, 16]: *cluster, swap,* and *multiagent contracts,* and all the above, including the original contracts, combined (*OCSM-contracts*). All of these new contract types allow more than one task to be transferred between the agents participating in the contract.

In this paper different sequences of the elementary contract types, *i.e.,* original, cluster, swap, and multiagent contracts are studied. The total time of contracting is divided into five intervals. In each of these intervals any of these contract types could be applied. All possible combinations of sequences of contract types were investigated, that is, all the $4 \times 4 \times 4 \times 4 \times 4 = 1024$ sequences of contract types were applied to all TSP instances.

In each interval, all contracts that are possible to construct with the contract type in question were tried.[4] Because of this, the length of the intervals varied for different contract types and task allocations. A contract was only performed if it was individually rational to all the agents participating in the contract.

The contracts included in the empirical study are described in the following sections. They are followed by a technical description of the sequencing of the contracts within each interval.

3.1 Original Contracts (O-contracts)

The most common contracts used in contract net implementations and analyses of contracting games are contracts in which only one task is considered at a time. These O-contracts are conducted between two agents where one task is transferred from one of the agents to another. A side payment may be paid between the agents to compensate the party that is worse off after the transfer of the task, *i.e.,* the agent taking on the task will be paid to do so. Formally, O-contracts are defined as follows:

Definition 2. [16] An *O-contract* is defined by a pair $\langle T_{i,j}, \rho_{i,j} \rangle$, where $|T_{i,j}| = 1$. $T_{i,j}$ is the task set (including one task) that agent i gives to agent j, and $\rho_{i,j}$ is the contract price that i pays to j for handling the task set.

---

[4] The possible contracts depend on the current allocation of tasks among the agents.

If the agents carry out a full lookahead, *i.e.*, consider the tree of all possible sequences of future contracts, these O-contracts would suffice to reach the globally optimal task allocation [16]. However, this generally cannot be accomplished, except for small problem instances, because of the complexity of exploring the tree of future contracts. On the other hand, the global optimum is not necessarily reached if the agents are individually rational and myopic when contracting. Such agents may get stuck in a local optimum since they will not accept a temporary decrease of their payoffs, which may be necessary to reach the global optimum. Individually rational contracting can be seen as hill-climbing in the task allocation space, where there is a risk of being trapped in a local optimum, and not reaching the globally optimal task allocation.

3.2 Cluster Contracts (C-contracts)

Cluster contracts allow the agents to exchange more than one task in each contract. We define a C-contract as a contract where at least two tasks are moved from one agent to another agent, potentially together with a side payment:

Definition 3. [16] A *cluster contract (C-contract)* is defined by a pair $\langle T_{i,j}, \rho_{i,j} \rangle$, where $|T_{i,j}| > 1$. $T_{i,j}$ is the task set that agent i gives to agent j, and $\rho_{i,j}$ is the contract price that i pays to j for handling the task set.

C-contracts avoid some of the local optima that O-contracts do not avoid, while at the same time, O-contracts avoid some of the local optima that C-contracts do not avoid. If the agents are individually rational and myopic, neither O- nor C-contracts, applied alone or together, are sufficient for reaching a global optimum in the space of task allocations [16]. This holds for C-contracts even if the agents can carry out lookahead instead of being myopic.[5]

3.3 Swap Contracts (S-contracts)

Even when both O-contracts and C-contracts are used, there may be other contract types that increase the social welfare even more, since the best that is reached via O- and C-contracts solution may be a local optimum. For example, there may be beneficial swaps of tasks to be made between two agents. In a swap contract, one agent gives one task to another agent and at the same time it receives a task from the same agent. A side payment may also be paid between the agents to compensate for any value difference between the tasks. Formally:

Definition 4. [16] A *swap contract (S-contract)* is defined by a 4-tuple $\langle T_{i,j}, T_{j,i}, \rho_{i,j}, \rho_{j,i} \rangle$, where $|T_{i,j}| = |T_{j,i}| = 1$. $T_{i,j}$ is the task set (including one task) that agent i gives to agent j. $T_{j,i}$ is the task set (including one task) that agent j gives to agent i. $\rho_{i,j}$ is the amount that i pays to j, and $\rho_{j,i}$ is the amount that j pays to i.

---

[5] In the auction of airwave bandwidth, the Federal Communication Commission used a simultaneous ascending auction to provide for the bidders the possibility to cluster the frequencies for which they were bidding, without explicit cluster contracts [10].

S-contracts, applied alone or together with one or both of the O- and C-contracts, are necessary but not sufficient for reaching the global optimum when the agents are individually rational and myopic [16]. The same holds for S-contracts alone even if the agents are not myopic. Also, S-contracts have a different set of local optima than O- and C-contracts.

3.4 Multiagent Contracts (M-contracts)

We define M-contracts as contract where at least three tasks are transferred between at least three agents. To differ from cluster contracts, no agent can give more than one task to the same agent, but an agent can give tasks to several different agents as well as receive tasks from several different agents. Side payments may be paid along with the tasks. Formally:

Definition 5. [16] A *multiagent contract (M-contract)* is defined by a pair $\langle \mathbf{T}, \rho \rangle$ of $|A| \times |A|$ matrices, where at least three elements of $\mathbf{T}$ are non-empty (otherwise this would be just a 2-agent contract), and for all i and j, $|T_{i,j}| \leq 1$. An element $T_{i,j}$ is the set of tasks that agent i gives to agent j, and an element $\rho_{i,j}$ is the amount that i pays to j.

M-contracts are also necessary but not sufficient for reaching the global optimum. This also holds for any combination of the contract types (O-, C-, S-, and M-contracts) discussed above [16]. If O-contracts are not included in such a combination, the statement holds even if the agents were able to carry out full lookahead. In these experiments the maximum number of agents $|A|$ participating in an M-contract was limited to three and each agent could only transfer one task to one other agent, $\sum_i |T_{i,j}| = 1$. These limitations were introduced so that the length of the intervals would be of the same order. If all possible M-contracts (with any $|A|$ and $|T|$) were to be checked in each interval, that interval would be much longer than the intervals for the other contract types [4].[6]

3.5 Sequencing of Contracts within an Interval

When searching for a good task allocation, the contract types used in the negotiation are applied repeatedly for all possible combinations of agents and tasks that suit the contract type. The local optimum is reached when no contracts of that type have been made for one period, that is, all possible contracts have been tried but none have been performed. In the following subsections the order of trying different contracts within each contract type is discussed. The agents are enumerated from 1 to $|A|$, and each agent's tasks from 1 to $|T_i|$.

---

[6] Sathi and Fox (1989) [19] studied a simpler version of multiagent contracts where bids were grouped into cascades.

Sequencing of Original Contracts An O-contract allows one agent to move one task to one other agent. In our experiments we sequenced the O-contracts as follows. First, agent 1's tasks are attempted to be moved, one at a time, to agent 2. If any contract (move of a task) is profitable, it is performed and the next contract is tried. After having tried to move all tasks (one at a time) from agent 1 to 2, agent 1 tries to move its tasks to agent 3. This continues until agent 1 has attempted to move all its tasks to all the other agents. Then the procedure continues with agent 2, which tries to move its tasks to agent 1, followed by all the other agents in increasing order. When agent $|A|$ has attempted to move all its tasks to all the other agents this interval is finished and the negotiation process is continued with the next contract type.

Sequencing of Cluster Contracts In an C-contract one agent moves at least two tasks to one other agent, and C-contracts were sequenced as follows. We start by trying out all combinations of two tasks followed by all combinations of three tasks, and so on.[7] If any contract is profitable, it is performed and the next contract is tried. After having tried to move all tasks (one at a time) from agent 1 to 2, agent 1 tries to move its tasks to agent 3. This continues until agent 1 has attempted to move all its tasks to all the other agents. Then the procedure continues with agent 2, which tries to move its tasks to agent 1, followed by all the other agents in increasing order. When agent $|A|$ has attempted to move its tasks to all other agents, this interval is finished and the negotiation process continues with the next contract type.

Sequencing of Swap Contracts In an S-contract, one agent transfers one task to another agent and it also receives one task from that agent. S-contracts were sequenced as follows. One at a time, agent 1 tries to move its tasks to agent 2, and in exchange agent 2 tries to move one task to agent 1. For every task agent 1 tries to move, agent 2 tries to move all its tasks to agent 1 (one at a time), before agent 1 continues with its next task. If any contract, *i.e.*, move of tasks, is profitable it is performed and the next contract is tried. When all contracts that include agent 1 and agent 2 have been attempted, all possible contracts including agent 1 and agent 3 are tried according to the procedure above. When agent 1 has attempted all contracts with all the other agents, agent 2 tries all contracts, according to the procedure above, with agent 1 followed by the other agents in increasing order. When agent $|A|$ has attempted to exchange tasks with all other agents, this interval is finished and the negotiation process is continued with the next contract type.

Sequencing of Multiagent Contracts In an M-contract three tasks are moved between three agents, and each agent can only move one task to one other agent. A discussion about how the agents participating in M-contracts are

---

[7] The order in which the tasks are tried to be moved is: $(1,2)$, $(1,3)$, $\ldots$, $(1, |T_1|)$, $(2,3)$, $(2,4)$, $\ldots$, $(|T_1|\text{-}1, |T_1|)$, $(1,2,3)$, $(1,2,4)$, $\ldots$

selected is followed by a description about how the tasks among those agents are chosen.

First, all combinations which include agent 1 are tried[8] until all combinations have been tried successively for all agents and then the interval is completed. Before the next combination of agents is tried all combinations of task transfers[9] are tried for the current combination of agents. When all combinations have been tried, or after a contract has been performed the next combination of agents is considered.

4 Algorithms and Evaluation

In principle the implementation of a contracting system can solve the multia-gent optimization TSP for any number of agents and tasks. In the simulations, the problem instances consisted of eight agents and eight tasks. One thousand randomly generated TSP instances were solved (initial locations of cities and start locations for the salesmen in each TSP instance were randomly chosen in the Euclidean unit square). Each problem instance was solved for each of the *protocols* (*i.e.* sequences of contract types) in the simulation. In addition, an exhaustive enumeration of task allocations was conducted in order to find the globally optimal allocation.

4.1 Algorithms for Solving the TSP

In the experiments, each problem instance was tackled in two phases: first all possible TSPs (*i.e.* TSPs with any of the salesmen getting any combination of cities to visit[10]) were solved and then simulations using different contracting protocols were conducted to solve the task allocation problem. This way the agents did not have to recalculate the TSPs every time a different contracting algorithm (protocol) was applied on the same problem instance. The IDA* search algorithm [9] was used to solve the TSPs. To ensure that the optimal solution was reached, an admissible $\hat{h}$-function was used. It was constructed by under-estimating the cost function of the remaining nodes by the minimum spanning tree of those nodes, *i.e.*, nodes not yet on that path of the search tree, the last city of that path of the search tree, and the finish (=start) location of the salesman [7].

---

[8] They are tried in the following order: $(1,2,3)$, $(1,2,4)$, ..., $(1,2,|A|)$, $(1,3,2)$, $(1,3,4)$, ..., $(1,|A| - 1,|A|)$. When all those combinations have been tried, all combinations of agents including the next agent (agent 2) are tried: $(2,1,3)$, $(2,1,4)$, ..., $(2,1,|A|)$, $(2,3,1)$, $(2,3,4)$, ..., $(2,|A| - 1,|A|)$.

[9] The order in which the tasks are tried are (from the first agent to agent no., from the second agent to agent no., from the third agent to agent no.): $(2,1,1)$, $(2,1,2)$, $(2,3,1)$, $(2,3,2)$, $(3,1,1)$, $(3,1,2)$, $(3,3,1)$, $(3,3,2)$. If one of the agents does not have the task needed, that combination is skipped.

[10] Salesman 1 visits city 1, salesman 1 visits city 2,..., salesman 1 visits cities 1 and 2,..., salesman 2 visits city 1,..., salesman 8 visits all eight cities.

4.2 Evaluation Criteria

To be able to compare the different protocols, the ratio bound (ratio of the welfare of the obtained local optimum for a given contract type to the welfare of the global optimum) was used. The ratio bounds, CPU-time usage, number of contracts tried, and performed were calculated using an average over the 1000 problem instances. The variances for the listed measures were also computed in order to calculate the confidence intervals [6].

Let x_j^l denote the social welfare (negative sum of the agents' total costs) of the jth problem instance, $j \in 1, \ldots, n$ (n=1000), after task reallocation has been performed until a local optimum has been reached using contract type $l \in \{$O, C, S, M, G$\}$, where G indicates the global optimum (or equivalently OCSM-contracts). The ratio bound, r_j^l, for the jth problem instance using l-contracts is given by the ratio of the social welfare of the local optimum obtained using l-contracts over the social welfare of the global optimum:

$$r_j^l = \frac{x_j^l}{x_j^G}$$

The average of the ratio bounds of the different contract types $l \in \{$O, C, S, M$\}$ is:

$$\bar{r}^l = \frac{1}{n}\sum_{j=1}^{n} r_j^l$$

5 Results

In order to investigate which sequences of the contract types performed best, all the 1024 sequences studied were ordered according to ascending ratio bounds. The 15 best contracts, are shown in Table 1. The reached social welfare for the best sequences are very close to each other (Table 1 and Figure 2): the best protocol is 3.1% off the global optimum social welfare and the 12 best protocols are all between 3% and 4% off the global optimum. In a broader perspective 24 protocols are less than 5% off the optimum, and 181 less than 10%.

If the same contract type is applied in all the five intervals the social welfare will be much worse, see Table 2. The two worst sequences both consisted of only one contract type: S-, and M-contracts, respectively. The sequence with only O-contracts performed better, but is still not among the best half. The same is true for C-contracts, which after the five intervals still are doing worse than the O-contracts. In neither of these cases O- or C-contracts reached their local optima, so this result says that it is better to switch to another protocol even before reaching the local optima using one contract type. If the O- and C-contracts were allowed to continue their computation until a local optimum arises, C-contracts would be better than the O-contracts, with the ratio bounds 1.13557 and 1.2025, respectively [4]. This can also be seen if the curves in question for the two sequences are extrapolated in Figure 3. So even if the local optimum is

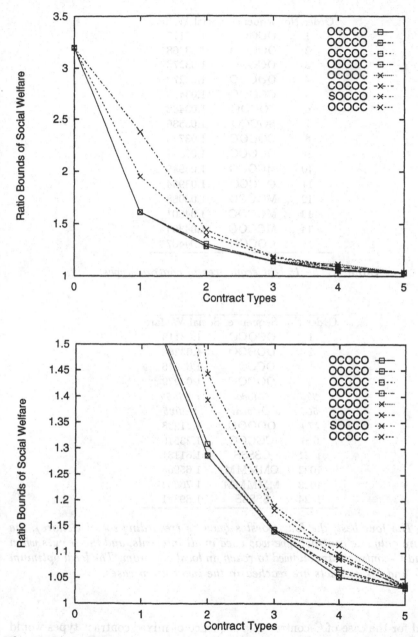

Fig. 2. *Ratio bound of social welfare (performance profiles). The bottom graph is a zoom of the top graph.*

Order No.	Sequence	Social Welfare
1	OCOCO	1.03113
2	OOCCO	1.03268
3	OCCOC	1.03276
4	OOCOC	1.03279
5	OCOOC	1.03413
6	SOCOC	1.03488
7	SOCCO	1.03536
8	COCOC	1.03755
9	OCOCC	1.03857
10	MCOCO	1.03945
11	OCCCO	1.03954
12	MOCCO	1.03988
13	MOCOC	1.04001
14	MCCOC	1.04304
15	COCCO	1.04407

Table 1. *The 15 best sequences of contract types.*

Order No.	Sequence	Social Welfare
1	OCOCO	1.03113
2	OOCCO	1.03268
3	OCCOC	1.03276
4	OOCOC	1.03279
375	*C-local*	*1.13557*
565	*O-local*	*1.2025*
579	OOOOO	1.21298
696	CCCCC	1.23515
1021	CSSSS	1.61181
1022	CMMMM	1.65965
1023	MMMMM	1.76634
1024	SSSSS	1.89321

Table 2. *The four best, the four worst sequences (regarding social welfare), the cases where only one contract type was used in all intervals, and the results when the O- and C-contracts are allowed to reach an local optimum. The local optimum for the S- and M-contracts are reached in the two bottom cases.*

computed for the case of C-contracts, a sequence of mixed contract types would achieve a lower result in a shorter amount of time. In Figure 3 we can see that the local optimum is already reached after the first and second interval with the S-, and M-contracts, respectively.

Studying the number of contracts tried and performed for the C-contracts (Figure 4) we can see that more contracts are tried and performed in the second interval than in the first interval (the curve is convex). This is because after the

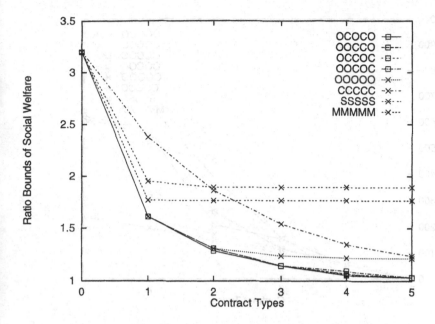

Fig. 3. *Ratio bound of social welfare (performance profiles) for the four best sequences and the cases in which only one contract type were applied.*

first interval of C-contracts the resulting task allocation makes more C-contracts possible to perform, because the C-contracts concentrate the tasks among a smaller number of agents [2]. In the subsequent intervals (of C-contracts) the number of individually rational C-contracts become fewer and fewer, resulting in fewer contracts being performed (curve is concave).

In Figure 5 we can see how the social welfare increases as more contracts are tried. The number of contracts tried for the different sequences differ greatly because of the varying task allocations among the agents and the different possible contracts to form with the different contract types. The expected diminishing returns with computation are also clearly illustrated in Figure 5.

The study shows the intuition that if two contract types are mixed in a sequence, the social welfare will never be worse than both of the social welfares obtained if the different contract types were not mixed. Also, the more mixture (not the same contract type applied several times in a row) between the contract types, the greater the social welfare will be. In fact, it is likely that if the social welfare for a mixed sequence is worse than the better social welfare of the the contract types applied alone, the mixed sequence consists mostly of one contract type.

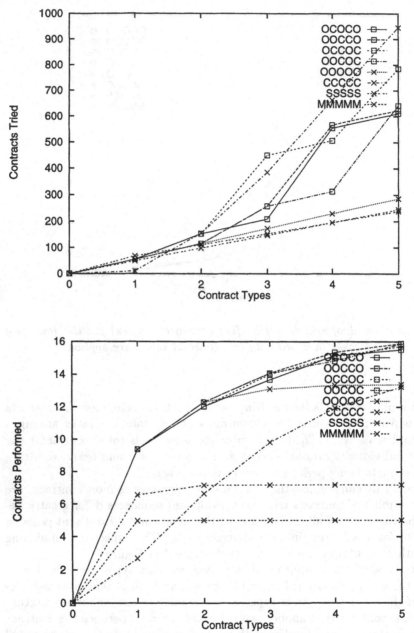

Fig. 4. *Contracts tried (top) and contracts performed (bottom) for the four best sequences and the cases in which only one contract type were applied.*

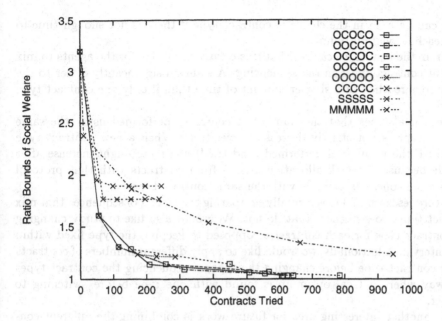

Fig. 5. *Ratio bound of social welfare (performance profiles) for the four best sequences and the cases in which only one contract type were applied.*

6 Conclusions

The current most widely used contract type allows for only one task to be moved from one agent to another at a time (O-contracts). Recently new contract types, cluster (C), swap (S), multiagent (M), and OCSM-contracts (all the other contract types combined) have been introduced. They are all based on the idea of moving several tasks in a single contract, which reduces the number of local optima in the search space of task allocations for hill-climbing-based contracting algorithms.

OCSM-contracts guarantee that a global optimum is reached in a finite number of steps when used in any hill-climbing algorithm. Although this is a powerful result for small problem instances, in large-scale problems the number of steps needed to reach the global optimum may be impractically large. In these problems it is more important to obtain the best achievable solution in a bounded amount of time than it is to reach the global optimum.

To be able to construct algorithms which obtain the best achievable solution in a bounded amount of time, we compared sequences of five contract types in an example problem: a multiagent version of the TSP. The results regarding the social welfare of the local optima of the different contract types provide guidelines to system builders regarding what contract types to use in different environments when computation is limited. We also presented timing results which can be used in the choice of contract type if there is not enough time to even reach a local optimum.

¿From the results we can see that it is clearly profitable for the agents to mix different contract types in the sequencing. A solution significantly closer to the optimum is reached in a shorter amount of time than if only one contract type is used.

We can also see that the number of contracts performed using the same contract type is not strictly decreasing over time. When a new contract type is applied, the number of performed (and tried) contracts might increase after a while because the task allocation arising from contracts with that protocol makes more contracts possible with the same contract type.

Future research includes formally comparing the results of sequences that mix contract types to sequences that do not. We would also like to study changing the contract type for each contract as opposed to keeping the type fixed within each interval. Additionally, we would like to apply different numbers of contracts of one contract type before changing the type, or sequencing the contract types in a way where a local optimum is found with one type before switching to another.

Yet another interesting area for future work is combining the different contract types, thus forming atomic contracts having characteristics of more than one of the O-, C-, S-, and M-contracts, but not all of them (unlike OCSM-contracts). These composite contract types would not guarantee that individually rational agents will reach the global optimal task allocation, but they would lead to a local optimum faster then OCSM-contracts, and to higher average social welfare than O-, C-, S-, or M-contracts.

Finally, we would like to study agents that may lie about their marginal costs of handling the task sets under negotiation [14, 12], and the use of backtracking in contracting, which is nontrivial to implement among self-interested agents [17].

References

1. M. R. Andersson. Performance of leveled commitment protocols for automated negotiation: An empirical study. Master's thesis, Royal Institute of Technology, Stockholm, Sweden, 1998.
2. M. R. Andersson and T. W. Sandholm. Contract types for optimal task allocation: II experimental results. Technical Report WUCS-97-36, Washington University, Department of Computer Science, 1997.
3. M. R. Andersson and T. W. Sandholm. Leveled commitment contracting among myopic individually rational agents. Technical Report WUCS-97-47, Washington University, Department of Computer Science, 1997.
4. M. R. Andersson and T. W. Sandholm. Contract types for satisficing task allocation: II experimental results. In *AAAI Spring Symposium Series: Satisficing Models*, pages 1–7, Stanford University, CA, Mar. 1998.
5. M. R. Andersson and T. W. Sandholm. Leveled commitment contracting among myopic individually rational agents. In *Proceedings of the Third International Conference on Multi-Agent Systems (ICMAS-98)*, Paris, France, July 1998.

6. P. R. Cohen. *Empirical Methods for Artificial Intelligence.* MIT Press, 1995.

7. T. H. Cormen, C. E. Leiserson, and R. L. Rivest. *Introduction to Algorithms.* MIT Press, 1990.

8. R. Kalakota and A. B. Whinston. *Frontiers of Electronic Commerce.* Addison-Wesley Publishing Company, Inc, 1996.

9. R. E. Korf. Depth-first iterative-deepening: an optimal admissible tree search. *Artificial Intelligence*, 27(1):97–109, 1985.

10. R. P. McAfee and J. McMillan. Analyzing the airwaves auction. *Journal of Economic Perspectives*, 10(1):159–175, 1996.

11. H. Raiffa. *The Art and Science of Negotiation.* Harvard Univ. Press, Cambridge, Mass., 1982.

12. J. S. Rosenschein and G. Zlotkin. *Rules of Encounter.* MIT Press, 1994.

13. T. W. Sandholm. An implementation of the contract net protocol based on marginal cost calculations. In *Proceedings of the National Conference on Artificial Intelligence*, pages 256–262, Washington, D.C., July 1993.

14. T. W. Sandholm. Limitations of the Vickrey auction in computational multiagent systems. In *Proceedings of the Second International Conference on Multi-Agent Systems (ICMAS-96)*, pages 299–306, Keihanna Plaza, Kyoto, Japan, Dec. 1996.

15. T. W. Sandholm. *Negotiation among Self-Interested Computationally Limited Agents.* PhD thesis, University of Massachusetts, Amherst, 1996. Available at http://www.cs.wustl.edu/~sandholm/dissertation.ps.

16. T. W. Sandholm. Contract types for satisficing task allocation: I theoretical results. In *AAAI Spring Symposium Series: Satisficing Models*, pages 68–75, Stanford University, CA, Mar. 1998.

17. T. W. Sandholm and V. R. Lesser. Advantages of a leveled commitment contracting protocol. In *Proceedings of the National Conference on Artificial Intelligence*, pages 126–133, Portland, OR, Aug. 1996. Extended version appeared as University of Massachusetts at Amherst, Computer Science Department technical report 95-72.

18. T. W. Sandholm and F. Ygge. On the gains and losses of speculation in equilibrium markets. In *Proceedings of the Fifteenth International Joint Conference on Artificial Intelligence*, pages 632–638, Nagoya, Japan, Aug. 1997.

19. A. Sathi and M. Fox. Constraint-directed negotiation of resource reallocations. In M. N. Huhns and L. Gasser, editors, *Distributed Artificial Intelligence*, volume 2 of *Research Notes in Artificial Intelligence*, chapter 8, pages 163–193. Pitman, 1989.

20. S. Sen. *Tradeoffs in Contract-Based Distributed Scheduling.* PhD thesis, Univ. of Michigan, 1993.

21. R. G. Smith. The contract net protocol: High-level communication and control in a distributed problem solver. *IEEE Transactions on Computers*, C-29(12):1104–1113, Dec. 1980.

Agent-Mediated Integrative Negotiation
for Retail Electronic Commerce

Robert H. Guttman and Pattie Maes

MIT Media Laboratory
20 Ames Street, E15-301
Cambridge, MA 02139
{guttman,pattie}@media.mit.edu
http://ecommerce.media.mit.edu

Abstract. Software agents help automate a variety of tasks including those involved in buying and selling products over the Internet. Although shopping agents provide convenience for consumers and yield more efficient markets, today's first-generation shopping agents are limited to comparing merchant offerings only on price instead of their full range of value. As such, they do a disservice to both consumers and retailers by hiding important merchant value-added services from consumer consideration. Likewise, the increasingly popular online auctions pit sellers against buyers in distributive negotiation tug-of-wars over price. This paper analyzes these approaches from economic, behavioral, and software agent perspectives then proposes integrative negotiation as a more suitable approach to retail electronic commerce. Finally, we identify promising techniques (e.g., multi-attribute utility theory, distributed constraint satisfaction, and conjoint analysis) for implementing agent-mediated integrative negotiation.

1. Introduction

Online marketplaces are both an opportunity and a threat to retail merchants. They are an opportunity because they offer traditional merchants an additional channel to advertise and sell products to consumers thus potentially *increasing sales*. Forrester Research estimates that online retail sales were at about $600 million USD in 1996, will exceed $2 billion USD in 1997, and will reach $17 billion USD by 2001 [1]. In addition, online markets are more efficient than their physical-world counterparts thus *lowering transaction costs* for both merchants and consumers. For example, low transaction costs is one reason why Amazon.com [2], a virtual bookstore, can offer a greater selection and lower prices than its physical-world competitors.

1.1. Cross-Merchant Product Comparisons

As in the physical world, an online merchant prefers to have consumers shop only at its own Web site as depicted in Figure 1(a). There are an increasing number of software agent tools available to merchants for enhancing and differentiating their product offerings online such as Firefly Network's recommendation system [3, 8] and PersonaLogic's buying guides [4]. These tools help consumers make buying decisions within a specific merchant's site. However, consumers also compare product offerings across merchant boundaries as depicted in Figure 1(b). Due to the lower transaction costs of online marketplaces and with the help of software *shopping agents*, consumers can easily perform cross-merchant product comparisons (whether merchants want this or not).

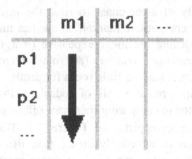

(a) Within-Merchant Product Comparisons

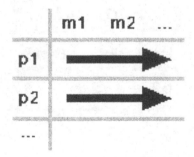

(b) Cross-Merchant Product Comparisons

Fig. 1. Merchants prefer that consumers shop for products only within their own store (a). However, on the Internet, software shopping agents make it very easy for consumers to cross merchant boundaries and perform cross-merchant product comparisons (b).

1.2. Value-Added, Merchant Differentiation and Market Power

Although cross-merchant product comparisons are a threat to merchant profitability, they are characteristic of the retail marketplace and are here to stay. Knowing this, retailers add value to manufacturers' products to distinguish themselves from their competitors. These *value-added services* include extended warranties, forgiving return policies, wide product selections, brand reputation, extensive service contracts, special gift services, high product availability, superior customer service and support, diverse payment, loan and leasing options, fast delivery times with low costs, promotions and coupons, cross-manufacturer product configurations, etc. Depending on the product, these value-added services can be critical to a consumer's buying decision regardless of the manner of shopping.

Merchant differentiation through added value is necessary for merchants to exercise *market power*, the ability of a merchant to raise the price of a product above its marginal cost. In a fully competitive market, no one has market power forcing prices down to the cost of producing the most expensive (marginal) unit [5]. Therefore, without merchant differentiation, retailers (and other intermediaries) are reduced to competing on marginal costs leaving little room for profit.

Unfortunately for online retailers, all of today's first-generation cross-merchant shopping agents are limited to comparing merchant offerings only on price instead of their full range of value as depicted in Figure 2. This makes it hard (if not impossible) for merchants to effectively differentiate themselves. This results in inappropriately competitive retail markets and forces merchants to compete almost entirely on marginal costs.

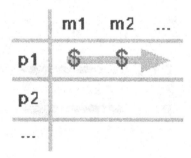

Fig. 2. First-generation Cross-Merchant Shopping Agents.

This paper suggests a reversal of this problematic trend in cross-merchant shopping agent approaches in order to restore merchant differentiation and thus their market power. With so much money at stake, this problem warrants attention. Although free markets are inherently "nature red in tooth and claw" [6], this need not be the relationship between retailers and their customers. Rather, we propose that a more cooperative and personalized integrative negotiation approach differentiates retailer's offerings in online markets better than today's limited price-comparison shopping agents and unnecessarily hostile distributive negotiation (e.g., auction) approaches.

1.3. Consumer Buying Behavior Model

Consumer Buying Behavior (CBB) marketing research builds descriptive theories and models for analyzing consumers' actions and decisions involved in buying and using goods and services. Guttman et al augment traditional CBB research with concepts from Software Agents research to accommodate electronic markets [7]. Table 1 lists all six stages of this CBB model and gives representative examples of agent systems that fall within this space.

	Persona Logic	Firefly	Bargain Finder	Jango	Kasbah	Auction Bot	Auction Web
1. Need Identification							
2. Product Brokering	√	√		√			
3. Merchant Brokering			√	√	√		
4. Negotiation					√	√	√
5. Purchase and Delivery							
6. Product Service and Evaluation							

Table 1. The six stages of the CBB model with representative examples of agent mediators [7].

Briefly, the *Product Brokering* stage comprises the retrieval of information to help determine *what* to buy. This encompasses the evaluation of product alternatives based on consumer-provided criteria. The result of this stage is the "consideration set" of products. The *Merchant Brokering* stage combines this "consideration set" with merchant-specific information to help determine *who* to buy from. This includes the evaluation of merchant alternatives based on consumer-provided criteria (e.g., price, warranty, availability, delivery time, reputation, etc.). The *Negotiation* stage is about *how* to determine the terms of the transaction. In traditional retail markets, price and other aspects of the transaction are often fixed leaving no room for negotiation. In other markets (e.g., stocks, automobile, fine art, local markets, etc.), the negotiation of price or other aspects of the deal are integral to product and merchant brokering.

As noted in [7], this analysis of retail electronic commerce represents an approximation and simplification of complex behaviors. CBB stages often overlap and migration from one to another is sometimes nonlinear and iterative.

2. Price-Only Shopping Agents and Distributive Negotiation Agents

There are several types of software shopping agents that assist consumers in making buying decisions. Table 1 gives representative examples of agents that play different roles in mediating online transactions. See [7] for a treatment of agent systems playing in the Product Brokering stage of the CBB model.

2.1. Price-comparison Shopping Agents

After Product Brokering comes Merchant Brokering in the CBB model shown in Table 1. Andersen Consulting's **BargainFinder** [9] was the first merchant brokering shopping agent. Given a specific music CD, BargainFinder requests its price (including shipping) from each of nine different online music catalogs using the same requests as a web browser. BargainFinder then presents its results to the consumer. As would be expected from the discussion in section 1, several of the merchants preferred not to participate and blocked all price requests from BargainFinder as shown in Figure 3.

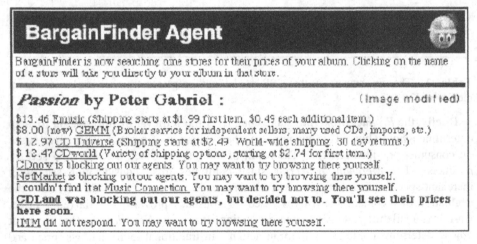

Fig. 3. BargainFinder requests prices of a given music CD from nine separate merchants and displays them to the consumer for a price comparison. However, three of the nine merchant sites are blocking BargainFinder's price requests.

It's also interesting to note that CDLand initially blocked BargainFinder agents but eventually decided to compete on price. However, a visit to their site indicates that it has been deactivated for the past seven months due to "new management" and "some initial transition difficulties" [10]. We can only presume that a lack of merchant differentiation and market power lead to their demise.

However, is merchant differentiation still relevant for commodity-like and low-price markets such as music CDs?   Although there may be less of a need, properly presented merchant differentiation can help consumers make more educated buying decisions even in these markets.   For instance, when buying music CDs, consumers may still want to consider product availability, delivery times and costs, gift services, return policies, customer service, as well as promotions and coupons.

Excite's **Jango** [11, 12] is similar to BargainFinder but with more product features to search across and more shopping categories.   The following sidebar describes the limitations of using Excite's Jango Shopping Agent to buy a specific notebook computer.

An Experience with Excite's Jango Shopping Agent

Product	CPU	RAM	Hard Drive	CD-ROM	Store		Price
MORE PRODUCT INFO					STORE HOMEPAGE		
APPLE PB 3400C/200 2GB 16MB 12X CD	PowerPC 200	16 MB	2.0GB	12X	CDW	$3579.88	Buy!
PowerBook 3400C/200 16MB/2.0GB/12X CD-ROM	PowerPC 200	16 MB	2.0GB	12X	Micro Warehouse	$3799.00	Buy!

Above are the results from Excite's Jango of a search for an Apple PowerBook 3400C/200 notebook computer with 16 MB of RAM, a 2.0 GB hard drive, and a 16x CD-ROM drive. Assuming I'm considering buying this computer (and know what these features mean), who do I buy it from? According to Excite's Jango, I can either buy the product from CDW for $3579.88 or from MicroWarehouse for $3799.00. All other things being equal (as Jango would have us believe), the rational decision is to buy the product from CDW for $219 less than from MicroWarehouse. But *are* all other things equal?

After a while of "manual" investigation, I discover that Apple is having a promotion. If I buy this product from MicroWarehouse within the next four weeks, I'll get a free 32MB RAM chip or a free Apple QuickTake Camera! It's not clear whether CDW honors this promotion. Such a differentiation makes the merchant offerings more comparable. Even if CDW also honors the promotion, it would have been useful if Jango informed me of it — perhaps enticing me to buy the product when I may not have otherwise.

More importantly, I also discover during my investigation that both merchants offer a 30 day return policy. However, if I'm unhappy with the product and return it to CDW, I'll be charged a 15% restocking fee. MicroWarehouse doesn't have a restocking fee. The $219 savings from buying it from CDW instead of from MicroWarehouse would have resulted in an extra $537 expense. It would have been useful if Jango allowed me to consider this information in my buying decision.

I'm still considering a purchase, but what are the reputations of these merchants? Do they offer extended warranties, service contracts, loan options, or gift services? Is the product even available? If so, how fast can it be delivered? How much will that cost? What other goods and services do I need to configure the product appropriately for my needs? A good sales agent would answer these questions to assist me in making a more educated buying decision and offer more products and options for consideration. Jango is not assisting me in considering any merchant value add in this buying decision.

2.2. Distributive Negotiation

Like the term "agent", there is no consensus on the definition of the term "negotiation." Economists, game theorists, business managers, political scientists, and artificial intelligence researchers each provide unique perspectives on its meaning. The business negotiation literature defines two types of negotiation: distributive negotiation and integrative negotiation [13]. *Distributive negotiation* is the decision-making process of resolving a conflict involving two or more parties over a single mutually exclusive goal. The economics literature describes this more specifically as the effects on market price of a limited resource given its supply and demand among self-interested parties [5]. The game theory literature describes this situation as a zero-sum game where as the value along a single dimension shifts in either direction, one side is better off and the other is worse off [14].

The benefit of dynamically negotiating a price for a product instead of fixing it is that it relieves the seller from needing to determine the value of the good a priori. Rather, this burden is pushed into the marketplace itself. A resulting benefit of this is that limited resources are allocated fairly _ i.e., to those buyers who value them most. As such, distributive negotiation mechanisms are common in a variety of markets including stock markets (e.g., NYSE and NASDAQ), fine art auction houses (e.g., Sotheby's and Christie's), flower auctions (e.g., Aalsmeer, Holland), and various ad-hoc haggling (e.g., automobile dealerships and commission-based electronics stores). More recently, software agents have been taught distributive negotiation skills (e.g., auctioneering and auction bidding skills) to help automate the Negotiation CBB stage of consumer-to-consumer and retail shopping over the Internet.

Kasbah [15, 16] is a Web-based multi-agent classified ad system where users create buying agents and selling agents to help transact goods. These agents automate much of the Merchant Brokering and Negotiation CBB stages for both buyers and sellers. A user wanting to buy or sell a good creates an agent, gives it some strategic direction, and sends it off into a centralized agent marketplace. Kasbah agents proactively seek out potential buyers or sellers and negotiate with them on behalf of their owners. Each agent's goal is to complete an acceptable deal, subject to a set of user-specified constraints such as a desired price, a highest (or lowest) acceptable price, and a date by which to complete the transaction.

Negotiation between buying and selling agents in Kasbah is bilateral, distributive, and straightforward. After buying agents and selling agents are matched, the only valid action in the distributive negotiation protocol is for buying agents to offer a bid to sellers. Selling agents respond with either a binding "yes" or "no". Given this protocol, Kasbah provides buyers with one of three negotiation "strategies": anxious, cool-headed, and frugal _ corresponding to a linear, quadratic, or exponential function respectively for increasing its bid for a product over time. The simplicity of these negotiation heuristics makes it intuitive for users to understand what their agents are doing in the marketplace.[1]   This was important for user acceptance as observed in a recent Media Lab experiment [15]. A larger Kasbah experiment is now underway at MIT allowing students to transact books and music [16].

AuctionBot   [19, 20] is a general purpose Internet auction server at the University of Michigan. AuctionBot users create new auctions to buy or sell products by choosing from a selection of auction types and specifying its parameters (e.g., clearing times, method for resolving bidding ties, the number of sellers permitted, etc.) as shown in Figure 4.   Buyers and sellers can then bid according to the multilateral distributive negotiation protocols of the created auction.   In a typical scenario, a seller would bid a reservation price after creating an auction and let AuctionBot manage and enforce buyer bidding according to the auction protocols and parameters.

AuctionBot also provides an application programmable interface (API) for users to create their own software agents to autonomously compete as buyers or sellers in the AuctionBot marketplace. This API permits AuctionBot to enforce auction protocols and provides a semantically sound communication interface to the marketplace. However, as with the similar Fishmarket system from the Artificial Intelligence Research Institute in Barcelona [21, 22], it is left to the buyers and sellers to encode their own bidding strategies.[2]

University of Michigan

AuctionBot™

The name of the good which you will auction is **Peter Gabriel's 'Passion'**, and it is described as **"This CD is in great condition."**.
The auction will follow the rules of the **Vickrey Auction**.
This auction will be displayed on the **public catalog** of auctions.
The auction will execute its final clear at **12:00:00 p.m.** on **December 30, 1997**.
The bid with the **earliest submission time** is filled first in the case of ties.
Users are notified of **price quotes**, and **new clearing prices**.
The **time of future price quotes**, and **the time of future clearing prices** will be made publicly available to users.
Goods are only sold in **discrete** units.
You are the **only** user allowed to place a selling bid in this auction.
Bidders are allowed to buy or sell **one unit at a time**.

Fig. 4. AuctionBot users create auctions by choosing from a selection of auction types and parameters.

---

[1] Unlike other multi-agent marketplaces [18], Kasbah does not concern itself with optimal strategies or convergence properties. Rather, Kasbah provides more descriptive strategies that model typical haggling behavior found in classified ad markets.

[2] Although not currently deployed as a real-world shopping system, Fishmarket has hosted tournaments to compare opponents' hand-crafted bidding strategies [23] along the lines of Axelrod's prisoner's dilemma tournaments [24].

Agent systems like Kasbah and AuctionBot are useful for building prescriptive theories for coordination among heterogeneous agents with (partially) predictable system-wide dynamics. However, as described next, distributive negotiation auctions are not well-suited for retail markets.

2.3. Auction Fever

Two of the original (non-academic) auction Web sites are OnSale [25] and eBay's **AuctionWeb** [26] and are still very popular. Likely reasons for their popularly include their novelty and entertainment value in negotiating the price of everyday goods, as well as the potential of getting a great deal on a wanted product. In any case, the popularity of OnSale and eBay's AuctionWeb has quickly spawned an already competitive and growing industry. Whereas once auctions were in themselves novel merchant differentiators, with the rapid proliferation of online auctions, this differentiation has waned. Yahoo! lists more than 90 active online auctions today [27]. Forrester Research reports that auctions will be core to making business-to-business transactions more dynamic, open and efficient [28]. online auctions like FastParts [29] and FairMarket [30] are already making this happen in the semiconductor and computer industries.

What's most relevant here is that many online auctions are augmentations to retail sites with retailers playing the roles of both auctioneer and seller (i.e., a sales agent). For example, First Auction [31] is a service of Internet Shopping Network, one of the first online retailers. Cendant's membership-driven retail site, netMarket [32], has also recently added auctions to its repertoire of online services. New auction intermediaries such as Z Auction [33] offer their auction services to multiple manufactures and resellers as a new sales channel.

With this much "auction fever," you would think that auctions are a panacea for retail shopping and selling. On the contrary, upon closer look we see that auctions have rather hostile characteristics. For example, although the protocols for the two most prevalent types of online auctions, first-price open-cry English and Yankee [34], are simple to understand and bid, determining the optimal bidding strategy is non-trivial[3] and, more importantly, can be financially adverse. In fact, in first-price open-cry auctions (i.e., highest bid wins the good for that price), the winning bid is always greater than the product's market valuation. This is commonly known as "winner's curse" as depicted in Figure 5. This problem is exacerbated in retail auctions where buyers' valuations are largely private[4]. Buyers with private valuations tend to (irrationally) skew bids even further above the product's true value.

---

[3] Factors to be considered include information asymmetry, risk aversion, motivation and valuation.

[4] The motivation of a buyer with private-valuation is to acquire goods for personal consumption (or for gifts). This is in contrast to a buyer with common-valuation (e.g.,

Fig. 5. "Winner's curse" is the paradox that the winning bid in an auction is greater than the product's market valuation. This occurs in all first-price, open-cry auctions _ the most prevalent type on the Internet.

Although winner's curse is a short-term financial benefit to retailers, it can be a long-term detriment due to the eventual customer dissatisfaction of paying more than the value of a product. Two universal auction rules that compound this problem are: (1) bids are non-retractable and, worse yet, (2) products are non-returnable. This means that customers could get stuck with products that they're unhappy with and paid too much for. In short, online auctions are less lucrative and far less forgiving than would be expected in retail shopping.

Another customer dissatisfaction problem owing to online auctions is the long delay between the start of the Negotiation CBB stage and the end of the Purchase and Delivery CBB stage. For example, due to communication latency issues and wanting a critical mass of bidders, the English and Yankee auction protocols as implemented over the Internet extend over several days. This means that after a customer starts bidding on a product, she/he must continuously bid for the product (or have a shopping agent do it as provided by AuctionWeb) up until the auction closes several days later. This does not cater to impatient or time-constrained consumers.[5]   To make matters worse, only the highest bidder(s) of an auction can purchase the auctioned good meaning that the other customers need to wait until the good is

---

in stock) where the motivation is to make money through the buying and later reselling of goods which have no other intrinsic value to the buyer.

[5] In fact, such delays are the antithesis to impulse buying.

auctioned again and then restart the Negotiation CBB stage.[6]   Additionally, since bids are non-retractable and binding, consumers are unable to reconsider earlier brokering decisions during this delayed negotiation stage.

There are other buyer concerns with English and Yankee style auctions such as shills. Shills are bidders who are planted by sellers to unfairly manipulate the market valuation of the auctioned good by raising the bid to stimulate the market. Although deemed illegal in all auctions, shills can be hard to detect especially in the virtual world where it is relatively inexpensive to create virtual identities (and thus virtual shills). Also, there is usually no negative consequence to the seller if one of his/her shills (accidentally) wins the auction.

Distributive negotiation auctions in retail markets also pose problems for merchants. Although auctions can relieve merchants of the burden of establishing prices for limited resources (e.g., fine art and stocks), this benefit is less realizable for production goods as in retail markets. Unlike fine art, for example, it is relatively easy to determine the marginal costs of production goods.[7]   If auctioning these goods, however, it is non-trivial for the merchant to determine the optimal size of the auctioned lots and the frequency of their auction [35]. Such a determination requires an understanding of the demand for the good since it directly affects inventory management and indirectly affects production schedule.[8]   Therefore, retailers are still burdened with determining the value of their goods a priori.

In addition, where sellers may have shills, buyers may collude by forming coalitions. A buyer coalition is a group of buyers who agree not to outbid one another. In a discriminatory (i.e., multi-good) auction, the result of this is that the coalition can buy goods for less than if they competed against one another thus unfairly cheating the seller. The coalition can then distribute the spoils amongst themselves (e.g., evenly, by holding a second private auction, etc.). As with shills, collusion through buyer coalitions is also considered illegal. However, as with shills, it can be hard to detect buyer collusion, especially in online markets where bidders are virtual. In fact, Multi-Agent Systems research has developed technologies that can efficiently form coalitions even among previously unknown parties [36] – posing an additional threat to online retail auctions.

As explained, online auctions are unnecessarily hostile to customers and offer no long-term benefits to merchants. Essentially, they pit merchant against customer in

---

[6] Even in traditional static catalog retail (as well as Continuous Double Auctions), consumers can purchase products immediately.

[7] Granted, the pricing of retail products can get involved. This is where marketing tactics come into play such as branding, market segmentation, price discrimination, etc.

[8] This relates directly to the just-in-time (JIT) concept for manufacturing, inventory, and retailing [37]. However, it is not yet clear how best to gauge demand in JIT (e.g., through negotiation or sales).

price tug-of-wars. This is not the type of relationship merchants prefer to have with their customers [38]. Unlike most consumer-to-consumer and commodity markets, merchants often care less about profit on any given transaction and care more about long-term profitability. This ties directly to customer satisfaction and long-term customer relationships. The more satisfied the customer and intimate the customer-merchant relationship, the greater the opportunity for repeat customer purchases and additional purchases through direct referrals and indirectly through positive reputation.

And as with price-only shopping agents, distributive negotiation auctions focus the consumers' attention solely on a product's price rather than its full range of value. This is a disservice to both consumers and merchants because, as with price-comparison shopping agents, it hides important merchant added value from consumers' consideration.[9] Also, by only negotiating over price, merchants lose an opportunity to differentiate themselves during the earlier Merchant Brokering and Product Brokering CBB stages. Ultimately, by shortsightedly succumbing to "auction fever," retail merchants may be instrumental in bringing about their own demise. By promoting auctions as appropriate retail negotiation mechanisms, it strips themselves of differentiation and exposes their markets to greater competition thus nullifying their market power and profit.

3. Integrative Negotiation Agents

There is a tremendous amount of literature on how to sell retail products. No one approach is correct as it depends upon a number of factors including the type of product and demographics of its intended audience. Likewise, there is no one correct way to shop. People have different goals, knowledge, preferences, constraints, influences, and attitudes during any given shopping experience. One type of shopping is cross-merchant product comparisons (see section 1.1). It assumes a (partially) rational shopper who is concerned with buying the merchant offering that best meets his/her needs given an invested amount of time and effort.

Cross-merchant product comparisons are conducive to software agent mediation by assisting the shopper in any of the Product Brokering, Merchant Brokering, and Negotiation stages of the Consumer Buying Behavior model. However, some agent-mediation approaches are better than others. We argue in section 2.1 for shopping agents that can perform value-comparisons, not just price-comparisons. In section 2.3, we argue for sales agents that can negotiate over the full range of a merchant's added value rather than just price.

---

[9] For example, Gerry Heller, CEO of FastParts - an online auction for semiconductors, was quoted in a recent Forrester Research report as admitting that even in this commodity-like market "availability is more important than price" when it comes to auctioning semiconductors.

We propose an integrative negotiation approach to cross-merchant product comparisons. This approach promotes negotiation between consumer-owned shopping agents and merchant-owned sales agents across each product's full range of value. The rest of this section discusses integrative negotiation and identifies promising techniques for its implementation.

3.1. Integrative Negotiation

As introduced in section 2.2, the business negotiation literature defines two types of negotiation: distributive negotiation and integrative negotiation. Integrative negotiation is the decision-making process of resolving a conflict involving two or more parties over multiple interdependent, but non-mutually exclusive goals [13]. The study of how to analyze multi-objective decisions comes from economics research and is called multi-attribute utility theory (MAUT) [40]. The game theory literature describes integrative negotiation as a non-zero-sum game where as the values along multiple dimensions shift in different directions, it is possible for all parties to be better off [14].

In essence, integrative negotiation is a win-win type of negotiation. An example of this is depicted in Figure 7. This is in stark contrast to distributive negotiation which is a win-lose type of negotiation as discussed in section 2.2. Also as discussed, all auctions are forms of distributive negotiation and are therefore win-lose types of negotiation.

Desired retail merchant-customer relationships and interactions can be described in terms of integrative negotiation – the cooperative process of resolving multiple interdependent, but non-mutually exclusive goals. A merchant's primary goals are long-term profitability through selling as many products as possible to as many customers as possible for as much money as possible with as low transaction costs as possible. A customer's primary goals are to have their personal needs satisfied through the purchase of well-suited products from appropriate merchants for as little money and hassle (i.e., transaction costs) as possible. An integrative negotiation through the space of merchant offerings can help maximize both of these sets of goals. From a merchant's perspective, integrative negotiation is about tailoring its offerings to each customer's individual needs resulting in greater customer satisfaction. From a customer's perspective, integrative negotiation is about conversing with retailers to help compare merchant offerings across their full range of value resulting in mutually rewarding and hassle-free shopping experiences.

3.2. Multi-Objective Decision Analysis and Multi-Attribute Utility Theory

Multi-objective decision analysis prescribes theories for quantitatively analyzing important decisions involving multiple, interdependent objectives from the perspective of a single decision-maker [40]. This analysis involves two distinctive features: an uncertainty analysis and a utility (i.e., preference) analysis. Techniques such as bayesian network modeling aid uncertainty analysis. Multi-attribute utility theory (MAUT) analyzes preferences with multiple attributes.

Examples of uncertainty in retail shopping are "will she like this product as a gift?" and "how much do I trust this merchant?" Such uncertainties weighed against other factors play a part in consumers' buying decisions. From a merchant's perspective, analyzing an uncertainty like "what will be the demand for this product?" is vital for pricing products and managing inventory.

Often, decisions have multiple attributes that need to be considered. For example, in retail shopping, the price of a product could be important, but so could its delivery time. What is the relationship and tradeoff between these two? Figure 6 gives a simple example of this.

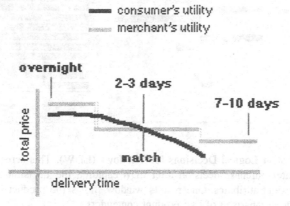

Fig. 6. This graph plots a consumer's and a merchant's multi-atribute utilities for a product's total price vs. delivery time (in days). In this example, the merchant offers three delivery options at different price points of which the "2-3 days" option best matches the consumer's utility profile.

Multi-objective decision analysis and MAUT can (and have) been used to tackle many different types of decision problems including electrical power vs. air quality, airport location, heroin addiction treatment, medical diagnostic and treatment, business problems, political problems, etc. These theories have also been instantiated in computer systems. The PERSUADER system at Carnegie Mellon University, for example, integrates Case-Base Reasoning and MAUT to resolve conflicts through negotiation in group problem solving settings [39]. Logical Decisions for Windows (LDW) by Logical Decisions, Inc. [41] is a general-purpose decision analysis tool for helping people think about and analyze their problems. Figure 7 shows LDW at work on a retail purchase decision problem.

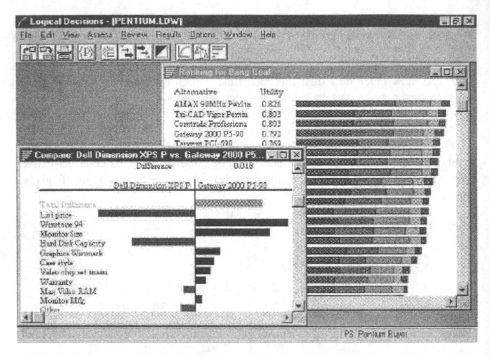

Fig. 7. A screenshot of Logical Decisions for Windows (LDW). This screenshot shows the results of a computer purchase decision after LDW captured the decision-maker's utilities across multiple product attributes. One results window shows the product rankings and the other a side-by-side comparison of two product contenders.

LDW falls within the Product Brokering stage of our CBB model. However, MAUT tools such as LDW can also be applied to the Merchant Brokering CBB stage by formulating a new problem to analyze merchant value add for the winning product (i.e., considered set) of the Product Brokering stage. If certain pragmatic issues concerning MAUT's appropriateness for real-time Internet-based bilateral negotiations can be allayed, then MAUT techniques are contenders for decision support in agent-mediated integrative negotiation strategies for online retail markets.

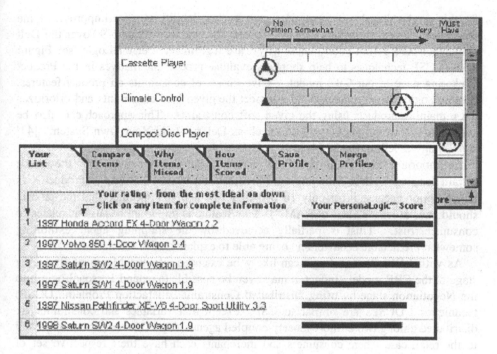

Fig. 8. Screenshots of PersonaLogic assisting a customer select automobile features with results.

3.3. Distributed Constraint Satisfaction

MAUT analyzes decision problems quantitatively through utilities. Constraint Satisfaction Problems (CSPs) analyze decision problems more qualitatively through constraints. A CSP is formulated in terms of variables, domains, and constraints. Once a decision problem is formulated in this way, a number of general purpose (and powerful) CSP techniques can analyze the problem and find a solution [42].

Finite-domain CSPs are one type of CSP and are composed of three main parts: a finite set of variables, each of which is associated with a finite domain, and a set of constraints that define relationships among variables and restricts the values that the variables can simultaneously take. The task of a CSP engine is to assign a value to each variable while satisfying all of the constraints. A variation of these "hard" constraints is the ability to also define "soft" constraints (of varied importance) which need not be satisfied. The number, scope, and nature of the CSP's variables, domains, and constraints will determine how constrained the problem is and, for a given CSP engine, how quickly a solution (if any) will be found.

Many problems can be formulated as a CSP such as scheduling, planning, configuration, and machine vision problems. In retail markets, CSP techniques can be used to encode hard constraints such as "I'm not willing to spend more than $2,000 for this product," and soft constraints such as "availability is more important to me than price." Even constraints such as "I prefer the Gateway 2000 P5-90 over the Dell Dimension XPS P (but I don't know why)" are legitimate. PersonaLogic (see Figure 8) uses CSP techniques to help shoppers evaluate product alternatives in the Product Brokering stage of our CBB model. Given a set of constraints on product features, PersonaLogic filters products that don't meet the given hard constraints and prioritizes the remaining products using the given soft constraints. This approach can also be applied to sales configuration systems such as Dell's "Build Your Own System" [43] and Trilogy's Selling Chain[a] [44].

An important side-benefit of CSPs is that they can clearly explain why they made certain decisions such as removing a product from the results list (e.g., "Product X is not an option because it has only 16 MB of RAM and you specified that the product should have at least 32 MB of RAM."). This feature is important because it relates to consumer trust. Trust is partially achieved by the shopping agent exhibiting somewhat predictable behavior and being able to explain its decisions.

As with LDW, PersonaLogic can likely be extended into the Merchant Brokering stage of the CBB model. In fact, it may even be possible to extend PersonaLogic into the Negotiation stage by using Distributed Constraint Satisfaction Problem (DCSP) techniques. DCSPs are similar to CSPs except that variables and constraints are distributed among two or more loosely-coupled agents [45]. This appears to map well to the retail case where consumers and merchants each have their respective set of constraints on merchant offerings.

However, DCSPs have been designed for fully cooperative group problem solving situations. Although integrative negotiations are far more cooperative than distributive negotiations, DCSP techniques may require more cooperation than is appropriate for merchant-customer interactions. For example, a customer may not be willing to divulge her reservation value (e.g., a willingness to pay up to $2,000 for a computer) to a merchant for fear of first-degree price discrimination with the merchant (unfairly) capturing all of the surplus in the market. However, first-degree price discrimination is tenuous in markets with monopolistic competition – i.e., a market with a large number of firms selling similar but differentiated products with no significant barriers to entry – which characterizes most retail markets [5]. This suggests that DCSP techniques may not be overly cooperative for bilateral integrative negotiations in retail markets.[10]

3.4. Conjoint Analysis and Machine Learning

Conjoint analysis is a popular marketing tool to help identify and market new product features [46]. The approach involves repeatedly surveying respondents for the preferred

---

[10] Full cooperation does not necessitate full disclosure. For example, merchants need not divulge their profit margins. However, full cooperation does assume soundness of trust - i.e., false advertising isn't permitted.

product given two or more product choices. This is in contrast to rating products (e.g., in automated collaborative filtering) or specifying requirements on product attributes (e.g., in constraint satisfaction). Rather, respondents jointly consider[11] and relatively rank product choices. Conjoint analysis then infers which product attributes are most important to the consumer relieving the consumer of specifying these features explicitly. Also, by being forced to make product decisions, consumers avoid unreasonable product attribute combinations – e.g., the most robust feature set and the lowest price. This is a benefit over CSPs which allow consumers to specify unreasonable product attribute combinations resulting in an empty "considered set" of products.[12]

However, in order to make a product selection, consumers need to identify differences in product attributes. It may be better for a user to just express these attribute preferences rather than spend time making a series of product choices which will (at best) infer the same preferences. Conjoint analysis also suffers from not dealing well with noisy or inconsistent data (which are very common in user surveys), not being conducive to changes in product preferences, and being time-consuming, redundant, and boring for the consumer. As such, although conjoint analysis is appropriate for identifying new product features and segmenting markets, it appears less appropriate as the sole mechanism for extracting utility preferences for integrative negotiations in retail electronic markets.

There are numerous statistical, search, and heuristic approaches that can also learn preferences and patterns of user behavior. In fact, a tenet of artificial intelligence (AI) is learning. Specific AI fields of inquiry include inductive learning, genetic algorithms, classifier systems, case-based reasoning, neural networks, and a variety of other machine learning and adaptive behavior theories and technologies [47, 48].

4. Conclusion

This paper analyzed the state-of-the-art in agent-mediated retail electronic commerce. We first looked at how price-only shopping agents are a disservice to both consumers and retailers by hiding important merchant value add from consumer consideration. We then explored how distributive negotiation techniques (e.g., online auctions) are considerably more hostile to both consumers and merchants than would be expected in retail markets (in spite of their increasing popularity).

Finally, we proposed a new integrative negotiation approach to retail electronic commerce. We described how techniques such as multi-attribute utility theory, distributed constraint satisfaction, and conjoint analysis could be harnessed for allowing consumer's to integratively negotiate over a product's full range of value.

---

[11] Conjoint is a contraction of "consider jointly."

[12] However, there are CSP techniques to automatically relax constraints in over-constrained problems.

From a merchant's perspective, integrative negotiation is about tailoring its offerings to each customer's individual needs resulting in greater customer satisfaction. From a customer's perspective, integrative negotiation is about conversing with retailers to help compare merchant offerings across their full range of value resulting in mutually rewarding and hassle-free shopping experiences.

Acknowledgements

We would like to thank Alex Kleiner III, Fernanda Viegas, Natalia Marmasse, and Alexandros Moukas for their help with this paper.

References

[1] Forrester Research Report. On-Line Internet Spending. 1997.

[2] Amazon.com URL: <http://www.amazon.com/>

[3] Firefly Network URL: <http://www.firefly.com/>

[4] PersonaLogic URL: <http://www.personalogic.com/>

[5] R.H. Frank. Microeconomics and Behavior, 3rd ed. McGraw-Hill, Inc., 1996.

[6] A. L. Tennyson. "In Memoriam" (LVI, 15).

[7] R. Guttman, A. Moukas, and P. Maes. "Agent-mediated Electronic Commerce: A Survey." To appear, Knowledge Engineering Review, June 1998.

[8] U. Shardanand and P. Maes. "Social Information Filtering: Algorithms for Automating 'Word of Mouth'." Proceedings of the Computer-Human Interaction Conference (CHI'95), Denver, Colorado, May 1995.

[9] BargainFinder URL: <http://bf.cstar.ac.com/bf>

[10] CDLand URL: <http://www.cdland.com/>

[11] Jango URL: <http://www.jango.com/>

[12] R. Doorenbos, O. Etzioni, and D. Weld. "A Scalable Comparison-Shopping Agent for the World Wide Web." Proceedings of the First International Conference on Autonomous Agents (Agents'97). Marina del Rey, CA, February 1997.

[13] R. Lewicki, D. Saunders, and J. Minton. Essentials of Negotiation. Irwin, 1997.

[14] J. Rosenschein and G. Zlotkin. Rules of Encounter: Designing Conventions for Automated Negotiation among Computers. MIT Press, 1994.

[15] A. Chavez, D. Dreilinger, R. Guttman, and P. Maes. "A Real-Life Experiment in Creating an Agent Marketplace." Proceedings of the Second International

Conference on the Practical Application of Intelligent Agents and Multi-Agent Technology (PAAM'97). London, UK, April 1997.

[16] Kasbah URL: <http://kasbah.media.mit.edu/>

[17] D. Friedman and J. Rust, eds. The Double Auction Market: Institutions, Theories, and Evidence. Addison-Wesley, New York, 1993.

[18] C. Sierra, P. Faratin, and N. Jennings. "A Service-Oriented Negotiation Model Between Autonomous Agents." Proceedings of the Eighth European Workshop on Modeling Autonomous Agents in a Multi-Agent World (MAAMAW'97). Ronneby, Sweden, May 1997.

[19] P. Wurman, M. Wellman, and W. Walsh. "The Michigan Internet AuctionBot: A Configurable Auction Server for Human and Software Agents." To appear, Proceedings of the Second International Conference on Autonomous Agents (Agents'98), May 1998.

[20] AuctionBot URL: <http://auction.eecs.umich.edu/>

[21] Fishmarket URL: <http://www.iiia.csic.es/Projects/fishmarket/newindex.html>

[22] J. Rodriquez, P. Noriega, C. Sierra, and J. Padget.. "FM96.5: A Java-based Electronic Auction House." Proceedings of the Second International Conference on the Practical Application of Intelligent Agents and Multi-Agent Technology (PAAM'97). London, UK, April 1997.

[23] J. Rodriguez, F. Martin, P. Noriega, P. Garcia, and C. Sierra. "Competitive Scenarios for Heterogeneous Trading Agents." To appear in Proceedings of the Second International Conference on Autonomous Agents (Agents'98).

[24] R. Axelrod. The Evolution of Cooperation. Harper Collins, 1984.

[25] OnSale URL: <http://www.onsale.com/>

[26] eBay's AuctionWeb URL: <http://www.ebay.com/aw>

[27] Yahoo! online Auction URL: <http://www.yahoo.com/Business_and_Economy/Companies/ Auctions/online_Auctions/>

[28] Forrester Research Report, Business Trade and Technology Strategies: Sizing Intercompany Commerce, vol. 1, no. 1. July 1997.

[29] FastParts URL: <http://www.fastparts.com/>

[30] FairMarket URL: <http://www.fairmarket.com/>

[31] First Auction URL: <http://www.firstauction.com/>

[32] netMarket URL: <http://www.netmarket.com/>

[33] Z Auction URL: <http://www.zauction.com/>

[34] P. Milgrom. "Auctions and Bidding: A Primer." Journal of Economic Perspectives, pp. 3-22. Summer 1989.

[35] C. Beam, A. Segev, and J. G. Shanthikumar. "Electronic Negotiation through Internet-based Auctions." CITM Working Paper 96-WP-1019, December 1996.

[36] T. Sandholm and V. Lesser. "Coalition Formation among Bounded Rational Agents." 14th International Joint Conference on Artificial Intelligence (IJCAI'95), Montreal, Canada, 1995.

[37] G. Morgenson. "The Fall of the Mall." Forbes, May 24, 1993.

[38] Forrester Research Report. "Affordable Intimacy Strengthens On-Line Stores." September, 1997.

[39] K. Sycara. "The PERSUADER." In The Encyclopedia of Artificial Intelligence. D. Shapiro (ed.), John Wiley and Sons, January, 1992.

[40] R. Keeney and H. Raiffa. Decisions with Multiple Objectives: Preferences and Value Tradeoffs. John Wiley & Sons, 1976.

[41] Logical Decisions URL: <http://www.logicaldecisions.com/>

[42] E. Tsang. Foundations of Constraint Satisfaction. Academic Press, 1993.

[43] Dell "Build Your Own System" URL: <http://www.dell.com/store/index.htm>

[44] Trilogy's Selling Chain URL: <http://www.trilogy.com/prodserv/products/main.html>

[45] M. Yokoo and E. Durfee. "Distributed Constraint Satisfaction for Formalizing Distributed Problem Solving." Proceedings of the 12th IEEE International Conference on Distributed Computing Systems, 1992.

[46] Crane, M. "Conjoint Analysis: A Guide for Designing & Interpreting Conjoint Studies." Austin Texas: IntelliQuest, Inc., 1991.

[47] J. Carbonell (ed.). Machine Learning: Paradigms and Methods. MIT Press, 1990.

[48] S. Russell and P. Norvig. Artificial Intelligence: A Modern Approach. Prentice Hall, 1995.

A Multi-agent System for Coordinating International Shipping[1]

Steven Y. Goldsmith, Laurence R. Phillips, Shannon V. Spires

Sandia National Laboratories, Albuquerque, NM 87185
{sygolds, lrphill, svspire}@sandia.gov

Abstract: Moving commercial cargo across the US-Mexico border is currently a complex, paper-based, error-prone process that incurs expensive inspections and delays at several ports of entry in the Southwestern US. Improved information handling will dramatically reduce border dwell time, variation in delivery time, and inventories, and will give better control of the shipment process. The Border Trade Facilitation System (BTFS) is an agent-based collaborative work environment that assists geographically distributed commercial and government users with transshipment of goods across the US-Mexico border. Software agents mediate the creation, validation and secure sharing of shipment information and regulatory documentation over the Internet, using the World-Wide Web to interface with human actors. Agents are organized into Agencies. Each agency represents a commercial or government agency. Agents perform four specific functions on behalf of their user organizations: (1) agents with domain knowledge elicit commercial and regulatory information from human specialists through forms presented via web browsers; (2) agents mediate information from forms with diverse ontologies, copying invariant data from one form to another thereby eliminating the need for duplicate data entry; (3) cohorts of distributed agents coordinate the work flow among the various information providers and they monitor overall progress of the documentation and the location of the shipment to ensure that all regulatory requirements are met prior to arrival at the border; (4) agents provide status information to human actors and attempt to influence them when problems are predicted.

1. Introduction

A simple model of commerce divides a commercial transaction into three phases: negotiation, delivery, and settlement. This paper focuses on an agent-based electronic commerce system, the Border Trade Facilitation System (BTFS), built to expedite the

---

[1] Sandia is a multiprogram laboratory operated by Sandia Corporation, a Lockheed Martin Company, for the U.S. Department of Energy under contract DE-AC04-94AL85000

regulation, control, and execution of commercial trans-border shipments during the delivery phase. The system is targeted towards the rapidly growing manufacturing industry centered around the US/Mexican border. The North American Free Trade Agreement (NAFTA) has fueled this growth to a large extent. Managing the logistics of trans-border shipments is a daunting task complicated by import/export regulations and documentation requirements promulgated by both the US and Mexico. Drug smuggling activities and drug interdiction efforts have made shipping even more difficult. The primary goal of the BTFS is to improve information handling and documentation processes for legitimate stakeholders without furthering opportunities for smuggling and other criminal activities.

The BTFS features a number of innovations, including a distributed object substrate that supports authenticated transactions among agents, a general-purpose agent development framework, agent integration with the World-Wide Web, and a collaborative agent architecture that supports open trading over the Internet. In this paper we provide only an overview of this complex information system.

2. Background

Each day several thousand commercial trucks cross the US-Mexico border at six major ports of entry along the US/Mexico border. The majority carry cargo to and from the *maquilas* in Mexico. A *maquila*, or "twin plant," typically provides inexpensive labor for the assembly of parts or subassemblies into finished goods that are then re-shipped to the US for consumption. Passage of the North American Free Trade Agreement (NAFTA) has increased maquila traffic at ports of entry along the Southwestern US border significantly since 1993. Maquila border crossings are projected to be in the thousands daily by the year 2000. Ironically, the increased border traffic has provided drug smugglers with a crowded street in which to disappear, creating a tension among US government agencies responsible for the facilitation of trade and the interdiction of drugs. The governments of the United States and Mexico currently have projects under way or planned that will expand the physical capacity of existing ports of entry. The US recently opened a new port at Santa Teresa, New Mexico. Plans to increase the capacity for handling information necessary to document the increasing number of border crossings have not been made, largely because the majority of the information handling resides in the commercial sector.

A significant fraction of commercial trucks currently arrive at ports of entry with either incorrect or incomplete documentation. These trucks are summarily pulled over to a primary inspection area, and sometimes subsequently to a secondary inspection area, where they are often completely unloaded. Primary and secondary inspections take a minimum of 15 minutes and can last several hours or even days if problems are found. Delays typically cost both the transport provider and the manufacturer. Truck and driver costs can exceed $100/hour. Maquila plants are increasingly operated in just-in-time mode, so receival delays at the maquilas can result in work stoppage, idling dozens of workers and halting production lines costing thousands of dollars per minute to run. Paper documents currently carry the information needed to cross the border. Truck drivers carry the documents and present them to inspectors at the ports of entry and exit. Many factors can cause delays at the port, including drug interdiction campaigns and fugitive alerts. Proper documentation in and of itself cannot prevent delays, but improper documentation is virtually certain to cause them.

The root causes of documentation errors are deeply buried in the complex preparations that precede a border crossing. The required regulatory documents for each leg of the trip are numerous and bilingual. Additional NAFTA requirements have complicated the documentation further while increasing the cross-border traffic, leading to the expansion of the import/export brokerage industry in both the US and Mexico. For example, a typical package prepared by a Mexican broker includes the original invoice; the Shipper's Export Declaration; a Spanish language invoice called the *factura*; an import *pedimento* (Mexican import/export declaration document); an English manifest and a Spanish *manifiesto* describing the physical nature of the shipment for the trucking firms; a packing list, describing how the shipment is actually arranged on the truck; and any of several possible Mexican regulatory compliance documents. NAFTA documents must be on file certifying the firm as a maquila, and the *pedimento* must be registered by the firm in some manner to satisfy year-end material-balancing regulations. The driver and the vehicle must be properly licensed and certified. Further complications stem from the maquilas' ability to consolidate several invoices/*facturas* under a single *pedimento*. Shipment into the US involves several additional US import documents. The documents are syntactically distinct, although there is significant semantic overlap. For example, the "total shipment value" given on many of these documents is not necessarily called the same thing between any given pair nor will the value necessarily be computed on the same basis; in particular, valuations are two different currencies.

Customshouse brokers assist manufacturers with preparing the documents for a given shipment and generally pay any duty assessed. Brokers also provide additional assurance to their clients by remaining up to date on the latest regulations regarding trade between the US and Mexico. They are essentially brokers of specialized knowledge and information, operating between government regulators and the commercial world. Brokers prepare regulatory forms from an initial manifest that may be presented by a client in a variety of forms, including "sneaker net," fax machine, Electronic Data Interchange (EDI), and most recently Internet email. Although segments of the process are computerized, transcription of information from paper to computer and back occurs often even in advanced brokerage houses. Fortunately both the US and Mexican customs services have (separate) computerized entry systems that accept document filings by modem. Nonetheless, errors occur with great regularity and brokers maintain troubleshooters on site at the ports of entry to handle such incidents.

A successful border crossing is the result of a coordinated effort on the part of the manufacturer, the consignee, and carriers and brokers on both sides of the border. For example, a nominal southbound (US to Mexico) maquila shipment involves the owner of the goods ("the firm"), the firm's US shipping facility, at least one US trucking company (perhaps owned by the firm), US customs, a US export broker (sometimes an employee of the firm), Mexican customs, a Mexican import broker (also sometimes an employee of the firm), a Mexican trucking company, and finally the maquila plant itself. Although new port facilities are planned and expansion of old ports is has begun, traffic at the border is often backed up several miles. Often the customs district maintains several alternative ports in the same area. However, drivers cannot effectively choose an alternative port prior to enqueuing for two reasons: (1) the intended port of entry is declared on the paper document he carries and cannot be changed without resubmission to the US Customs Automated Cargo System; and (2) the driver cannot determine the traffic load (nor, therefore, estimate the delay) at the port until arrival.

Border-crossing stakeholders have noted that "the most frequent cause of legitimate freight being pulled over for inspection is improper or incomplete documentation [Godfrey 1998]." In a recent border process survey [Parker and Icerman 1996], 78% of US and Mexican firms doing business across the border cited "automated documentation" as a priority technology, the highest percentage for any technology in the survey. Stakeholders were concerned, however, that a highly-accessible electronic documentation scheme might make their proprietary information vulnerable. Commercial stakeholders were adamant that the system be decentralized; they considered a central database administered by a national government highly undesirable. The second-most frequently cited technology, "Container/conveyance tracking," was cited by 60%. In all, technologies that the stakeholders identified as high-priority appear to address the root causes of their delays: correct, complete, and timely electronic documentation; computer-based sharing of shipment information among stakeholders; protection of proprietary information; and timely shipment status information.

Simulations of the new Santa Teresa port of entry by Science Applications International Corporation [SAIC 1997] show that computerized documentation and tracking technology would cut time spent waiting to cross the border by 33% (from 18 to 12 minutes) at 30% technology penetration and four times the current traffic, and by 52% (from 47 to 20 minutes) at 60% penetration and six times the current traffic (saturation level)[2]. These reduced waiting times would be enjoyed by all vehicles, not just those with advanced technology. If a dedicated lane for advanced technology vehicles is added in the latter case, those vehicles enjoy a reduction in waiting time of 75%.

In 1997 the Advanced Information Systems Laboratory (AISL) at Sandia National Laboratories completed a prototype of the Border Trade Facilitation System (BTFS), a collaborative information processing environment that operates on the Internet and World-Wide Web. The BTFS comprises multiple autonomous software agents that assist human actors in conducting international shipping transactions by creating, documenting, monitoring, and coordinating shipment transactions in information space. The BTFS attacks the border-crossing problem in the three problem areas with the highest potential for improving the border-crossing process: (1) manual entry of redundant information throughout the process by different organizations; (2)

---

[2] "Current traffic" refers to 1995-96 levels; traffic grew 80% during the 1996-97 year and is thus already at twice the "current traffic" level

incomplete regulatory documents; and (3) lack of timely status information regarding the location of the vehicle and the progress of the documentation. We discuss the conceptual design and implementation of the BTFS in the remainder of this paper.

3. System Concept

The essential concept of the BTFS is that the physical trans-border shipment of goods and the required accompanying certification are entirely represented as a set of events in information space, the state of which both controls and certifies events in physical space. The BTFS information system contains a real-time transaction-centric model of the physical border-crossing process. This leads to a two-component system: (1) a physical sensor system that reports state of health and location data via satellite [Schoeneman and Fox 1996]; and (2) a secure electronic commerce system that interfaces with the humans responsible for documenting commercial and regulatory information. We will focus on the secure electronic commerce system for the remainder of this paper.

Coordination of the shipping process to improve the timeliness and correctness of the information requires a collaborative information processing network that spans government and commercial entities, involves both the US and Mexico, and passes Spanish and English-language documents. Security to protect proprietary information is of paramount importance to commercial entities. Security is also critical to government agencies; an insecure system on the open Internet could be used to spoof regulatory agencies at the border and thereby lend support to criminal activities such as drug smuggling.

The ultimate objective of the system is to ensure that the US and Mexican Customs databases contain validated documents when the truck arrives at the border. The truck cargo must have a unique ID code that identifies it with its counterpart (representation) in information space. An enforcement officer must use this code to reference the documents and make an inspection decision. The flow of data through the system is transaction-centric; each new shipment instance is a new transaction. A transaction is initiated by the ultimate customer—the manufacturer—on either the shipper side or the consignee side. A transaction may be open for long periods, many days in some cases.

To achieve the level of integration and information quality envisioned by the border stakeholder community, the BTFS is based on multi-agent concepts and technology. Software agents elicit specialized information from human informants, monitor overall progress of the documentation task, monitor the location of the shipment via tracking sensors, coordinate the work flow, and attempt to influence human actors when problems are predicted or detected. Agent functions are realized by goal-directed agents specializing in various tasks in the import/export domain.

The BTFS design is based on three general concepts: (1) creation of a distributed object programming environment with an underlying secure network infrastructure; (2) a distributed object representation of a shipping transaction; and (3) insertion of knowledgeable software agents at critical points in the information flow. Since the stakeholders in the trans-border shipping domain are geographically distributed independent organizations, the Internet provides a ready-made communications infrastructure to integrate their operations. Using the open Internet as the communications infrastructure accommodates any commercial organization with access. Security is provided by public-key encryption and authentication techniques. Our initial approach suggested that the Internet, with its high ramification and ubiquity, would be well suited for the BTFS if security issues were addressed. Assuming this can be accomplished, the Internet goes well beyond merely satisfying BTFS requirements; with the BTFS in place, one could conduct international commerce from any site with an Internet connection and a web browser. The Web, nearly as far-flung as the Internet itself, also suggested HTML as the *lingua franca* of the BTFS, thus obviating the user interface dilemma and neatly solving the client end of the system. In the BTFS, a highly specialized agent converts HTML from the client into the central ontology and back.

Overlying the secure Internet is a distributed object programming system that provides a seamless design methodology for networked object environments [Spires 1997]. The distributed object system is essential to networking agents in a collaborative environment. Distributed object technology also supports a shared fragmented workpiece object. The information needed to effect a single shipment is captured in a complex distributed information structure with compositional semantics called the Maquila Enterprise Transaction (MET). The components of a given MET are distributed among the agencies involved in a particular shipment. The MET is shared via proxy; when a given agent needs information in the MET, it is handed the proxy to the MET. Since the MET is distributed, no one agent or agency has access to all components. Access is permitted based on task requirements and controlled by electronic signature. BTFS agents interact with the border-crossing process by collecting and organizing information and posting it in the MET. Control of the distributed computation is decentralized and opportunistic. Each agent computes new information components based on its internal knowledge base and the state of the MET. Changes in the components trigger computations in a manner reminiscent of blackboard systems [Englemore and Morgan 1987].

Agents improve the border crossing process in the following manner:

- Document quality is improved by elicitation agents. Elicitation agents interface with human informants and specialists to elicit highly structured forms-based data, ensuring that proper documents are entered into the system. Elicitation agents have significant knowledge about the domain and the forms, and they are able to present partially-instantiated documents through use of a case-based reasoning mechanism. Elicitation includes mediation of information from other documents to remove the opportunity for redundant data entry. Invariant data from previously completed documents, having been validated by other elicitation agents and not the responsibility of the current human informant, is translated into the target document's ontology and copied into a non-editable field of the target document.

- Timeliness of documentation and integration of shipment information is improved by an agent collective comprising agents from different organizations that monitor status and coordinate work flow. The collective correlates the physical state of the shipment with its information state to maintain registration and reference, mediates the agency's work on the transaction, updates the transaction, notifies collaborators of updates, and enforces selective data sharing. Monitoring is accomplished by each agent independently and focuses on the interests of its parent organization. Agents respond to requests for status information by users.

- An open decentralized trading regime is ensured by negotiation agents. Negotiation agents are the points of contact for each trading organization. They inspect each incoming transaction before committing to accept the transaction, first validating customer and supplier relationships, and analyzing the ability of the organization to perform the requested services. Upon accepting a transaction, negotiation agents dispatch potential transactions to agents representing knowledge workers for further processing.

Figures 1-3 show elicitation, delegation, and negotiation in *use case* notation [Jacobson 1992] (the agents are distinguished as spherical). Elicitation and mediation are performed within the same context by an elicitation agent. Figure 1 shows the Elicitation Agent working with **form A instance** connected by its inherent slot structure to the **shared workpiece** (this is the MET in the BTFS). The **Export plan** requires that a form of each type named as one of the "Required forms [0 ... n]" be properly filled out. The agent interacts with the **Human actor** object, an internal representation of the individual, which in turn communicates with the person via the **Web browser**. Another *Elicitation agent* (the italicized links) that needs access to the same information gets it from the **shared workpiece**, which is the transaction record.

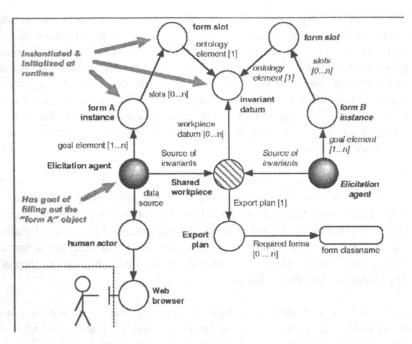

Fig. 1. Elicitation and Mediation.

   Negotiation and delegation behaviors provide coordination of the workflow and timely completion of all documents. Agents coordinate their activities through direct communications and explicit cooperative control [Lesser 1991]. Customer agents negotiate task specifications with supplier agents. When a contract is negotiated and the supplier agent commits to perform the services, the customer agent delegates the task to the supplier. Throughout the negotiations, each proposed new version of the task is signed by the proposing agent with a cryptographic digital signature (Figure 2). Agent "A" signs with the signature denoted "A;" agent "B" signs with signature "B." The final contract is signed by both agents. The basis of coordinated negotiation and delegation is very similar to a joint intentions protocol [Levesque et al. 1990; Cohen and Levesque 1991]. We have added public-key digital signatures to all negotiated forms and tasks for accountability and non-repudiability. This is an essential feature for commercial trading applications. Delegation is shown schematically in Figure 3. A goal or task is passed from a "boss agent," who retains responsibility for the goal, to a "worker agent," who must commit to achieve the goal or report defaulting. If the delegate defaults, the delegator is responsible for finding another qualified delegate.

4. Implementation of Agents

Agent populations are organized into *agencies*, collectives of agents of various competencies, that have ongoing high-level goals stated in business terms. In particular, the BTFS is a distributed set of agencies specialized on the commercial functions of the various stakeholders in the border-crossing process.

The agents that populate the BTFS are realized as instances of speciated agent classes whose behavioral envelope is defined by the Standard Agent Framework [Goldsmith 1997]. The Standard Agent Framework is an object-oriented framework that enables the exploratory development of multiagent systems that interact with human users. The Standard Agent Framework provides a means for constructing and customizing multiagent systems by specialization of base classes (architecture-driven) and by composition (data-driven).

The framework comprises two associated abstract classes: *agent* and *agency*. An *agency* identifies an independent locus of processes, activities, and knowledge typically associated with an company, organization, department, site, household, machine, or some other natural partitioning of the application domain. The underlying assumption is that the application is naturally modeled as a group of interacting agencies. The agency provides a containing context for a collection of agents. The activities of the agency are conducted by its constituent agents. Agents inhabit an agency for the express purpose of providing *services*, including interagency communications, that maintain the functioning of the agency and lead to satisfaction of the ultimate objectives of the agency. An agent performs domain-specific tasks on behalf of human actors and other agents.

Actual agent systems are implemented by the specialization and instantiation of four concrete classes: (1) Standard Agency, (2) Standard Agent, (3) Human Actor, and (4) Resources. The class Standard Agency is an elaboration of the agency concept that includes human activities within the agency and devices for data-oriented activities such as storage and communications. An instance of Standard Agency is a persistent, identity-bearing composite object that contains collections of the component classes Standard Agent, Human Actor, and Resources.

The class Standard Agent implements instances of agents that have specific attributes: autonomy, social ability, reflexivity, and pro-activeness [Wooldridge and Jennings 1995]. The primary Standard Agent protocols are: An interface mechanism that enables interaction with other agents and human actors, a reflexive action mechanism for rapidly responding to event objects in the agent's environment, and a generic inference mechanism for achieving explicit goals. The interaction and inference protocols can be specialized with methods that implement other agent architectures and mechanisms. Agents are self-contained threads of execution that execute both periodically and through immediate scheduling.

100

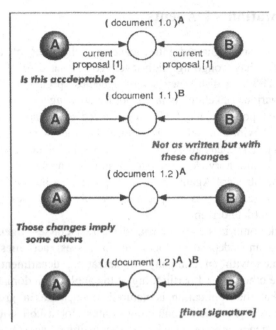

Fig. 2. Negotiation between two agents.

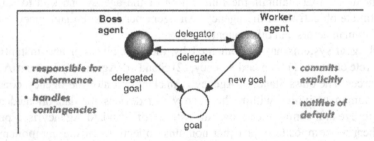

Fig. 3. Delegation.

Human Actors are people that inhabit the agency through an interface device and interact with agents to accomplish tasks. Human actor objects are temporary objects that contain an interface address, an interface object that captures the display, data entry and control functions currently available to the person, and a persistent person object that holds personal data, passwords, email address, and an account object that provides access to past and current workspaces. A workspace object contains objects created and stored by the person during work sessions.

Agents and human actors have access to *resources* such as databases, fax machines, telephones, email handlers, and other useful services. Resource objects provide concurrency control and access protocols for agency resources. Subclasses of the resource class implement objects representing data bases, fax machines, printers, email ports, EDI ports and other commonplace legacy devices in the agency environment.

The Standard Agent Framework supports distributed agent systems. Agency objects may be distributed in a network environment to create a collaborative enterprise structure of interconnected agencies. The fundamental activity conducted among distributed agencies is the trading of domain objects through proxy agents that represent one agency within the agent collection of another agency. These proxy objects delegate all messages (except for a local request for identifying information about the represented agency) to the appropriate domain or task agent residing in the agency. Public proxies are registered in an agency network phonebook with a well-known address. To find other agencies, an agent issues one or more queries to the phonebook and is returned the proxy objects matching the query. The agent proxies interned within an agency form a persistent network of agencies. Such networks are called *durable proxy networks*.

An *electronic commerce agency* (ECA) is a specialized subclass of an agency that implements architectural features specific to electronic commerce applications. An ECA has the additional attributes of *transactions* and *organizations*. The transactions attribute holds a collection of open and closed transaction objects. The organizations attribute holds a collection of public proxy objects pointing to agencies that represent trading partners.

The BTFS agent society comprises several federated ECAs analogous to the interested business entities. Each ECA is populated by a heterogeneous collective of speciated agents, each of which is able to perform a fragment of the information tasks needed to effect trans-border shipment. Their exact duties are based on the idiosyncratic business rules of the actual businesses involved, so an operational ECA must be tailored and situated for each business. Constructing the ECA and the agents that make it up consists in specializing agents from a set of standard agent classes constructed for commerce. ECA classes are also pre-defined for the various required roles: originator, receiver, transport provider, and import/export broker.

In addition to domain and task specialists, several varieties of housekeeping agents perform maintenance tasks for the ECA. Security agents control access by human actors to each agency within the parent organization. A human actor logged into the ECA "inhabits" the agency for the duration of the work session. An agent handles all interactions with the human actor. Task agents initiate requirements to obtain information based on activated goals, monitor the appropriate information sites to see whether the goals have been achieved, and take corrective or contingency measures when failures occur. Dispatch agents allocate new transactions to the appropriate agents. Supervisory agents allocate work to task agents, deal with rejected goals, collate agency-level data, and respond to outside requests for task status information. Various agents incorporate reporting facilities for human actors, including government customs on both sides of the border.

5. Meta-comments on the state of agent-mediated commerce

Work presented at the Workshop on Agent-mediated Electronic Trading discusses, among others, the following:

- Task reallocation,
- Contract type selection,
- Trading/bidding strategy selection and evolution,
- Algorithms for negotiation,
- Realization infrastructures for multi-agent trading,
- Representation strategies and logics for trade, and
- Encoding standards and integration with existing systems.

We have observed a tendency to concentrate on the formation of mechanisms to support observed practice, which may not be sufficiently visionary for the coming paradigm shift.

If we have any criticism of the field as a whole, it is that there seems to be an overemphasis on negotiation for individual consumer-to-business transactions, especially auctions, with the concomitant underemphasis on delivery and settlement. Negotiation establishes the pipeline for the flow of goods and payment; delivery and settlement fill that pipeline, and agent-based systems are as valuable here. In large-scale commercial operations, the negotiation phase of a given transaction has often already been accomplished. The issue in general is more likely to be a matter of accessing the negotiated terms. These usually reside in a document, e.g. a contract or Trading Partner Agreement (TPI). Agents must know how to formulate, populate, and access these (to be sure, the formulation and population will involve negotiation). The existence of secure, agent-readable documents is a crucial aspect of business-to-business ecommerce.

The stock exchange is an example of a multi-buyer, multi-seller environment that agents will certainly make more efficient due to their ability to communicate and act nearly instantaneously. Commodity values will be less affected by local market forces and perception. Large-scale price effects—often undesireable ones—have been observed in practice as so-called "robots" automatically buy and sell huge amounts of stock based on computed economic indicators. The implication is that blind (or at least uninformed) automation is at best a risky strategy for commerce automation. It seems clear that a more reflective mechanism that better understands the ramifications of its actions needs to be employed.

Representation of various market bidding, auction, and trading environments can enable agents to choose behaviors that are instantaneously optimal based on information they hold at decision time. Theories of realization and optimal behavior are engendering realization mechanisms that make agent systems increasingly easy to implement. Representational standards, especially in describing customer needs and product attributes, are making it easier for general automated mechanisms to communicate without significant co-engineering, thus also enabling a trading environment that is more reliable and more likely to be able to handle any given transaction. Some of our work [Phillips *et al.*] has addressed formation of interlinguae to enable transactions among diverse business stakeholders. The business community has embraced the well-developed Electronic Data Interchange (EDI) standard, albeit in several specialized versions, to enable electronic transactions without prior communication. To be sure, the EDI standards are so broad that ongoing business relationships must be supported by a Trading Partner Agreement (TPI) that bounds the kind and content of electronic communication between the partners.

As an aside, there is a natural residence for such interlinguae once they exist: the broker. When commercial transactions require a broker, it is often at least partially because one party or the other is not familiar with the language of the transaction, and the broker serves not only to cause the transaction to occur but also to dynamically translate the terms back and forth among the parties involved. This has direct benefits for referential integrity and parsimony, because every party doesn't require the ability to translate every other parties' terms. Workload may be distributed among several brokers if necessary.

We have observed much consternation over the question of how to decide whether an agent standing on your figurative doorstep is trustworthy or not. Two comments: First, trust is born out of reliable delivery and settlement practices. Information must be unavailable to those who aren't supposed to see it and available to those who are; the intended effects of permitted, purposeful actions must occur reliably, and forbidden or accidental actions must have no effect. These notions are encompassed by the word "surety." Our assessment is that agents participating in a mechanism with surety will automatically engender trust because they will be trustworthy and reliable.

Second, and notwithstanding surety, we suggest that trust of an agent is not based on any inherent property of the agent; rather it is based on the agency that the agent represents. What is needed is an agent bonding or certification mechanism so that we can instantly recognize the affiliation of an agent. This implies the existence of an *agency*, discussed herein, a concept not new in domains needing surety (e.g. certificate issuers). We trust and use Automated Transaction Machines (ATMs) not because we believe each machine to be trustworthy but because it has on it the name of a known financial institution. We don't go to the ATM to complain about failures; we go to its bank. In short, you can't create trust, but you can engineer surety, and trust devolves from surety.

6. Conclusions

The BTFS prototype demonstrates a multi-agent approach to coordinating a complex, knowledge-intensive shipping process. We have demonstrated the following agent behaviors: elicitation, mediation between ontologies, negotiation, delegation, monitoring, and goal satisfaction. We have demonstrated an authenticated negotiation protocol for commercial contracts.

The most challenging aspects of integrating a diverse enterprise such as border trade are: (1) knowledge-intensive elicitation of form information, (2) mediation and ontological leveling of information across multiple organizations, (3) knowledge engineering in general, and (4) secure distributed object computing.

The BTFS system is currently being evaluated for commercialization.

Acknowledgements

The authors express their gratitude to John Wagner of the New Mexico Alliance for Transportation Research for his support of this project.

References

[1] Cohen, P. R. and Levesque, H. J. (1991). Confirmation and Joint Action, *Proceedings of the International Joint Conference on AI*.

[2] Godfrey, J. B. (1998). *Advanced Technologies for International and Intermodal Ports of Entry (ATIPE) Final Report*, Sandia National Laboratories Technical Report, publication pending 1998, Albuquerque, NM

[3] Goldsmith, S. (1997). *The Standard Agent Framework*, Sandia National Laboratories, Advanced Information Systems Laboratory Technical Report, Albuquerque, NM

[4] Engelmore, R. and Morgan, T., (Eds.). (1988). *Blackboard Systems*. Addison-Wesley, Reading, Massachusetts.

[5] Jacobson, I. (1992). *Object-Oriented Software Engineering*, ACM Press.

[6] Lesser, V. (1991). A Retrospective View of FA/C Distributed Problem Solving. *IEEE Transactions on Systems, Man, and Cybernetics , 21* (6): 1347-1362.

[7] Levesque, H. J., Cohen, P. R., and Nunes, J. (1990). On Acting Together, *Proceedings of the National Joint Conference on AI*.

[8] Parker, S. K. and Icerman, L. (1996). *Stakeholder Identification of Advanced Technology Opportunities at International Ports of Entry*, Sandia National Laboratories Technical Report, Albuquerque, NM.

[9] Phillips, L. R.; Goldsmith, S. Y.; and Spires, S. V. (1998) Capturing and Using Precise Semantics for Complex Transactions, *Proc. ECOOP Wkshp of Precise Behavioral Semantics,* July, 1998

[10] SAIC. (1997). unpublished communication, Science Applications International Corporation.

[11] Schoeneman, L. and Fox, E. (1996). *Authenticated Tracking and Monitoring System (ATMS)*, Sandia National Laboratories Technical Report VST-071, Albuquerque, NM

[12] Spires, S. (1997). *The DCLOS Distributed Object System*, SNL AISL Technical Report

[13] Wooldridge, M. and Jennings, N. (1995). Intelligent Agents: Theory and Practice, *Knowledge Engineering Review* 10(2).

Bid Evaluation and Selection in the MAGNET Automated Contracting System

Erik Steinmetz, John Collins, Scott Jamison, Rashmi Sundareswara,
Bamshad Mobasher, and Maria Gini

Department of Computer Science and Engineering
University of Minnesota

Abstract. We present an approach to the bid-evaluation problem in
a system for multi-agent contract negotiation, called MAGNET. The
MAGNET market infrastructure provides support for a variety of types
of transactions, from simple buying and selling of goods and services to
complex multi-agent contract negotiations. In the latter case, MAGNET
is designed to negotiate contracts based on temporal and precedence constraints, and includes facilities for dealing with time-based contingencies.
One responsibility of a customer agent in the MAGNET system is to
select an optimal bid combination. We present an efficient anytime algorithm for a customer agent to select bids submitted by supplier agents in
response to a call for bids. Bids might include combinations of subtasks
and might include discounts for combinations. In an experimental study
we explore the behavior of the algorithm based on the interactions of
factors such as bid prices, number of bids, and number of subtasks. The
results of experiments we present show that the algorithm is extremely
efficient even for large number of bids.

1 Introduction

The combination of electronic commerce and autonomous intelligent agents has
the potential to deliver enormous economic benefits. Primitive examples are
already being deployed on the Internet, in the form of automated shopping
agents [8] and auction services [17,26]. More complex economic activities remain
outside the reach of the current generation of automated agents.

The overall research goal of the MAGNET project [6,7] is to develop a semantic model for the integration of planning, contracting, scheduling, and execution
in a multi-agent market domain, such as the Internet. In particular, we are interested in how an agent that has a goal to satisfy can construct a plan, issue a
call for bids to other self-interested agents, award contracts, and monitor their
execution. We call this process *Plan Execution by Contracting*.

MAGNET includes a market infrastructure and a set of agents that can
make use of this environment to carry out Plan Execution by Contracting activities. The market infrastructure provides an environment with explicit support
for complex agent interactions. The market acts as a trusted third party to reduce opportunities for fraud and misrepresentation. It also manages and enforces

the negotiation protocol between agents, from the negotiation and contracting phases through the full cycle of contract commitment, execution, and settlement.

All the agents in the MAGNET environment are assumed to be self-interested. In other words, they exhibit limited rationality in the sense that they will do what is in their own best interests within the limits of their reasoning capabilities. Agents are also heterogeneous; they are not assumed to have the same capabilities, nor do they necessarily embody similar decision processes. In general, they are motivated to engage in contracting behavior because they do not have direct access to the resources needed to execute their plans.

The main focus of this paper is a bid-evaluation mechanism for MAGNET agents. We start by providing an overview of the MAGNET market architecture and a negotiation protocol for Plan Execution by Contracting, and then proceed to discuss bid evaluation. Because the evaluation of bids must take into account plan feasibility as well as cost factors, straightforward auction mechanisms are inadequate for the MAGNET domain. We describe an anytime bid-evaluation algorithm that attempts to find the lowest-cost feasible plan, within the limits of available time and computing resources. Finally, we describe how our work relates to other efforts in the general area of automated negotiation and contracting.

2 The MAGNET Architecture

The MAGNET architecture is a distributed set of objects that can support electronic commerce in a variety of domains, from the simple buying and selling of goods to situations that require complex multi-agent negotiation and contracting. The fundamental elements of this architecture are the *exchange*, the *market*, and the *market session*, as outlined below.

2.1 The Exchange

An *Exchange* is a collection of domain-specific markets in which goods and services are traded, along with some generic services required by all markets, such as verifying identities of participants in a transaction, or a Better Business Bureau that can provide information about the reliability of other agents based on past performance. Architecturally, an exchange is a network-accessible resource that supports a set of markets and common services, as depicted in Figure 1.

2.2 Markets

Each *Market* within an exchange is a forum for commerce in a particular commodity or business area. We envision markets devoted to banking, publishing and printing, construction, transportation, industrial equipment, electronic assembly, etc. Each market includes a set of domain-specific services and facilities, as shown in Figure 2, and each market draws upon the common services of the exchange.

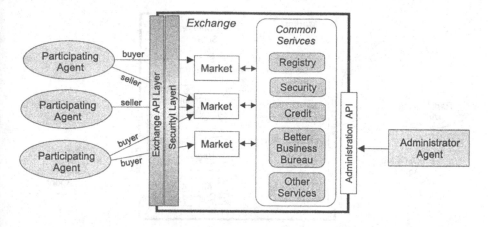

Fig. 1. The Structure of an Exchange. ©1988 by ACM, Inc., appeared in [7]

An important component of each market is a set of current *Market Sessions* in which the actual agent interactions occur. Agents participating in a market may do so as either session initiators, or as clients, or both. As detailed in the next section, each session is initiated by a single agent for a particular purpose, and in general multiple agents may join an existing session as clients. Important elements of the market include:

- An *Ontology* that is specific to the domain of the market, specifying the terms of discourse within that domain. In a commodity-oriented domain, it would include terms for the products or services within the domain, as well as terminology for quality, quantity, features, terms and conditions of business, etc. In a planning-oriented domain, specifications of services would be in a form that supports planning.
- A *Protocol Specification* that formalizes the types of negotiation supported within the market. Within a planning-oriented market domain, these specifications include limits on parameters of the negotiation protocol, such as the maximum decommitment penalty, whether bids can be awarded before the bid deadline, etc.
- A *Registry* of market clients who have expressed interest in doing business in the market. Entries in this registry would include the identity of a client, a catalog (or a method for accessing a catalog) of that client's interests, products or capabilities, which can be used to locate clients to meet requests for new session participants, and a client agent that is empowered to negotiate contracts on behalf of the supplier. Client catalogs are required to express their interests and offerings in terms of the market's ontology.

2.3 Market Sessions

A *Market Session* (or simply a session) is the vehicle through which market services are delivered dynamically to participating agents. It serves as an encap-

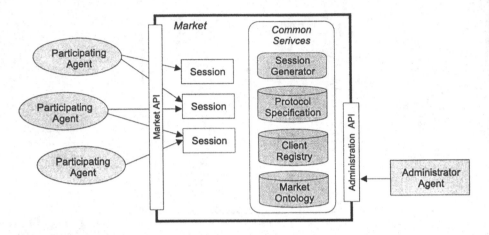

Fig. 2. The Structure of a Market within the Exchange. ©1988 by ACM, Inc., appeared in [7]

sulation for a transaction in the market, as well as a persistent repository for the current state of the transaction.

We have chosen the term "session" to emphasize the temporally extended nature of many of these interactions. For example, in a construction-oriented market, if an agent wishes to build a new house, it initiates a session and issues a call-for-bids. The session extends from the initial call-for-bids through the negotiation, awards, construction work, paying of bills, and final closing. In other words, the session encloses the full life of a contract (or possibly a set of related contracts). The session mechanism ensures continuity of partially-completed transactions, protects against fraud by verifying the identity of agents, limits counterspeculation by enforcing negotiation rules, and relieves the participating agents from having to keep track of detailed negotiation status themselves.

Agents can play two different roles with respect to any session. The agent who initiates a session is known as the *session initiator*, while other participating agents are known as *session clients*. A session can be initiated either for the purpose of buying or selling, depending on the type of market. In the above example of building a house, the initiating agent was the buyer or customer, and the other participants would be sellers or suppliers, whether they were supplying materials, labor, advice, credit, or other services. A session could also be initiated to sell items or services at auction.

At any given time, a session can be *open* to new participants, or *closed*. A public auction would typically be open to new participants, while the house-building session described above would be closed once the contracts were let. The market maintains a list of open sessions which may be accessed (and potentially joined) by participating agents.

Figure 3 shows the structure of a session. Two APIs are exposed, one for the session initiator and one for session clients.

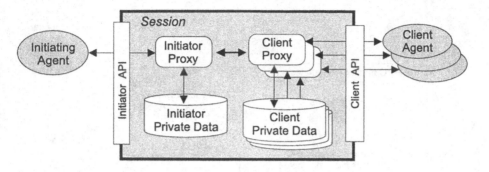

Fig. 3. The Structure of a Market Session. ©1988 by ACM, Inc., appeared in [7]

Each session contains an Initiator Proxy that implements the Initiator API and persistently stores the current state of the session from the standpoint of the initiator.

A Client Proxy is provided for each client that similarly provides a Client API to the client agent, and persistently stores the current state of the session from the standpoint of the client. Proxies are market entities that act on behalf of the agents and enforce market rules.

There are two reasons for the existence of the proxy components. The first is related to security: client proxy components cannot see the private data of the initiator or of other clients. The second is that in a distributed system environment, the processing and persistent data elements of the initiator and clients could be instantiated at different locations in the network to maximize performance.

3   The MAGNET Protocol

In this section we briefly describe a protocol that supports the Plan Execution by Contracting model. As outlined in the interaction diagram in 4, the negotiation portion of the protocol is a finite 3-step process that begins when a customer agent initiates a session and issues a Call For Bids. This diagram does not deal with decommitment or settlement.

The Plan Execution by Contracting protocol begins after the session has been initiated by a customer agent: the customer issues a call-for-bids, suppliers reply with bids, and the customer accepts the bids it chooses with bid-accept messages.

Another set of messages, including release, completion, and decommitment, are used to manage the progress of the plan once bids have been awarded. We have avoided the need for open-ended negotiation by means of bid break downs and a time-based decommitment penalty as described below.

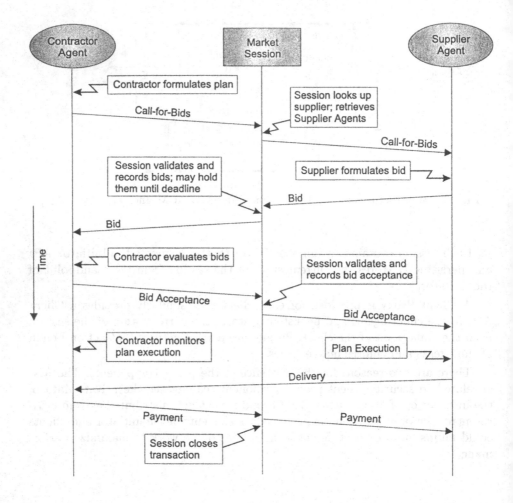

Fig. 4. A Typical Session-Mediated Negotiation

3.1 Call for bids

Once the customer has developed a plan of subtasks chosen from the market's ontology, it will send a call-for-bids message. The call-for-bids message will include, for each subtask listed, a time window during which the work must be done. The call-for-bids message will also include, among other information:

1. a bid deadline, or the time by which the suppliers must respond with bids,
2. the time at which the customer will begin considering the bids,
3. the earliest time at which bid acceptances will be sent,
4. penalty functions for each subtask, which will be assessed against the supplier if the supplier commits to work, but fails (or decides not) to do it. These penalty functions are piecewise-linear functions of time that are intended to

encourage suppliers to perform the work they commit to. If a supplier is unable to perform, the increasing value of the penalty function encourages it to explicitly decommit as early as possible.

This call-for-bids message, once created, is passed to the market session, which makes it available to all of the appropriate suppliers (those who are registered with the market, and are able to perform the necessary tasks.)

In this sense, the call-for-bids message is public, while all of the remaining messages are private. Before forwarding it, the market session may check the message to make sure that it conforms to all market and exchange rules which may exist.

3.2 Bidding

Each supplier will inspect the call-for-bids, and will decide whether or not it should respond with a bid, according to its resources, time constraints, and knowledge of the work to be done, according to the catalog of services provided by the market agent.

If it chooses to respond, it will send a bid message, which will be private (i.e. other suppliers will not see the contents of the bid). This bid message can include a combination of subtasks, which must be a subset of the subtasks listed in the call-for-bids. The content and number of bid messages will be monitored and may be recorded by the market session, before they are validated and forwarded to the customer.

In the bid, the supplier must indicate the cost (to the customer), the time window, and the estimated duration of the work for the whole subtask combination, and this same data for each of the separate subtasks (please see the explanation for this in the next section). The bid-accept deadline must also be included, as well as a penalty function for each subtask which the customer will have to pay if it commits to giving this supplier the work but then decides to decommit. This penalty function will have the same structure as the supplier penalty function.

Each supplier can send multiple bids for each call-for-bids, each including different costs and time windows, but each supplier will be awarded only one bid combination (or part of one). This is to enable the supplier to send many bids, but not over commit itself.

This bid is a commitment by the supplier to do work listed in the bid, should the customer accept it. If the supplier sends no bid message before the customer's bid deadline, the customer will assume that the supplier has decided not to send a bid for this particular call for bids. Thus, rejection is passive.

3.3 Bid acceptance

Having received the bids, the customer must decide which of the bids to accept, using knowledge about the bids, the task and subtask values, its own time constraints and the bidder (perhaps provided by the market agent). After completing this process, the customer must decide to do one of three things for each bid that it has received:

1. accept the whole bid,
2. accept a subset of the subtasks in the bid, or
3. reject the bid (passive rejection).

The motivation for these choices is to make open-ended negotiation unnecessary. If no acceptable set of bids together would cover every subtask to the satisfaction of the customer, then the customer can avoid negotiation because it knows how the supplier will break down the costs of the accepted subtasks, should it become necessary for the customer to accept a subset of the original bid combination.

This scheme in conjunction with the time-based decommitment penalty functions makes it possible to avoid open-ended negotiation without loss of generality.

The bid-accept message will be sent through the market session, which will verify, validate and time-stamp it before forwarding it to the customer. Note that either of the first two choices are commitments to give the supplier the work and at the point in time that this message is sent (according to the market session's time stamp), both the supplier and the customer penalty functions will be set into effect.

A failure to send a bid-accept message means the customer is rejecting the supplier's bid.

Once commitments have been made, an agent may determine that it cannot do the tasks it has committed to, or that it would disadvantageous to do so. In these situations, the agent must send a decommitment message to the other agent, describing what parts of its commitment it will not be satisfying. Included in the decommitment messages will be an acknowledgment of the penalty that the agent will be paying as a result of the decommitment.

3.4 Release

As the plan progresses, Release messages are used to inform supplier agents that they may begin work on portions of the plan for which they have been awarded bids. Failure to release prior to the suppliers latest start time constitutes decommitment on the part of the customer, and a penalty will be assessed by the Session.

3.5 Decommitment

Once bids are awarded, either party may choose to decommit and pay a penalty. The ability to decommit makes this a "leveled commitment" protocol. This is a requirement in many real-world contracting domains, and Sandholm and Lesser [21] have shown that the ability to decommit permits agreements to be reached in situations where no agreement would otherwise be possible.

Decommitment is only valid prior to delivery, and the penalty is not discounted in the case where a discounted multi-element bid was awarded.

3.6 Delivery and acceptance

The protocol is completed with messages that signify delivery by the supplier and acceptance of delivery by the customer. Failure to deliver prior to the deadline agreed to in the bid constitutes supplier decommitment, and the supplier will be assessed the decommitment penalty by the Session. For present purposes, we will assume that settlement is outside the scope of the system.

4 An Algorithm for Bid Evaluation

In this section we consider the specific problem of evaluating bids in a Plan Execution by Contracting situation. In general it is not enough to merely compare prices, because the set of bids accepted must constitute a complete and feasible plan. We have chosen a local improvement search [22,27] over a constructive search for three reasons:

– There is a straightforward mechanism for constructing a baseline feasible solution.
– The time-dependent nature of the negotiation protocol requires that the search be completed within a fixed period of time. Boddy and Dean [3] have characterized this type of search as an anytime search. In [2], Boddy has further characterized the requirements for anytime problem solving using performance profiles.
– Since the search space for this problem is well-structured, a systematic, domain-specific search algorithm such as the one we propose here appears more suited than the generic methods described in [16].

We consider a typical contracting situation in which the customer's call-for-bids is comprised of a group of subtasks. We use bid break-downs to avoid open-ended negotiation among agents, but for simplicity, we do not consider temporal factors such as bid deadlines or time-based decommitment penalties. Accordingly, a bid by a supplier is a subset of these subtasks with an associated cost or price for the whole bid.

In addition, each bid includes a cost for individual subtasks that make up the bid. The bid cost may represent a *discount* over the sum of the costs of individual subtasks contained in the bid. To satisfy a subtask the customer agent has the option of choosing the whole bid from a given supplier, or selecting individual bid elements from various suppliers.

A typical contracting situation is depicted in Figure 5, where the customer agent has issued a call-for-bids comprised of four subtasks S_1, S_2, S_3, and S_4. Suppliers have submitted 3 bids, each containing a subset of these subtasks. Finally, the customer, after evaluating the bids, has accepted parts of bids 1 and 3 and all of bid 2. In this case, the customer would pay the full price for subtasks S_1 and S_4 as specified by bids 1 and 4, respectively. However, subtasks S_2 and S_3 may have been obtained at a discount price since the customer has accepted the complete bid.

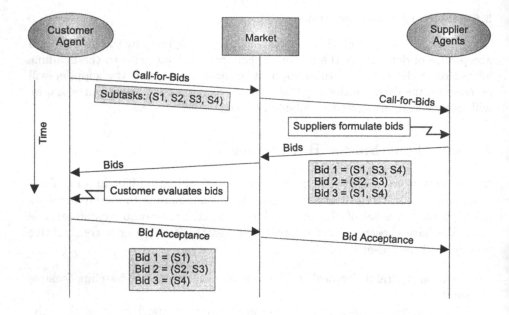

Fig. 5. A Typical contracting situation

We now present our bid selection algorithm. The goal is to find the best combination of bids and parts of bids (selecting only some of the subtasks from a bid, and ignoring the discount) to cover the entire set of subtasks specified by the call-for-bids.

The algorithm has two phases. First, we build an initial solution from the best individual subtask prices. If there are no bids for one or more of the subtasks, no initial solution can be constructed and the algorithm terminates. If a solution exists, we try to improve the initial solution by applying discounts from the various bids. Because each bid represents a single discount, we conduct our search by bid, not by subtask.

Each solution is represented by a node in a list of feasible solutions. We start the list by creating an initial solution, storing it in what we call the origin node, and placing the origin node in the feasible solution list.

Each node, which represents a solution to the problem, includes a list of subtasks, the price of each subtask, which bid is covering each subtask, whether each subtask is part of a discount (false for all subtasks in the origin node), and the total discount amount (zero in the origin node).

In the algorithm, we use the notation $node.bidID[i]$ to indicate the bid identifier of subtask i in the node $node$, $node.price[i]$ to indicate the price of subtask i, $node.discount?[i]$ to indicate if subtask i is part of a discount. $node.TotalDiscount$ indicates the total discount, $node.DiscountedPrice$ the discounted price, and $node.TotalPrice$ the total price of the solution. We will use a similar notation to indicate the components of a bid.

```
/* initialize origin node */
create origin node;
origin.TotalDiscount ← 0;
for each subtask ∈ SetofTasks do
    origin.bidID[subtask] ← unassigned
    origin.price[subtask] ← ∞
    origin.discount?[subtask] ← false

/* construct an initial solution (if one exists) */
for each bid ∈ SetofBids do
    for each subtask covered in bid do
        if     origin.bidID[subtask] = unassigned
               or bid.price[subtask] < origin.price[subtask]
        then origin.price[subtask] ← bid.price[subtask]
               origin.bidID[subtask] ← bid.bidID[subtask]
solution? ← true
for each subtask ∈ SetofTasks do
    if origin.bidID[subtask] = unassigned then solution? ← false
if solution? = false then exit /* no solution exists */
add origin to SolutionList /* a solution exists */

/* improve the initial solution by applying one or more discounts */
for each bid ∈ SetofBids do
    for each node in SolutionList do
        discounted? ← false
        for each subtask covered in bid do
            if node.discount?[subtask] = true then discounted? ← true
        if     discounted? = false
               /* there is no subtask overlap for the discounts */
        then create a new node current
               for each subtask in bid do
                   current.price[subtask] ← bid.price[subtask]
                   current.bidID[subtask] ← bid.bidID[subtask]
                   current.discount?[subtask] ← true
               current.TotalDiscount ← node.TotalDiscount + bid.discount
               current.TotalPrice ← ∑_{subtask∈SetofTasks} current.price[subtask]
               current.DiscountedPrice ←
                   current.TotalPrice − current.TotalDiscount
               if     current.DiscountedPrice < node.DiscountedPrice
               then add current to TemporaryList
               else  discard it
    add the nodes from TemporaryList to SolutionList
    sort SolutionList in decreasing order by DiscountedPrice
the first node in SolutionList is the best solution
```

Let us now consider a detailed example of this procedure. In this example, we consider a call-for-bids on four subtasks. Suppose that, in response to the call-for-bids, three bids are received by the customer agent:

1. Bid 1 covers subtasks 1, 3 and 4 for 130 units with subtask 1 at 50 units, subtask 3 at 50 units and subtask 4 at 45 units (15 units discount).
2. Bid 2 covers subtasks 2 and 3 for 95 units with subtask 2 at 60 units and subtask 3 at 70 units (35 units discount).
3. Bid 3 covers subtasks 1 and 4 for 95 units with subtask 1 at 75 units and subtask 4 at 40 units (20 units discount).

The origin node is formed by taking the smallest individual price for each subtask, thus:

Origin		Parent Node: None	
subtask	bidID	price	discount?
1	1	50	false
2	2	60	false
3	1	50	false
4	3	40	false
total price:		200	
total discount:		0	
discounted price:		200	

We now try to form a child node for each node in the list using the Bid 1 discount. Since there is only one node in the list, and none of its subtasks are marked as discounted, we make a child node:

Node 1		Parent Node: Origin	
subtask	bidID	price	discount?
1	1	50	true
2	2	60	false
3	1	50	true
4	1	45	true
total price:		205	
total discount:		15	
discounted price:		190	

Since the discounted price is indeed less than the discounted price of its parent, we add this node to the list. We now try to create children using the Bid 2 discount. From the Origin Node we can make a child:

Node 2			Parent Node: Origin
subtask	bidID	price	discount?
1	1	50	false
2	2	60	true
3	2	70	true
4	3	40	false
total price:		220	
total discount:		35	
discounted price:		185	

Since the discounted price is less than the discounted price of its parent, we add this node to the list. We cannot, however, make a child node from Node 1 (because there is a discount overlap on subtask 3).

We now move on to Bid 3. We can make a node from the Origin Node:

Node 3			Parent Node: Origin
subtask	bidID	price	discount?
1	3	75	true
2	2	60	false
3	1	50	false
4	3	40	true
total price:		225	
total discount:		20	
discounted price:		205	

This node is not added to the list. Its discounted price is actually above the price of its parent (in this case the origin node).

We cannot make a child from Node 1 using Bid 3 because of the overlap on subtasks 1 and 4. We can, however, make a child of Node 2:

Node 4			Parent Node: Node 2
subtask	bidID	price	discount?
1	3	75	true
2	2	60	true
3	2	70	true
4	3	40	true
total price:		245	
total discount:		55	
discounted price:		190	

This node is not added to the list, because though it is cheaper than the Origin Node, it is not cheaper than its parent node (Node 2).

There are now a total of three nodes in the list, and the cheapest price can be found in Node 2. Though that node contains higher subtask prices than the origin node, it contains enough discount to make it the least expensive combination.

The number of nodes created by this algorithm is highly dependent on the interaction between the number of bids, subtasks, price variation, and discount. We shall examine the results of some of these interactions in the next section.

Our algorithm conducts a systematic search on a finite space, so the algorithm is complete. It finds the optimal solution because it creates all non-conflicting discount combinations. Combinations which are not considered as solutions are rejected because they increase the total price. Since the algorithm starts with a solution and only combinations that decrease the price are considered, the algorithm has an anytime behavior. The algorithm can be terminated any time and will return the best solution found so far. Given additional time, it will produce a better solution, if one is available.

5   Experimental Evaluation

In order to observe the behavior of this algorithm under different circumstances, we constructed a set of experiments using the following parameters:

- The number of subtasks in the call-for-bids. We tried 10, 20 or 30 subtasks.
- The number of bids (suppliers). We tried 10, 20, or 30 suppliers.
- The mean percentage of subtasks that suppliers will include in their bids. This percentage was fixed at 30% for one set of experiments, and was varied randomly within the 10 to 60% range, for another set of experiments.
- The price range that suppliers can bid for each subtask. We tried allowing the price to vary widely (10-100) or narrowly (80-100).
- The percentage discount that suppliers will offer in their bids. This was picked with a uniform distribution within the range 0-40%.

All of the subtasks were considered to be of equal importance and were bid by the suppliers up to a price of 100 units each. Subtask ordering and other temporal considerations were ignored. For each experiment, ten different bid sets were produced with the same parameters, and the number of nodes examined to complete the search was computed.

Figures 6 and 7 illustrate the results for these experiments. Figure 6 shows the results for two sets of experiments, one in which the percentage of subtasks per bid was fixed at 30% and another with the percentage varying in the range of 11-60%. In both cases, the bid prices varied from 10 to 100 units. Figure 7 shows the results of another two sets of experiments using the same subtask percentage parameters, but using a bid price range of 80-100 units.

Comparing Figures 6 and 7, we can see that when pricing is allowed to fluctuate widely, the number of nodes searched decreases as the number of bids increases. When prices are constrained in their range, however, the number of nodes increases as the number of bids increases. This is due to the fact that, in the unconstrained scenario, there is an increased chance of bids being overpriced with

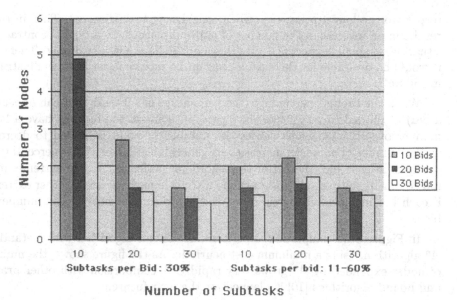

Fig. 6. Price varying from 10 to 100 unit

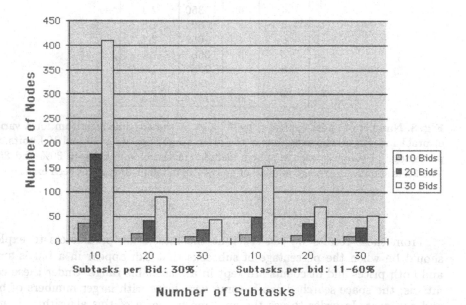

Fig. 7. Price varying from 80 to 100 unit

respect to the lowest price, even when considering their discount. This, in turn, results in an increase in the number of nodes discarded. In a typical contracting situation we should expect the price range not to have a large variance. Therefore it would be desirable for the customer agent to receive fewer bids, as illustrated in Figure 7.

When the subtask percentage (the percentage of subtasks that can appear in a bid) is allowed to vary up to sixty percent, some of the bid sets have a large number of subtasks, which causes the number of nodes searched to decrease as the number of subtasks increases. In general, the larger is the percentage of subtasks in each bid, the better the algorithm performs. At one extreme, if no bid contains multiple subtasks only one node is expanded. At the other extreme, if each bid includes all the subtasks, the algorithm is linear in the number of bids.

In Figure 8 we compared the performance of this algorithm with a standard A^* algorithm, using a minimum cost heuristic. As the figure shows, the number of nodes expanded by A^* grows very rapidly. A comparison with other branch and bound algorithms [10] is planned for the near future.

No. of Subtasks	No. of Bids	A^*	Anytime Algorithm
4	4	137	2.6
4	6	350	2.3
4	8	695	1.8
6	4	659	2.7
6	6	3682	2.1
6	8	7367	1.9
7	4	4830	2.3
7	6	22104	1.5

Fig. 8. Number of nodes expanded by A^* and by the anytime algorithm for a variety of problems. For all the experiments the price range is between 10 and 100 units, the percentage of subtasks each suppliers includes in the bids is between 30% and 80%. The table shows the average number of nodes expanded in 10 runs for each experiment.

From these results we can see that the interesting parameters to explore should be when the percentage of subtasks that can appear in a bid is small and both prices and discounts are kept in a reasonable range. Under these conditions, the space searched can become very large with larger numbers of bids and subtasks. In order to use the anytime property of this algorithm, it may become useful to sort the bids (and thus guide the search space) by the percentage discount given. When the algorithm is interrupted, it will have already tried to apply the better discounts, and so should produce a cheaper solution than looking at the bids in a random order.

In a further experiment, we limited the prices and discounts to a reasonable range. The prices were kept between 80% and 100% of the highest price, and discounts were allowed only up to 30% of the total price of a bid. Further, the subtask percentage was kept at 10%. We then looked at the effect of varying the number of bidders from 20 to 45 and the number of subtasks from 20 to 45.

The following table shows the results of our experiments. Each cell shows the mean number of nodes expanded for trials in which a feasible solution existed. Ten trials were attempted for each cell. Assuming that decisions to bid on individual subtasks are independent events, the probability that all subtasks will be bid on by at least one bidder is $\mathcal{P} = (1 - (1 - p)^m)^n$, where m is the number of bidders, n is the number of subtasks, and p is the probability that a bidder will bid on a subtask. It should be noted that the variance in these numbers is rather high; typically, $\sigma > 0.6\overline{X}$.

Bidders Subtasks	20	25	30	35	40	45
20	364	1352	8125	27591	72465	201827
25	2190	6827	15384	34064	66510	88380
30		1366	3271	19244	45595	85348
35		2767	9613	21659	31409	55318
40			4088	7493	21257	34133
45			4445	7167	16136	32795

Fig. 9. Number of nodes expanded by the anytime algorithm for a price range between 80 and 100 units, the probability of a subtask being included in a bid is 10%. Empty cells had no instances of full subtask coverage in 10 runs.

Under these conditions, it appears as though the number of nodes searched increases exponentially with the number of bidders when the number of subtasks is kept constant, approximately doubling with every five bidders added. The number of nodes searched decreases, however, as the number of subtasks increases for a constant number of bidders, which also increases the probability that some subtasks will be included in only one or a very small number of bids.

There are two ways this information could be used by a customer agent in the MAGNET system: before the Call For Bids is issued, and after bids are received:

– if a customer agent has a priori knowledge of the likely number of bidders and the bid density (expected number of subtasks per bid), then the structure of the Call For Bids could be manipulated to both increase the probability of achieving plan coverage, and to reduce the search effort. Such manipulation could be done by choosing plan expansions with more or fewer elements, or with different levels of hierarchical breakdown. The necessary a priori knowledge could be gathered by the Market as contracting activity proceeds under its jurisdiction;

– after bids are received, a simple measure of the bid density and degree of overlap could be used to estimate the required search effort. If the predicted effort was greater than the available time, then a different search strategy, such as simulated annealing, might be chosen in order to achieve broad coverage of the search space, while sacrificing detailed examination.

6 Related Work

In recent years, a variety of architectures have been proposed for electronic commerce and multi-agent automated contracting [4,9,13,15,17,24,25].

In addition to the work on virtual market architectures, several protocols have been developed and proposed that support automated contracting and negotiation among multiple agents in such markets [11,18–20]. Automated contracting protocols generally assume direct agent-to-agent negotiation. For example, Smith [23] pioneered research in communication among cooperating distributed agents with the Contract Net protocol. The Contract Net has been extended by Sandholm and Lesser [19] to self-interested agents.

In these systems, agents communicate and negotiate directly with each other. On the other hand, in the MAGNET system [7], the proposed architecture and the associated protocol for automated contracting utilize an external and independent market infrastructure to reduce fraud and counterspeculation among self-interested agents. In contrast to Sandholm's protocol [20], MAGNET avoids the need for open-ended negotiation by means of bid break-downs and time-based decommitment penalties, as described more in detail in [6].

A primary motivation behind the design of our proposed protocol and market framework is to support automated contracting. This sort of problem is often found in public contracting and it is useful, in general, in multi-enterprise manufacturing.

Existing architectures are generally designed for the kind of commercial activity that involves buying and selling of physical or electronic goods over a distributed electronic environment such as the Internet. They do not explicitly support more complex interactions such as those in a contracting domain where customer agents formulate plans and use the negotiation process to gain commitment from multiple supplier agents for the execution of these plans.

To the extent that we require the existence of an external market mechanism as an intermediary, our proposed framework is similar to that of Wellman's market-oriented programming used in AuctionBot [26]. AuctionBot supports a variety of auction types each imposing a set of market rules on the agent interactions. Hence, the auctions, themselves, become the intermediaries. The entity that sets up the auction can specify certain parameters for the auctions. In contrast, our framework provides explicit market mechanisms which can not only specify and enforce auction parameters, but also support more complex interactions. Furthermore, these market mechanisms also enforce general market rules and "social laws", such as government regulations, by which all participants must abide. Rosenschein and Zlotkin [18] showed how the behavior of the agents can be influenced by the set of rules that the system designers choose for the agents' environment.

In Rosenschein and Zlotkin' study [18] the agents are homogeneous, and the assumption is that there are no side payments. In other words, the goal is to share the work, not to pay for work. Sandholm's agents [19,20,1] redistribute work among themselves by a contracting mechanism. Unlike Rosenschein and Zlotkin, Sandholm considers agreements involving explicit payments.

7 Conclusions and Future Work

In this paper we have presented an overview of the MAGNET automated contracting system, and preliminary results of our work in developing an anytime algorithm that can choose the best combination of bids in real time on a reasonably sized problem. Our proposed algorithm has been developed as part of the MAGNET contracting market framework [7]. It compares favorably with algorithms that build solutions (for example, a constructive A^* search of the subtask space).

Our experimental evaluation suggests that the algorithm searches very efficiently and expands a small number of nodes before producing the optimal solution. The algorithm can be interrupted at any time and will return the best solution found so far. Our results also affirm the common sense notion that there is a tradeoff between cost of computation and opportunity for optimization.

It has been observed that there is often a form of *phase transition* situation that separates easy from hard problems [5]. This observation has produced significant results in the context of propositional satisfiability (SAT) problems (see, for instance, [14,12]. It would be worthwhile to explore if specific heuristics adapt better to either of these extremes, and to study the effect of alternative pruning tactics on hard problems in the domain we have described here.

There are extensions to this algorithm that we are considering. First, we plan on including other factors in the cost of bids, such as the reliability of the supplier, or the desirability of the customer to deal with a specific supplier, Second, we plan on extending the algorithm to include time considerations in addition to price. The best bid could be the one that accomplishes the task at the most appropriate time for the customer, not the one that has the lowest price.

References

1. Martin R. Andersson and Tuomas W. Sandholm. Sequencing of contract types for anytime task reallocation. In *1998 Workshop on Agent Mediated Electronic Trading*, Minneapolis, MN, May 1998.
2. Mark Boddy. Anytime problem solving using dynamic programming. In *AAAI91*, pages 738–743, 1991.

3. Mark Boddy and Thomas Dean. Solving time-dependent planning problems. In *International Joint Conference on Artificial Intelligence*, pages 979–984, 1989.

4. Anthony Chavez and Pattie Maes. Kasbah: An agent marketplace for buying and selling goods. In *Proc. of the First International Conference on the Practical Application of Intelligent Agents and Multi-Agent Technology*, London, UK, April 1996.

5. P. Cheeseman, B. Kanefsky, and W. M. Taylor. Where the really hard problems are. In *Proceedings of the 12th International Joint Conference on Artificial Intelligence*, pages 331–337, 1991.

6. John Collins, Scott Jamison, Maria Gini, and Bamshad Mobasher. Temporal strategies in a multi-agent contracting protocol. In *AAAI-97 Workshop on AI in Electronic Commerce*, July 1997.

7. John Collins, Ben Youngdahl, Scott Jamison, Bamshad Mobasher, and Maria Gini. A market architecture for multi-agent contracting. In *Proceedings of the Second International Conference on Autonomous Agents*, pages 285–292, May 1998.

8. Robert Doorenbos, Oren Etzioni, and Daniel Weld. A scalable comparison-shopping agent for the world-wide web. In *Proceedings of the First International Conference on Autonomous Agents*, pages 39–48, 1997.

9. Joakim Eriksson, Niclas Finne, and Sverker Janson. SICS Marketspace – an agent-based market infrastructure. In *1998 Workshop on Agent Mediated Electronic Trading*, pages 33–48, Minneapolis, Minnesota, May 1998.

10. Freuder and Wallace. Partial constraint satisfaction. *Artificial Intelligence*, 58:21–70, 1992.

11. Robert H. Guttman and Pattie Maes. Agent-mediated integrative negotiation for retail electronic commerce. In *1998 Workshop on Agent Mediated Electronic Trading*, pages 77–90, Minneapolis, Minnesota, May 1998.

12. Larrosa and Meseguer. Phase transition in MAX-CSP. In *Proceedings of the European Conference on Artificial Intelligence*, pages 190–194, 1996.

13. S. McConnell, M. Merz, L. Maesano, and M. Witthaut. An open architecture for electronic commerce. Technical report, Object Management Group, Cambridge, MA, 1997.

14. D. Mitchell, B. Selman, and H. Levesque. Hard and easy distributions of SAT problems. In *Proceedings of the National Conference on Artificial Intelligence*, pages 459–465, 1992.

15. Tracy Mullen and Michael P. Wellman. The auction manager: Market middleware for large-scale electronic commerce. In *1998 Workshop on Agent Mediated Electronic Trading*, pages 113–128, Minneapolis, Minnesota, May 1998.

16. Colin R. Reeves. *Modern Heuristic Techniques for Combinatorial Problems*. John Wiley & Sons, New York, NY, 1993.

17. J. A. Rodriguez, Pablo Noriega, Carles Sierra, and J. Padget. FM96.5 - a Java-based electronic auction house. In *Second Int'l Conf on The Practical Application of Intelligent Agents and Multi-Agent Technology (PAAM'97)*, London, April 1997.

18. Jeffrey S. Rosenschein and Gilad Zlotkin. *Rules of Encounter*. MIT Press, Cambridge, MA, 1994.

19. Tuomas Sandholm and Victor Lesser. Issues in automated negotiation and electronic commerce: Extending the contract net framework. In *1st International Conf. on Multiagent Systems*, pages 328–335, San Francisco, 1995.

20. Tuomas W. Sandholm. *Negotiation Among Self-Interested Computationally Limited Agents*. PhD thesis, University of Massachusetts, 1996.

125

21. Tuomas W. Sandholm and Victor R. Lesser. Advantages of a leveled commitment contracting protocol. In *Proceedings of the Thirteenth National Conference on Artificial Intelligence*, pages 126–133, Portland, Oregon, July 1996. AAAI.
22. Bart Selman, Hector Levesque, and David Mitchell. A new method for solving hard satisfiability problems. In *Proceedings of the Tenth National Conference on Artificial Intelligence*, pages 440–446, Menlo Park, CA, 1992. AAAI, AAAI Press.
23. R. G. Smith. The contract net protocol: High level communication and control in a distributed problem solver. *IEEE Trans. on Computers*, 29(12):1104–1113, December 1980.
24. J. M. Tennenbaum, T. S. Chowdhry, and K. Hughes. eCo System: CommerceNet's architectural framework for internet commerce. Technical report, Object Management Group, Cambridge, MA, 1997.
25. Maksim Tsvetovatyy, Maria Gini, Bamshad Mobasher, and Z. Wieckowski. MAGMA: An agent-based virtual market for electronic commerce. *Journal of Applied Artificial Intelligence*, 11(6), 1997.
26. P.R. Wurman, M.P. Wellman, and W.E. Walsh. The Michigan Internet Auctionbot: A configurable auction server for human and software agents. In *Second Int'l Conf. on Autonomous Agents*, pages 301–308, May 1998.
27. Monte Zweben, Brian Daun, Eugene Davis, and Michael Deale. Scheduling and rescheduling with iterative repair. In Monte Zweben and Mark S. Fox, editors, *Intelligent Scheduling*, chapter 8, pages 241–256. Morgan Kaufmann, San Francisco, CA, 1994.

Evolutionary Computing and Negotiating Agents

Noyda Matos and Carles Sierra

IIIA - Artificial Intelligence Research Institute
CSIC - Spanish Council for Scientific Research
Campus UAB, 08193 Bellaterra, Catalonia, Spain.
{noyda, sierra}@iiia.csic.es,
http://www.iiia.csic.es/~{ noyda, sierra}

Abstract. Automated negotiation has been of particular interest due to the relevant role that negotiation plays among trading agents. This paper presents two types of agent architecture: *Case-Based* and *Fuzzy*, to model an agent negotiation strategy. At each step of the negotiation process these architectures fix the weighted combination of tactics to employ and the parameter values related to these tactics. When an agent is provided with a Case-Based architecture, it uses previous knowledge and information of the environment state to change its negotiation behaviour. On the other hand when provided with a Fuzzy architecture it employs a set of fuzzy rules to determine the values of the parameters of the negotiation model. In this paper we propose an evolutionary approach, applying genetic algorithms over populations of agents provided with the same architecture, to determine which negotiation strategy is more successful.

1 Introduction

Negotiation in multi-agent systems is one of the main research lines in multi-agent systems [18] and has been studied from different points of view: economics [22], dialectics [27] or coordination [4]. Recent growing interest in autonomous agents and their application in areas such as electronic commerce has given more importance to the problem of automated negotiation. Agents negotiate to coordinate their activities and come to a mutual agreement. In many cases, this automated negotiation requires different behaviours for different negotiation situations. We not present any experiments results, we only made an outline proposal.

We explore an existing model of negotiation [15] based on a set of mutually influencing two-parties, many-issues negotiation. This model relies on strategies and tactics to define the agent's negotiation behaviour (i.e. to determine which offers should be accepted and which rejected, what counter-offers should be generated and when). The model has been already applied upon a real-world business process management system [15] in which the agents need to agree as to who should perform a particular service under what terms and conditions.

Since this model can operate in a wide range of environments and has a large number of parameters, Genetic Algorithms (GA) appear to be a good means of determining its performance through an empirical evaluation (see previous results in [19]).

In this paper we extend this previous work by exploring the combination of an evolutionary approach with two types of agent architecture: *Case-Based* and *Fuzzy*. Both architectures determine, at each step of the negotiation, which combination of tactics is more useful and which are the best tactic parameters. Over a family of agents with the same architecture we use an evolutionary approach to determine which individual instantiation of each type of architecture is preferred.

Case-Based Reasoning has received a lot of attention over the last years, and has been employed with good results in many areas, including negotiation [24]. We use this technique to determine the combination of tactics and the parameter values to use at each moment of the negotiation by looking at the similarity of the current negotiation to previous cases kept in a case base. The successful negotiations that an agent performs following a specific role (seller or buyer) are kept in the case base for later retrieval. The most similar case is adapted to the current situation by a set of adaptation fuzzy rules.

As an alternative route, we propose agents that use a set of fuzzy rules to model the strategy of the negotiation process for an agent. A subset of these rules determines the general behaviour of the agent, and the other adjusts the weights and the parameters of the tactics considering the information of the agent's mental state. With the combination of both kind of rules we obtain a weighted combination of tactics and their associated parameter values.

Over these architectures we make an evolutionary approach using GAs to analyse the behaviour of both kinds of agents architecture. This approach was chosen because GAs have been shown to find good solutions for problems of this nature [3]. The long term goal of this research is to study the dynamics of agents populations.

This paper presents a preliminary view of these two types of architectures, not the experimental results and is structured as follows: Section 2 summarises the service-oriented negotiation model presented in [23]. Section 3 gives an example of scenarios in which we apply this model. Sections 4 and 5 describe the two agent architectures. Section 6 describes the general steps of the GA. Section 7 places our work in context and Section 8 outlines the avenues of further research.

2 The service-oriented negotiation model

This section outlines the main components of the service-oriented negotiation model presented in [23]. The majority of the justification for particular design choices and much of the detailed explanation of the negotiation behaviour has been omitted.

This multi-lateral negotiation model is based on a set of mutually influencing two-parties, many-issues negotiations. In service-oriented negotiations, agents can adopt two possible roles that are, in principle, in conflict. Let *Agents* denote the set of agents in the system and let the conflicting roles be denoted by the set of agents: *Sellers* and *Buyers*.

Negotiations can range over a number of quantitative (e.g. price, duration, and cost) and qualitative (e.g. type of reporting policy, and nature of the contract) issues. The set of issues used by each agent can change during the negotiation process, increasing or decreasing the number of issues. Quantitative issues in negotiation are defined over a real domain (i.e $x[j] \in \mathcal{D}_j = [min_j, max_j]$). Qualitative issues are defined over a totally ordered domain (i.e $x[j] \in \mathcal{D}_j = \langle q_1, \cdots, q_n \rangle$). When an agent receives an offer ($x = (x[1], \cdots, x[n])$) where n is the total number of issues), it rates it by using a function that combines the scores of the different issues. For the purposes of this paper we can see it as a linear combination:

$$V^a(x^t) = \sum_{1 \leq j \leq n} w_j^a(t) V_j^a(x^t[j])$$

where $w_j^a(t)$ is the importance of issue j for agent a at time t[1].

Each agent has a scoring function $V_j^a : \mathcal{D}_j^a \to [0,1]$ that gives the score agent a assigns to a value of issue j in the set of its acceptable values $\mathcal{D}_j^a$. For convenience, scores are kept in the interval $[0,1]$, and scoring functions are monotonous for quantitative issues. If the score of the received offer is greater than the score of the counter offer the agent would send at this point, then the offer is accepted. If the pre-established constant deadline (t_{max}^a) at which the negotiation must have been completed by agent a is reached, the offer is rejected by a. Otherwise, a counter offer is submitted.

Let $x_{a \to b}^t$ represent the vector of values proposed by agent a to agent b at time t, and $x_{a \to b}^t[j]$ be the value for issue j proposed from a to b at time t. Given any two agents negotiating we will call agent a to the agent that initiate the negotiation process and b to the other agent. A *Negotiation Thread* between agents $a, b \in Agents$, at time $t_n \in Time$, noted $X_{a \leftrightarrow b}^{t_n}$, is any finite sequence of length n of the form $(x_{a \to b}^{t_1}, x_{b \to a}^{t_2}, x_{a \to b}^{t_3}, \dots)$ with $t_1 < t_2 \cdots < t_n$, where for each issue j, $x_{a \to b}^i[j] \in \mathcal{D}_j^a, x_{b \to a}^{i+1}[j] \in \mathcal{D}_j^b$ with $i = 1, 3, 5, \dots$, and optionally the last element of the sequence being one of the particles $\{accept, reject\}$. $last(X_{a \leftrightarrow b}^{t_n})$ is a function returning the last element in a sequence.

Offers and counter-offers are generated by lineal combinations of functions called *tactics*. A tactic generates a value for a single negotiation issue based upon a single criterion: time remaining, resources remaining and/or the behaviour of the opponent. If multiple criteria are important in determining the value of a negotiation issue, then multiple tactics can be applied to the issues. In this case, the tactics are assigned a weight to indicate their relative importance. As the negotiation proceeds, new criteria may become relevant and the relative importance of existing criteria may vary. To reflect this fact, an agent has a

---

[1] The weights associated to the issues are defined by each agent at the beginning of the negotiation, but can change later due to external causes or to the agent's interests. We assume the weights are normalised.

strategy which varies the weights of the different tactics over time in response to various environmental and negotiation cues (section 2.3).

2.1 Quantitative Case

Time-dependent tactics These tactics model the fact that the agent is likely to concede quicker as the deadline for the negotiation approaches. We model the offer of agent a to agent b for issue j at time $0 \leq t \leq t^a_{max}$, by a function $\alpha^a : t \to [0,1]$,

$$x^t_{a \to b}[j] = \begin{cases} min^a_j + \alpha^a(t)(max^a_j - min^a_j) & \text{If } V^a_j \text{ is decreasing} \\ min^a_j + (1 - \alpha^a(t))(max^a_j - min^a_j) & \text{If } V^a_j \text{ is increasing} \end{cases}$$

A wide range of functions can be defined simply by varying the way in which $\alpha^a(t)$ is computed. Here we use a family of polynomial functions parameterised by a value $\beta \in \mathbb{R}^+$ that determines the convexity of the curve:

$$\alpha^a(t) = \left(\frac{t}{t^a_{max}} \right)^{\frac{1}{\beta}}$$

This expression represents an infinite number of possible tactics, one for each value of β. However, to better understand their behaviour, we have classified them into two sets which show clearly different patterns of behaviour: **Boulware** (don't start conceding until the deadline is nearly up) with $\beta \ll 1$, and **Conceder** (start giving ground fairly quickly) with $\beta \gg 1$.

Resource-dependent tactics These tactics generate counter-offers depending on how a particular resource, in this case the time, is being consumed; they become progressively more conciliatory as the quantity of resource diminishes:

$$\alpha^a(t) = e^{-(t^a_{max} - t)}$$

Behaviour-dependent or Imitative tactics These tactics base their actions on the behaviour of their negotiation opponent [2]. The new offer is calculated in the following way:

$$x^{t_n+1}_{a \to b}[j] = \begin{cases} min^a_j & \text{if } P \leq min^a_j \\ max^a_j & \text{if } P > max^a_j \\ P & \text{otherwise} \end{cases}$$

The tactics differ depending on which aspect of the opponent's behaviour they imitate and to what degree, determine by the factor P.

1. **Relative Tit-For-Tat** (Relative-TFT)
   The agent reproduces, in percentage terms, the behaviour that its opponent has performed $\delta \geq 1$ steps ago:

$$P = \frac{x^{t_n-2\delta}_{b \to a}[j]}{x^{t_n-2\delta+2}_{b \to a}[j]} x^{t_n-1}_{a \to b}[j]$$

2. **Absolute Tit-For-Tat** (Random-TFT)

The same as *Relative TFT* except that the behaviour is imitated in absolute rather than percentage terms.

$$P = x_{a \to b}^{t_n-1}[j] + x_{b \to a}^{t_n-2\delta}[j] - x_{b \to a}^{t_n-2\delta}[j]$$

3. **Averaged Tit-For-Tat** (Average-TFT).

The agent uses the average of the percentage change in a window of size $\lambda \geq 1$ of its opponents history to determine its offer.

$$P = \frac{x_{b \to a}^{t_n-2\lambda}[j]}{x_{b \to a}^{t_n}[j]} x_{a \to b}^{t_n-1}[j]$$

2.2 Qualitative Case

In this work we admit only ordered qualitative variables $\mathcal{D}_j = \langle q_1, \cdots, q_n \rangle$. For this kind of variables the aforementioned tactics need some transformation. We must redefine values like min_j^a or max_j^a. When we need to use a qualitative issue's value in a tactic equation, we use instead of the qualitative value, the score related to the value. In the same way the min_j^a and max_j^a values are related to the maximum and minimum scoring of the variable. For instance for the *Relative Tit-For-Tat* tactics:

$$x_{a \to b}^{t_n+1}[j] = \begin{cases} min_j^a & \text{if } P \leq min_j^a \\ max_j^a & \text{if } P > max_j^a \\ P & \text{otherwise} \end{cases}$$

the transformation is the following:

$$P = \frac{V_j^a(x_{b \to a}^{t_n-2\delta}[j])}{V_j^a(x_{b \to a}^{t_n-2\delta+2}[j])} V_j^a(x_{a \to b}^{t_n-1}[j]), \ min_j^a = \min_{q \in \mathcal{D}_j^a}\{V_j^a(q)\}, \ max_j^a = \max_{q \in \mathcal{D}_j^a}\{V_j^a(q)\}$$

For the qualitative case, each tactic give as a result an score value, $x_{a \to b}^{t_n+1}[j] \in [0, 1]$. In the next section we explain how the agent conform the qualitative offer.

2.3 Strategies

The aim of a negotiation strategy is to determine the best course of action to reach an agreement. When agent a receives an offer from agent b, it becomes the last element in the current negotiation thread between the agents. If the offer is unsatisfactory to a, the agent a generates a counter-offer. In generating its counter-offer, a may use the information of mental state and different weighted combinations of tactics for each of the negotiation issues. More formally, an agent (a) has a representation of its mental state (MS_a^t) at time t, which contains information about its beliefs, its knowledge of the environment (time, resources, etc.), and any other attitudes (desires, goals, obligations, intentions, etc.).

Given a negotiation thread between agents a and b at time t_n, $X^{t_n}_{a \leftrightarrow b}$, over domain $\mathcal{D} = \mathcal{D}_1 \times \cdots \times \mathcal{D}_p$, with $last(X^{t_n}_{a \leftrightarrow b}) = x^{t_n}_{b \to a}$, and a finite set of m tactics[2] $T^a = \{\tau_i | \tau_i : MS_a \to \mathcal{D}\}_{i \in [1,m]}$, where MS_a is the representation of its mental state for all time t, a *weighted counter proposal*, $x^{t_{n+1}}_{a \to b}$, is a linear combination of the tactics given by a matrix of weights

$$\Gamma^{t_{n+1}}_{a \to b} = \begin{pmatrix} \gamma_{11} & \gamma_{12} & \cdots & \gamma_{1m} \\ \gamma_{21} & \gamma_{22} & \cdots & \gamma_{2m} \\ \vdots & \vdots & \vdots & \vdots \\ \gamma_{p1} & \gamma_{p2} & \cdots & \gamma_{pm} \end{pmatrix}.$$

defined in the following way:

$$\begin{aligned} x^{t_{n+1}}_{a \to b}[j] &= (\Gamma^{t_{n+1}}_{a \to b} * T^a(MS^{t_{n+1}}_a))[j,j] \\ &= \gamma_{j1}(\tau_1(MS^{t_{n+1}}_a))[j] + \gamma_{j2}(\tau_2(MS^{t_{n+1}}_a))[j] + \cdots + \gamma_{jm}(\tau_m(MS^{t_{n+1}}_a))[j] \end{aligned}$$

With $(T^a(MS^{t_{n+1}}_a))[i,j] = (\tau_i(MS^{t_{n+1}}_a))[j]$, $\gamma_{ji} \in [0,1]$ and for all issues j, $\sum_{i=1}^m \gamma_{ji} = 1$. The weighted counter proposal extends the current negotiation thread as follows:

$$X^{t_{n+1}}_{a \leftrightarrow b} = X^{t_n}_{a \leftrightarrow b}; x^{t_{n+1}}_{a \to b}$$

where ; is the sequence concatenation operation.

For qualitative case $x^{t_{n+1}}_{a \to b}[j]$ is the weighted combination of all tactics used by issue j. In subsection 2.2 we mention that the tactics gave as a result a scoring value. For that reason we apply a pseudo inverse function, $V_j^{a^{[-1]}}$, over this weighted counter proposal for obtain a qualitative offer.

$$V_j^{a^{[-1]}}(x^{t_{n+1}}_{a \to b}[j]) = \begin{cases} q & \text{if } \exists\, q \in D^a_j \text{ and} \\ & V_j^a(q) = x^{t_{n+1}}_{a \to b}[j] \\ \min_{q \in \mathcal{D}^a_j}\{|V_j^a(q) - x^{t_{n+1}}_{a \to b}[j]|\} & \text{otherwise} \end{cases}$$

This pseudo inverse function give the traditional inverse value if exist and the qualitative value that has the score more near to the $x^{t_{n+1}}_{a \to b}$ value.

Given a set of tactics, different types of negotiation behaviour can be obtained by weighting the tactics in a different way. That is, by changing the matrix Γ — particular to each negotiation thread.

A *Negotiation Strategy* for agent a is any function f such that, given a's mental state at time t_n, $MS^{t_n}_a$, and a matrix of weights at time t_n, $\Gamma^{t_n}_{a \to b}$, generates a new matrix of weights for time t_{n+1}, i.e.

$$\Gamma^{t_{n+1}}_{a \to b} = f(\Gamma^{t_n}_{a \to b}, MS^{t_n}_a)$$

The main point in every step of the negotiation process is then to determine both, which weighted combination of tactics to employ and the value of the

---

[2] This definition uses the natural extension of tactics to the multi-dimensional space of issues' values.

parameters associated with these tactics. Our goal is to make an evolutionary study of how two different agent architectures allow us to create a negotiation strategy and determine which strategy is more successful. In this paper we study two of these architectures: *Case-Based* and *Fuzzy*. In figure 1 their schemes are presented.

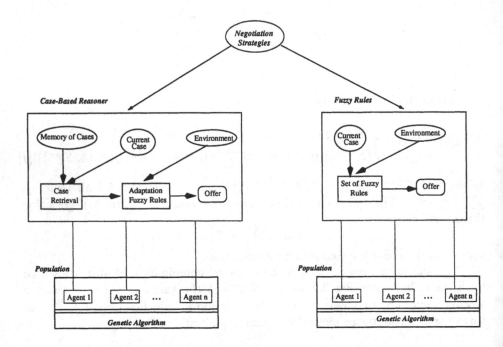

Fig. 1. Main components of the agent architecture.

3 Negotiation in a Real Estate Agency

In this section we describe a real domain, a Real Estate Agency, that will be used to exemplify our negotiation model. In a Real Estate Agency there is a set of properties that need to be sold. In this domain there are two main agent roles, *seller* that represents the interests of a Real Estate Agency and *buyer* that represents the interests of a customer. Seller agents need to sell a house (preferable the one with higher profit for the agency) and buyers want to buy a house with specific features.

In this example, artificial agents represent the interests of a human buyer or seller. If a person needs to buy a house he wants to visit as few properties as possible; this is why the person might be willing to instruct an agent with a set of features that represent his desires in order to obtain a house that meets his needs. The coordination of different buyer agents negotiating at the same time with different Real Estate Agencies is not treated here.

The agents so delegated negotiate over a set of issues that describe the characteristics of the house, for instance:

- *Surface*
- *District*
- *Number of rooms*
- *Floor number*
- *Garage*

- *Price*
- *Brightness*
- *Number of bathrooms*
- *Elevator*
- *Address*

The seller agent has a complete information of all the properties on sale at the Real Estate Agency. However, in some cases the buyer agent does not have a clear opinion on his preferences on the mentioned issues. The seller agent, during the negotiation, usually includes new issues to enrich the description of a house. Then, the buyer uses this new information to compare and discriminate better among the different offers made by the seller. That is, its utility function gets extended to consider the new issues introduced. In so doing, the buyer tries to obtain a complete description of the properties, negotiating over the set of issue mentioned before. Usually the agents try to adjust either the issues related to the description of the house and later the price issue. They negotiate until they obtain an agreement, in this case a property that satisfies both sides, if any exists, or one of them withdraws.

4 Case-Based Negotiating Agents

Case-based reasoning solve a new problem by adapting a previous similar situation [1, 25]. Using CBR terminology, a *case* in negotiation can be thought of as a negotiation process that has been stored in a specific way and that can be reused in solving new negotiation processes. The main tasks that a case-based negotiating agent has to deal with are the representation of the negotiation cases in its case base, the retrieval of a past case similar to the new one and the adaptation of its solution to the current negotiation process. In figure 1 we are described the main components old a CB reasoner. From the memory of cases the most similar case to the actual negotiation is retrieval. This selected case is then adapted considering the environmental information. Then the new offer is calculated using the weighted combination and the parameters gave by this case.

We denote by CB the $Case\ Base$. In CB we only keep track of the negotiation processes that reach an agreement, that is, that have the following final thread: $X_c^{t_n} = \{x_c^{t_1}, \cdots, x_c^{t_{deal}}, accept\}$ where $t_n = t_{deal} + 1$. Now we analyse in detail the main parts of the CBR cycle.

4.1 Case Representation

The *Case Base* for any agent a, is composed of a set of cases that represent past negotiation processes. This *Case Base* is extended by the negotiations performed by agent a and the negotiations performed by other agents with the same role as a (seller or buyer). An agent can communicate successful cases to agents following the same role when meeting during the evolutionary computation (see section 6). The cases that belong to other agents will be considered like a negotiation performed by agent a and, to simplify, we incorporate then in the case base by substituting the name of the other agent by a. We represent a case as a vector that keeps values of the following components:

1. Problem Description
   - *Good*: the good which was negotiated.
   - t_{deal}: the time that negotiation takes.
   - t_{max}: the maximum time for the negotiation, $t_{max} \geq t_{deal}$.
   - *Init*: this value determines who began the negotiation, 1 if agent a started, 0 otherwise.
   - *Issues*: the vector of the subsequent sets of issues involved in each step of the negotiation process, i.e. $Issues = [[j_1, j_2, j_3], [j_1, j_3], \cdots, [j_1, j_4]]$. The vector is indexed by time instants, i.e. $Issues[t_1] = [j_1, j_2, j_3]$, $Issues[t_2] = [j_1, j_3]$.
   - *Weights*: the vector of the subsequent vectors of relative importance values assigned by the agent to each issue during the negotiation, i.e. $Weights = [[w_{j_1}, w_{j_2}, w_{j_3}], [w_{j_1}, w_{j_3}], \cdots, [w_{j_1}, w_{j_4}]]$.
   - *Thread*: the vector that keeps offers and counter-offers made during the negotiation.
   - *Valuation*: the relative importance of this case. This value quantifies the contributions that this case made in the resolution of other cases ($Valuation \in [0, 1]$) The updating of this value is explained in section 4.4.
   - *Utility*: this quantity indicates how well the negotiation resulted by comparing the utility of final deal with the utility at the Nash equilibrium point [5].

$$Utility = \tanh\left(\frac{V^a(x_c^{t_{deal}})}{V^a(x_c^{Nash})}\right)$$

   where $x_c^{t_{deal}}$ is the final deal, and x_c^{Nash} represents the deal that would be made at the Nash equilibrium point. We use the monotonically increasing function $\tanh: \Re \to [0, 1]$ (hyperbolic tangent) to keep the value of utility in the interval [0,1].

2. Solution
   - *Gammas*: sequence of matrices of weights Γ employed by agent a during the negotiation.
     $Gammas = (\Gamma_1, \cdots, \Gamma_p)$ where p is the number of times that agent a participates (makes offers) during the negotiation.
   - *Parameters*: the vector that keeps the value of the parameters of each one of the tactics used in each step of the negotiation.
     $Parameters = [(Par_{\tau_1}^1, Par_{\tau_2}^1, ...Par_{\tau_m}^1), \cdots, (Par_{\tau_1}^p, Par_{\tau_2}^p, ...Par_{\tau_m}^p)]$
     where τ_i denote tactics from the families of tactics defined in Section 2.

Example: Now let us see an example of case representation for a negotiation process in a Real Estate Agency. Two agents, a seller b and a buyer a negotiate during 5 units of time. In the first steps of the negotiation process the set of issues was $S_1 = \{Address, Surface, Number\_of\_Rooms, Brightness, Price\}$ and later the seller agent b added a new issue $Garage$, so $S_2 = \{Address, Surface, Number\_of\_Rooms, Brightness, Price, Garage\}$. Agent a began the negotiation process and used only 3 tactics, from the following families: *Boulware*, *Conceder* and *Relative TFT*. The offers and counter-offers are shown in the following negotiation thread: $X_{a\leftrightarrow b}^{t5} = \{x_{a\rightarrow b}^{t_1}, x_{b\rightarrow a}^{t_2}, x_{a\rightarrow b}^{t_3}, x_{b\rightarrow a}^{t_4}, x_{a\rightarrow b}^{t_5}, accept\}$ where:

$$x_{a\rightarrow b}^{t_1} = [?, \quad 140m^2, 4, Very\_Bright, \quad £400k]$$
$$x_{b\rightarrow a}^{t_2} = [\#21, 60m^2, \quad 4, Slightly\_Bright, £400k]$$
$$x_{a\rightarrow b}^{t_3} = [?, \quad 120m^2, 4, Very\_Bright, \quad £400k]$$
$$x_{b\rightarrow a}^{t_4} = [\#69, 120m^2, 3, Bright, \quad £600k, true]$$
$$x_{a\rightarrow b}^{t_5} = [\#69, 120m^2, 3, Bright, \quad £500k, true]$$

The sign $=$ in the negotiation thread represents that the value of the component at this position is the same as the previous one in the vector. Then the representation of this negotiation process in the *Case Base* of agent a would be:

$$\left[House, \quad 5, \quad 7, \quad 1, \quad [S_1, S_1, S_1, S_2, S_2], \quad [[0.1, 0.23, 0.23, 0.14, 0.3], \quad =, \right.$$

$$Good, \quad t_{deal}, t_{max}, Init, \quad Issues, \quad Weight[t_1], \quad Weight[t_2],$$

$$=, \quad =, \quad [0.1, 0.2, 0.15, 0.1, 0.4, 0.05]],$$
$$Weight[t_3], Weight[t_4] \quad Weight[t_5]$$

$$[x_{a\rightarrow b}^{t_1}, x_{b\rightarrow a}^{t_2}, x_{a\rightarrow b}^{t_3}, x_{b\rightarrow a}^{t_4}, x_{a\rightarrow b}^{t_5}, accept], \quad 0.3, \quad 0.5$$
$$Thread^* \quad Valuation \quad Utility$$

$$\left([[0.4, 0.3, 0.3], [0.5, 0.2, 0.3], [0.5, 0.1, 0.4], [0.4, 0.4, 0.2], [0.7, 0.1, 0.2]], =, \right.$$

$$\Gamma^1, \quad \Gamma^2,$$

$$[[0.9, 0.05, 0.05], [0.9, 0.05, 0.05], [0.9, 0.05, 0.05], [0.9, 0.05, 0.05], [0.7, 0.1, 0.2],$$
$$\Gamma^3,$$

$$\left. [0.9, 0.05, 0.05]] \right) [(0.02, 5, 2), =, =] \left. \right]$$
$$Par^1 \quad Par^2 \; Par^3$$

The vector $Par^i = (0.02, 5, 2)$ contains the value of the parameters related with the tactics employed by agent a, in this case $(\beta_{boulware}, \beta_{conceder}, \delta_{relative})$. In the last step of the negotiation, agent a behaves in a more boulware way for all the issues for which it agrees on the value (agent a doesn't want to change these values) and only concentrates in adjusting the price of the house. That is shown in the value of the Γ matrix, $[0.9, 0.05, 0.05]$. The value ? for an issue j is handled like a *don't care* value which has scoring zero, $V_j^a(?) = 0$.

4.2 Case Retrieval

The case retrieval process is executed concurrently with the other activities of a case-based agent. When an agent sends an offer, it immediately begins to retrieve those cases that are more similar to the current negotiation from its *Case Base*. When it receives a counter-offer to its offer it is incorporated into the negotiation thread and used to finally select the most similar case from those that were obtained in the meantime. We denote by N the current negotiation represented in the same format used for the cases stored in the *Case Base CB*. The goal of this task is to find the case in *CB most similar* to N. We can see a graphical representation of this process in figure 2.

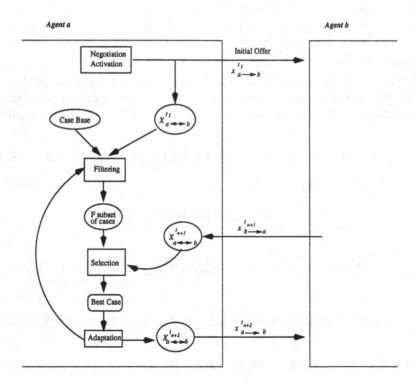

Fig. 2. Case Retrieval.

Filtering Not all cases stored in *CB* can be compared with N for different reasons. For instance, because the set of issues considered in each step of the negotiation and the duration of the negotiation are different. This is why we build a subset F selecting from *CB* those cases that satisfy all the following criteria:

1. **Class of t_{deal}.** We divide *CB* into two classes that depend on the value of t_{deal} with respect to a cut value θ:

- *Short t_{deal}*: $C \in F_1$ iff $C \in CB$ and $C[t_{deal}] \leq \theta$
- *Large t_{deal}*: $C \in F_1$ iff $C \in CB$ and $C[t_{deal}] > \theta$

The rationale here is that the negotiation strategies are radically different depending on how much time is available.

2. **Duration of negotiation.** With t being the time consumed so far in the current negotiation, we select the cases with a duration longer than the value of t, but not longer than the t_{max} defined in N. This is an important criterion, again because the negotiation strategies strongly depend on the time that the agent has to negotiate [10]. These conditions can be expressed by:

$C \in F_2$ iff $C \in CB$ and $t < C[t_{deal}] \leq N[t_{max}]$

3. **Sets of Issues.** We select the cases from CB that contain at least the set of issues of N for each step of the negotiation, to make the comparison between them possible.

$C \in F_3$ iff $C \in CB$ and $\forall k \leq t$ $S(N[Issues, k]) \subseteq S(C[Issues, k])$ where S is a function that transforms a vector into a set.

4. **Who began the negotiation?** Only the cases in which the agent that began the negotiation is the same as in N are considered. $C \in F_4$ iff $C \in CB$ and $C[Init] = N[Init]$.

Hence, we define F as the set of cases that satisfy all criteria, that is, $C \in F$ iff $C \in F_1 \cap F_2 \cap F_3 \cap F_4$

Final Selection The cases that satisfied all the aforementioned criteria compose the set F from where we will select the most similar case with respect to the current negotiation. The similarity at time t between the case N and all the cases $C \in F$ is measured in the following way:

$$Sim(N, C, t) = \rho_1 * \sum_{k=1}^{t-1} \frac{2k}{t(t-1)} * Sim\_Step(N, C, k) + \rho_2 * C[Valuation] +$$

$$\rho_3 * C[Utility]$$

In this similarity measure we take into account three factors:

- The similarity between the offers of both cases for all previous instance k of the negotiation ($Sim\_Step(N, C, k) \in [0, 1]$). With the factor $\frac{2k}{t*(t+1)}$ [3] we concede an increasing importance to the similarity of the offers in the last steps of the negotiation.
- The Valuation of the case, that shows how much this case has contributed to the solution of other cases ($C[Valuation] \in [0, 1]$).
- The utility obtained by this case during the negotiation ($C[Utility] \in [0, 1]$).

---

[3] $\sum_{k=1}^{t-1} \frac{2k}{t(t-1)} = 1$; so we employ this component as a weighting mechanism that produces a normalised output.

The factors $\rho_i \in [0,1]$, $i = 1,2,3$, determine the relative relevance of the three elements mentioned in the similarity measure and satisfy: $\rho_1 + \rho_2 + \rho_3 = 1$. The similarity of cases will change by varying the value associated with each ρ_i, for example: if we give more importance to ρ_3, associated with the $C[Utility]$, we prefer cases which are better off in the negotiation, i.e. whose scoring was better or nearest to the scoring at the Nash equilibrium point.

The similarity degree between two offers takes into account the similarity between the issues of both cases and is defined as:

$$Sim\_Step(N,C,k) = \sum_{j=i_1}^{i_n} AE\left(\frac{V_j^a(N[Thread,k,j])}{V_j^a(N[Thread,k+1,j])} * \frac{V_j^a(C[Thread,k+1,j])}{V_j^a(C[Thread,k,j])} \right)$$

$$* N[weights,k,j] * Sim\_Weight(N,C,k,j)$$

with $N[issues,k] = [i_1, \cdots, i_{n_k}]$ In this function we take into account:

- The similarity between the vector *Thread* for both cases. We consider a quotient between the scoring value for issue j in the step k and the scoring for the same issue in the step $k+1$. This quotient is computed for both cases, N and C, and then the quotient of both is the argument of the function $AE = Almost\_Equal$ that shows how close to 1 was the result. For example,

$$AE = \begin{cases} x & \text{if } x \le 1 \\ 1/x & \text{if } x > 1 \end{cases}$$

- The weight for issue j in N at step k ($N[weights,k,j] \in [0,1]$). We give more importance to the similarity between those issues that agent a considers more relevant in the current step of negotiation.
- The similarity between the vectors of weights of the case C and N ($Sim\_Weight(N,C,k,j) \in [0,1]$). The relative importance that the agents gave to the issues under the negotiation determine in some way how similar the strategies to adopt in each step of this process can be. For this reason we consider the similarity between the vectors of weights as a factor in the overall step similarity. We prefer cases with a similar importance to the issues. The similarity between the vectors of weight is calculated in the following way:

$$Sim\_Weight(N,C,k,j) = \frac{\left| N[weights,k,j] - \frac{C[weights,k,j]}{\aleph(N,C,k)} \right|}{n_k}$$

$$\aleph(N,C,k) = \sum_{j=i_1}^{i_n} C[weights,k,j]$$

with $N[issues,k] = [i_1, \cdots, i_{n_k}]$

The sets of issues for both cases are not necessarily the same. We compute the similarity related with the set of issues involved in the case N. For that reason we must normalise the weights of that set of issues for the case C, that is the factor $\aleph(N,C,k)$.

Incremental Computation of Similarity We use an incremental way of computing the similarity between cases in F and the current case N. This is done for efficiency reasons. Immediately after agent a sends an offer at time t, it begins to compute a provisional similarity $(Sim(N,C,t))$ to profit from the waiting time. When the counter part answers, the agent incorporates the new information, the offer just received, by actualising its thread and adjusting the similarity of the cases stored in F with the objective of selecting *the most similar case*.

The similarity between N and all the cases $C \in F$ is then computed in the following way:

$$Similarity(N,C,t) = \rho_1 * Sim(N,C,t) + \rho_2 * C[Valuation] + \rho_3 * C[Utility]$$
$$Sim(N,C,0) = 0$$
$$Sim(N,C,t) = \frac{t}{t+1} * Sim(N,C,t-1) + \frac{2}{t+1} * Sim\_Step(N,C,t)$$

Where $Sim\_Step(N,C,t)$ is as mentioned before. The value $Sim(N,C,t)$ is kept by each agent and is used in the next step t to avoid calculate the same quantity.

4.3 Adaptation

The case with the highest similarity contains the vector of $Parameters_{t+1}$ and the Γ_{t+1} matrix; these elements are to be used in the next step of the negotiation process. However, this solution can be improved by adapting the values of the $Parameters_{t+1}$ and the Γ_{t+1} to the current mental state (MS_a^{t+1}). This adaptation process is modelled by a set of *Adaptation Fuzzy Rules*. These rules represent conditions of the environment in which the agent acts and determine variations in the value of the parameters of the tactics and the γ_{ij}'s. In general these rules follow the following pattern:

$RULE_i$: **IF** x_1 is A_{i1} and ... and x_n is A_{in} **THEN** y is B_i

where $x_1, \cdots, x_n$ and y are the mental state variables and $A_{i1}, \cdots, A_{in}, B_i$ are linguistic labels of the variables $x_1, \cdots, x_n, y$ in the universe of discourse $U_1, \cdots, U_n, V$ of the variables. An example of linguistic labels could be:{$high$, $medium, low$}. These linguistic labels are characterised by their membership functions $A_{ij} : U_j \rightarrow [0,1]$, $j = 1, \cdots, n$; $B_i : V \rightarrow [0,1]$ and have a trapezoidal shape. For more details see [26].

In general the rule conditions express a state of the environment and the negotiation tactics. The rule consequents change the weighted combinations and the tactic parameters. A variation in a γ_{ij} generates automatically a normalisation of the rest of gammas.

Example: In the domain of the Real Estate Agency, we could have the following fuzzy rules:

IF *highway is near* and $\gamma_{price,boulware}$ *is medium* THEN $\Delta\beta_{boulware}$ *is*
$$negative\_small$$
IF *park is near* and $\gamma_{price,boulware}$ *is high* THEN $\Delta\gamma_{price,conceder}$ *is*
$$positive\_high$$

The linguistic labels *positive_high* represents a big positive number and *negative _small* a small negative number. If the first rule applies, the agent will behave in a more boulware fashion in all issues by decreasing its $\beta_{boulware}$ value. On the contrary (second rule) if a park is near the house and the agent's attitude to the price is mainly boulware, it will become more conceder, i.e. the $\gamma_{price,conceder}$ related to the conceder tactic increases the value and via the normalisation process $\gamma_{price,boulware}$ will decrease.

4.4 Retain

If the result of the negotiation is satisfactory, i.e. $last(X_N^{t_n}) = accept$, the new case is stored in *CB*. Moreover, the *Valuation* of all $C \in CB$ is updated by assigning a positive reinforcement to the cases that contributed to steps of the solution $(r = 0)$ and negative reinforcement if not $(r = 1)$:

$$C[Valuation] = C[Valuation] + \delta * (1 - C[Valuation])$$
$$\delta = k * (-1)^r * \tanh\left(\frac{V^a(x_N^{t_{deal}})}{V^a(x_N^{Nash})}\right)$$

where $\delta \in [0, 1]$, $x_N^{t_{deal}}$ is the final deal, and x_N^{Nash} represents the deal that would be made at the Nash equilibrium point and $k = 0.001$ is a reduction factor. Like explained before the function tanh keeps the value of the quotient in $[0, 1]$.

5 Fuzzy Rules

Systems based on fuzzy rules [8, 7] have proved to be an important tool to model complex systems. We had defined a type of agents that use a family of fuzzy rules to model the negotiation strategy. At each step of the negotiation process (figure 1) a set of fuzzy rules is applied to the parameters of the tactics involved in the negotiation step and the weighted combination of these tactics.

Each agent interacts in a specific domain; this is why they must represent this domain in a way that permits the interaction with other agents in the same domain. In other words, they need to use an ontology [12] that permits the representation of objects, concepts that exist in that domain and also relations between them. We assume, for the purpose of using GA as will be seen later in section 6, that this ontology is common, and that the fuzzy rules are built on top of it using the same syntax for all agents.

Similar to the adaptation fuzzy rules of the case-based agents, the rules follow the following pattern:

$RULE_i$:   **IF** x_1 is A_{i1} and ... and x_n is A_{in} **THEN** y is B_i
where $x_1, \cdots, x_n$ and y are the mental state variables and $A_{i1}, \cdots, A_{in}, B_i$
are linguistic labels of the variables $x_1, \cdots, x_n, y$ in the universe of discourse
$U_1, \cdots, U_n, V$ of the variables. These linguistic labels are characterised by their
membership functions $A_{ij} : U_j \to [0, 1]$, $j = 1, \cdots, n$; $B_i : V \to [0, 1]$ and have
a trapezoidal shape.

In general we can divide the set of fuzzy rules in two classes:

- *Rules of general behaviour.* These rules define the general conduct of the
  agent. They determine how an agent reacts during a negotiation, i.e. with a
  more boulware, conceder or imitative behaviour.
- *Rules of the Mental State.* These rules analyse the environment to adjust the
  parameters and the weighted combination of tactics. The mental state rules
  have a higher priority because are more specific, that is, more informed.

Example: In the domain of the Real Estate Agency we could have the following
rules:

1. *Rules of general behaviour.* Like in the adaptation fuzzy rules of the *Case
   Base* architecture, these rules change the value of the $\gamma_{i,j}$'s and the value of
   the parameters associated with each tactic. However, these rules take into
   account other aspects such as the general conduct of the agent. For instance,
   the following rules describe the behaviour (the dominant tactic) depending
   on the current of negotiation stance and the behaviour of the opponent.

   - IF *remaining_time is medium* THEN $\triangle \gamma_{j,tft}$ *is positive_high*

     If the remaining time that the agent has to negotiate is medium then the pos-
     sibilities to interact with the contrary are bigger. Under these conditions the
     imitative tactics have more opportunities to assess their opponents' behaviour
     and to respond appropriately, hence we increment the value of the $\gamma_{j,tft}$ for all
     issues j.

   - IF *average(last_opponent_offers) is high_conceder* and $\gamma_{j,conceder}$ *is high*
     THEN $\triangle \beta_{conceder}$ *is negative_small*

     The agent analyses the last offer received and if the opponent, in av-
     erage, has conceded, and if the conceder tactic is the domain tactic for
     all issues j, then the agent carries out a small decrease in its conceder
     behaviour to try to exploit the opponent.

2. *Rules of the Mental State.* These rules cause variations on the weighted combinations and the parameter values depending on the knowledge of the agent
   about the negotiation context.

− IF *agency is going_bankrupt* and $\gamma_{price,conceder}$ *is medium* THEN $\Delta\gamma_{price,boulware}$ *is positive_high*

If the Real Estate Agency is going bankrupt and we are not very tough in negotiating price, we change it by making the agent behave in a more boulware way, because it has, in such conditions, a higher opportunity of getting a lower price for a property.

− IF *time_on_sell is long* and $\gamma_{j,tft}$ *is high* THEN $\Delta\gamma_{j,boulware}$ *is positive_high*

If the Real Estate Agency has a property that wasn't sold for a long period we can obtain more profit by not conceding in the same way as the agency, because if the house has not been sold for a long time, means probably that its price is far beyond the reasonable one. In other words we should not imitate the conceding steps of the agency in the same amount, hence we increase our boulware behaviour for all issues.

− IF w_{bright} *is high* and *house is bright* and $\gamma_{surface,boulware}$ *is medium* THEN $\beta_{boulware}=1$

The agent behaves less boulware if it gives a lot of importance to brightness and it is a feature of the house being offered.

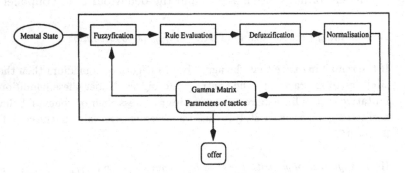

Fig. 3. Main Components of a Fuzzy Agent Architecture.

The handling of this set of rules is done by the following steps (see Figure 3):

1. *Fuzzification.* The membership functions of the input variables about the current negotiation thread and the weighted tactics are applied to their actual values to determine the truth degree of each condition.
2. *Rule Evaluation.* In this process the truth value of the premise of each rule is propagated to the conclusions. The result of this process is the assignment of a fuzzy subset to some output variables.

3. *Defuzzification.* Our goal is to determine a new matrix Γ and values for the parameters associated to each tactic, for this reason we need to obtain an exact value for these variables. There are several defuzzification methods to obtain a crisp value from a fuzzy subset and its associated truth degree, but we employ the centroid method, where the crisp value of the output variables corresponds to the value of the centre of gravity of the membership function of the fuzzy value [26].

4. *Normalisation.* Finally, a normalisation of the values of gamma, Γ, obtained by defuzzification is done.

6   Evolving the negotiation strategies

GAs generate a sequence of ever improving ("fitter") populations as the outcome of a search method modelled by a *selection mechanism, crossover* (recombining existing genetic material in new ways) and *mutation* (introducing new genetic material into the population by random modifications) [11]. In our case we employ the GA to make an evolutionary approach of the *Fuzzy Rules,* of fuzzy agents, and the *Case Base* and the *Adaptation Fuzzy Rules* associated with Cased-Based agents. We form a population, where each agent becomes an individual, and model as genetic material the different sets of rules and/or the case base. The overall aim of the search in all cases is to find a set of rules and a base of cases which are optimally adapted for particular negotiation situations. Even though we have two kinds of populations to analyse, *Fuzzy* and *Case-Based* (see Figure 4) the general steps for the GA are the same.

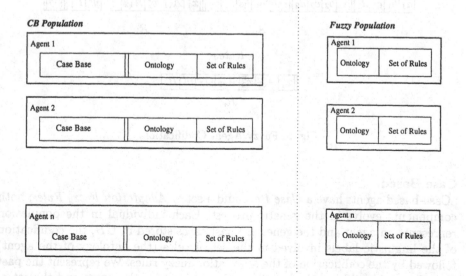

Fig. 4. Types of Populations

In this section we develop its basic schema —indicating how rules and cases are encoded as genes (section 6.1), how the fitness of the agents is computed (section 6.2), and how the search algorithm operates in detail (section 6.3).

6.1 Codification

Fuzzy. Every fuzzy agent has a set of *Fuzzy Rules*. Each individual in a population represents an agent, and the genes that conform it are the codification of the linguistic labels involved in the set of rules (the ontology of the agent) followed by the codification of its fuzzy rules (see Figure 5). Linguistic labels have the form of trapezoidal-shaped functions, and for each one we represent the 4-tuple (a_j, b_j, c_j, d_j) that describes its shape, that is, $A_{ij}, B_i \in \{A_1, \cdots, A_p\}$ where p is the maximum number of linguistic labels on the ontology, and $A_j = (a_j, b_j, c_j, d_j)$ $1 \le j \le p$.

The dimension of the set of fuzzy rules differs from one agent to another. We consider the length of the individual's genetic code to be equal to the cardinality of the biggest set of rules in the current population and denote it by

$$r = \max_{agent_i \in P^t} \{card(FR_{agent_i})\}$$

Where P^t is the population in the generation t. If the number of rules of an agent is smaller than r the remaining positions of the vector codifying them are filled in with zeros.

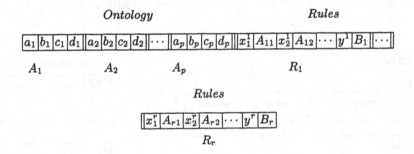

Fig. 5. Fuzzy Agent Codification.

Case-Based.

Case-based agents have a *Case Base* and a set of *Adaptation Fuzzy Rules*; both components evolve in the genetic process. Each individual in the population represents an agent and the genes are past cases stored in CB, the codification of the linguistic labels involved in the set of rules (the ontology of the agent) followed by the codification of the adaptation fuzzy rules. We represent the past cases by an identifier and we codified the ontology of the agent and the set of adaptation fuzzy rules in the same way as mentioned for the Fuzzy agents.

For the *Case Base* we have fixed a maximum number of cases (M_Cases). We controlled the number of cases in CB selecting those cases with the best *Valuation*. Cases stored in the *Case Base* are genes of the individuals in the population. The dimension of the *Case Base* differs between agents. We consider the length of the individuals' genetic code to be equal to the cardinality of the biggest *Case Base* in the current population

$$m_c = \min \left(M\_Cases, \max_{agent_i \in P^t} \{card(CB_{agent_i})\} \right)$$

If the number of cases of an agent is smaller than m_c the remaining positions of the vector codifying them are filled in with zeros.

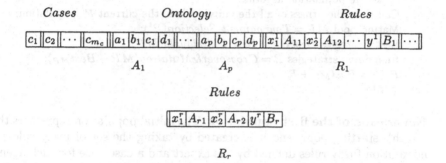

Fig. 6. Case-Based Agent Codification.

6.2 Measuring a strategy's fitness

An agent's fitness value indicates how well it performs in comparison to others in the same population. Following basic evolutionary ideas, fitness also determines the agent's chance of surviving to the next population generation —the higher the value, the more likely the agent will be to reproduce. To compute an agent's fitness we play a round-robin tournament in which each buyer $b \in Buyers$ negotiates with each seller $s \in Sellers$. Then, we score each agent with a value that measures how well it performed and this score becomes the agent's fitness.

The fitness function compares the utility associated with the deal and the utility associated with the Nash equilibrium point (the point at which the sellers' and the buyers' scoring functions are equal [5]). The more positive the difference, the more successful the agent's behaviour. The cost involved in attaining a deal is taken into consideration by associating a charge with each message interchange —the more messages exchanged in coming to a deal, the higher the associated cost. With these two components in place, a non-subjective, cost-adjusted fitness function (f_a) can be defined:

$$f_a(X_c^{t_n}) = \begin{cases} V^a(x_c^{t_{deal}}) - V^a(x_c^{Nash}) - \tau(X_c^{t_n}) & \text{if } last(X_c^{t_n}) = accept \\ -V^a(x_c^{Nash}) - \tau(X_c^{t_n}) & \text{otherwise} \end{cases} \quad (1)$$

where $x_c^{t_{deal}}$ is the final deal, and x_c^{Nash} represents the deal that would be made at the Nash equilibrium point. Communication cost is modelled as: $\tau(X_c^{t_n}) = q * |X_c^{t_n}|$ where q is a constant. Varying the value of q allows us to change the relative importance of the communication cost in the fitness computation.

6.3 Algorithm steps

The GA 's basic operation can be characterised by the following schema:

> P^0 population given by an expert;
> **While not**(Stopping Criterion) **do**
> > Make the population negotiate;
> > Calculate the fitness of all the individuals in the current P^t population;
> > Mating pool $MP = Tournament\_Selection(P^t)$;
> > Best strategies $Best_{MP} = Best\_Individuals(MP)$;
> > Remaining strategies $R = Crossover\&Mutation(MP - Best_{MP})$;
> > $P^{t+1} = Best_{MP} + R$
> **end while**

1. **Generation of the first population.** The initial population represents the search's starting point and it is created by taking the set of fuzzy rules or adaptation fuzzy rules defined by the expert and a case base for each agent.
2. **Selection Process.** All GAs use some form of mechanism to chose which individuals from the current population should go into the mating pool that forms the basis of the next population generation. To be effective, the selection mechanism should ensure that as diverse a range of fit agents make it into the mating pool as possible (especially in the early stages). A selection mechanism which is known to work well in such circumstances is *Tournament Selection* [6]. Tournament selection works in the following way: k individuals are randomly chosen from the population. The individual with the highest fitness among the selected k is placed in the MP. This process is repeated N times, where N is the size of the population. k is called the tournament size and it determines the degree to which the best individuals are favoured [20]. For this reason, it is the mechanism we employ to select from P^t those individuals that will reproduce. Tournament selection works in the following way: t individuals are randomly chosen from the population. The individual with the highest fitness among the selected t is placed in the mating pool. This process is repeated N times, where N is the size of the population. t is called the tournament size and it determines the degree to which the best individuals are favoured [20]. Once the mating pool has been created, H individuals with the highest fitness in the pool are selected. These individuals will definitely form part of the new population. The rest of individuals in the next population, R, are created by applying crossover and mutation to the remaining individuals in the mating pool. Thus, the next generation (P^{t+1}) is composed of the H best individuals of the old population plus a number of newly created ones.

3. **Crossover Process**. This mechanism exchanges genetic material between individuals. We randomly select two individuals from the population. c crossover points are then randomly chosen and sorted in ascending order. Then, the genes between successive crossover points are alternately exchanged between the individuals. For the characteristics of our codification, for fuzzy agents we set two crossover regions, one where the ontology of the agent is codified and the other where the fuzzy rules are codified (in Figure 5 the two regions are separated by |||). We give a different crossover probability to each region, that is $P_{ontology}$ and P_{rules}. We made this distinction because we want to make less variations (exchange) in the ontology of the agents, $P_{ontology} < P_{rules}$. Similarly for the case-based agents we define P_{cases}, $P_{ontology}$ and P_{rules}. These regions are separated by ||| (see Figure 6).

4. **Mutation Process**. Mutation is another technique to create individuals in new generations. For the *Case Base* we do not apply mutation because any variation in a component of a case will most probably produce an undesirable strategy.

   In the case of fuzzy rules, the genes related with the linguistic variables of an individual, that is, the ontology, are given a chance P_m of undergoing mutation. When a gene is selected for mutation we change the scaling factor of one linguistic label involved in the set of rules. This kind of variation affects directly all the rules that contain that particular linguistic label as part of a condition or in the conclusion. Thereby we consider a low probability of mutation.

5. **Stopping Criterion**. The simulations stop when the population is stable (95% of the individuals have the same fitness) or the number of iterations is bigger than a pre-determined maximum.

The concrete values for the probability of mutation and crossover are not mentioned in this paper because we are still at the experimental phase and we have not completely adjusted these values.

7 Related Work

In this paper we mention several topics from different research areas like negotiation, case-based reasoning, fuzzy logic and genetic algorithms. A complete review of all related literature is not possible here. Many works have been developed in each one of these areas, but up to our knowledge none combines these techniques to obtain a better performance for an agent during a negotiation process.

Research in negotiation models have been pursued in different fields like, game theory, social sciences and artificial intelligence, making assumptions that were pertinent for the objective of their study. Our interests lay in the study of the negotiation process among the agents and not on the outcome. In this work we employ a negotiation model and we concentrate on how can we find the best strategies in that model. For this propose we used case-based reasoning and fuzzy rules to model strategies.

In the area of case-based reasoning there are several works related with negotiation. For instance, Sycara [24] presented a model of negotiation that combines case-based reasoning and optimisation of the multi-attribute utilities of the agents. She provided a model of goal conflict resolution through negotiation implemented in the PERSUADER system, a program that resolves labour disputes, and tested her system using simulations of such domains. Our approach differs from this previous work in that we employ case-based reasoning to determine in each step of the negotiation the best performance of the agent by selecting the weighted proposal combinations and the parameters associated with a set of tactics. We also make to evolve the case base and the adaptation fuzzy rules trying to find the best performance. With this evolutionary process the agents interchange cases and rules to find an optimal set of cases and rules that allow to obtain a better scoring during the negotiations.

Many researchers have explored the use of genetic algorithms to tune fuzzy logic controllers. One of the pioneers on this was C. Karr [16], who used GAs to modify the membership function in the term sets of the variables used by a fuzzy controller. In the same line Herrera, Lozano and Verdegay [14], used a real encoding for a four-parameter characterisation of a trapezoidal membership value in each term set. Each rule used by the fuzzy control was represented by the concatenation of the membership values. The population was the concatenation of all rules so represented. In our case we use GAs to make evolve a set of fuzzy rules that model negotiation strategies in one case or that adapt the solution obtained by a case-based agent. We make genetic evolution over the linguistic labels (the ontology) of the agent and also, during the genetic process, the agents interchange rules to find an optimal performance.

Others researchers have also attempted to use GAs and co-evolutionary programming to find optimal interaction strategies. For example, Oliver [21] does consider negotiation strategies where each negotiating agent is a chromosome and the parameters of the negotiation model are genes in the chromosome. However, his negotiation model is much simpler. (Offers are accepted if they have a utility over a preset threshold and he encodes counter-offers as part of the genetic material which means they have limited sophistication.) The extra complexity required by our model means additional work was needed when designing the population evolution mechanism.

8 Conclusions and Further Work

In this paper we presented the main technical ideas of our current work on automated negotiation. We presented two agent architectures for negotiation, *Case-Based* and *Fuzzy*. Three basic techniques: *Case-Based Reasoning, Fuzzy Sets and Genetic Algorithms* are used as the basis to make an evolutionary analysis of negotiation strategies. Case-based agents, in each step of the negotiation, use it past information (case base) to retrieve a similar case to the current negotiation and adapt it by means of fuzzy rules. Fuzzy agents conduct their behaviour by means of a set of fuzzy rules. Over both architectures we make an evolutionary study applying GA, to determine the best strategy for the negotiation model mentioned in this paper.

Many aspects of these architectures need to be studied and adjusted during the experimental process that is currently ongoing. We think that this combination technique is a step forward the design of flexible and accountable trading agents.

9 Acknowledgements

The research reported in this paper is supported by the ESPRIT LTR 25500-COMRIS *Co-Habited Mixed-Reality Information Spaces* project and by the Agencia Española de Cooperación Internacional by means of Ph.D grant.

References

1. A. Aamodt and E. Plaza. Case-Based Reasoning: Foundational Issues, Methodological Variations, and System Approaches. AI Communications. IOS Press. (1994) vol 7 1 39–59
2. R. Axelrod. The Evolution of Cooperation. Basic Books, Inc., Publishers. (1984) New York, USA.
3. R. Axelrod. The Complexity of Cooperation. Princeton University Press. (1997)
4. M. Barbuceanu and M. S. Fox. COOL: A Language for Describing Coordination in Multi Agent Systems. J. Muller, M. Wooldridge. Spring Verlag. (1995) 1193, LNAI, 233-244,
5. K. Binmore. Fun and Games. A text on Game Theory. Heath. (1992)
6. T. Blickle and L. Thiele. A Comparison of Selection Schemes used in Genetic Algorithms. 11. May. TIK. (1995)
7. P. P. Bonissone and P. S. Khedkar and Y. Chen. Genetic Algorithms for Automated Tuning of Fuzzy Controllers: A Transportation Application. IEEE. (1996) 674-680
8. D. Dubois and H. Prade. What are fuzzy rules and how to use them. Fuzzy set and systems. (1996) 169-185
9. D. Dubois and H. Prade and F. Esteva and P. Garcia and L. Godo and R. López de Mántaras. Fuzzy set Modelling in Case-Based Reasoning. Iternational Journal of Intelligent Systems. 13 (1997) 345-373
10. P. Faratin and C. Sierra and N. R. Jennings. Negotiation Decision Functions for Autonomous Agents. Int. J. of Robotics and Autonomous Systems. 24 (1998) 159-182
11. D. Goldberg. Genetic Algorithms in Search, Optimisation and Matching Learning. Addison-Wesley Publishing Co (1989)
12. T. R. Gruber. Toward Principles for the Design of Ontologies Used for Knowledge Sharing. Formal Ontology in Conceptual Analysis and Knowledge Representation. (1993)
13. T. Haynes and R. Wainwright and S. Sen. Strongly Typed Genetic Programming in Evolving Cooperation Strategies. Proceedings of the 6th International Conference on Genetic Algorithms. Pittsburg, Pennsylvania (1995) 271–278
14. F. Herrera and M. Lozano and J.L. Verdegay. Tuning Fuzzy Logic Controllers by Genetic Algorithms. Technical Report DECSAI-93102. (1995)

15. N. R. Jennings and P. Faratin and M. J. Johnson and T. J. Norman and P. O'Brien and M. E. Wiegand . Agent-Based Business Process Management. Int Journal of Cooperative Information Systems. vol. 5 2–3 (1996) 105–130
16. C.L. Karr. Genetic algorithms for fuzzy controllers. AI Expert. (1991) 27-33
17. J. Koza. Evolution of Emergent Cooperative Behaviour using Genetic Programming. Computing with Biological Metaphors. (1992)
18. S. Kraus. Negotiation and cooperation in multi-agent environments. Artificial Intelligence. 94 (1997) 79–97
19. N. Matos and C. Sierra and N. R. Jennings. Determining Successful Negotiation Strategies: An Evolutionary Approach. Proc. 3rd. Int. Conf. on Multi-Agent Systems (ICMAS-98). (1998) 182–189
20. B. L. Miller and D. E. Golberg. Genetic Algorithms, Tournament Selection, and the Effects of Noise. Complex Systems. 3 Vol. 9 (1995) 193-212
21. J. R. Oliver. On Artificial Agents for Negotiation in Electronic Commerce. The Wharton School. (1994)
22. J. S. Rosenschein and G. Zlotkin. Rules of Encounter. MIT Press. (1994) Cambridge, MA
23. C. Sierra and P. Faratin and N. R. Jennings. A service-Oriented negotiation Model between Autonomous Agents. MAAMAW'97. M. Boman and W. Van de Velde. LNAI 1237 (1997) 17-35
24. K. Sycara. Resolving Goal Conflicts via Negotiation. In Proceedings of the Seventh National Conference on Artificial Intelligence. AAAI Press/The MIT Press. (1988) 245-250
25. I. Watson. Applying Case-Based Reasoning: Techniques for Enterprise Systems. Morgan Kaufmann Publishers, inc. (1997)
26. R. R. Yager and D. P. Filev.: Essentials of Fuzzy Modelling and Control. Wiley-Inter-science. (1994) New York, USA.
27. D. Zeng and K. Sycara. How can an agent learn to negotiate. Intelligent Agents III. Agents Theories, Architectures and Languages. J. Muller, M. Wooldridge. Spring Verlag. (1997) 1193, LNAI, 233-244,

Bidding Strategies for Trading Agents in Auction-Based Tournaments

Pere Garcia, Eduard Giménez, Lluis Godo, and Juan A. Rodríguez-Aguilar

Artificial Intelligence Research Institute, IIIA
Spanish Council for Scientific Research, CSIC
08193 Bellaterra, Barcelona, Spain.
{pere,duard,godo,jar}@iiia.csic.es
http://www.iiia.csic.es

Abstract. Auction-based electronic commerce is an increasingly interesting domain for AI researchers. In this paper we present an attempt towards the construction of trading agents capable of competing in multi-agent auction markets by introducing both a formal and a more pragmatic approach to the design of bidding strategies for buyer agents in auction-based tournaments. Our formal view relies on possibilistic-based decision theory as the means of handling possibilistic uncertainty on the consequences of actions (bids) due to the lack of knowledge about the other agents' behaviour. For practical reasons we propose a two-fold method for decision making that does not require the evaluation of the whole set of alternative actions. This approach utilizes global (market-centered) information in a first step to come up with an initial set of potential bids. This set is subsequently refined in a second step by means of the possibilisitic decision model using individual (rival agent centered) information induced from a memory of cases composing the history of tournaments.

1 Introduction

Auctions are an attractive domain of interest for AI researchers in at least two areas of activity. On the one hand, we observe that the proliferation of on-line auctions in the Internet —such as Auctionline[1], Onsale[2], InterAUCTION[3], eBay[4] and many others— has established auctioning as a main-stream form of electronic commerce. Thus, agent-mediated auctions, and more generally agent-mediated institutions[18], appear as a convenient mechanism for automated trading, mainly due to the simplicity of their conventions for interaction when multi-party negotiations are involved, but also to the fact that on-line auctions may successfully reduce storage, delivery or clearing house costs in many markets. This popularity has spawned AI research and development in auction servers[28,

---

[1] http://www.auctionline.com
[2] http://www.onsale.com
[3] http://www.interauction.com
[4] http://www.eBay.com

23] as well as in trading agents and heuristics[9, 16]. On the other hand, auctions are not only employed in web-based trading, but also as one of the most prevalent coordination mechanisms for agent-mediated resource allocation problems (f.i. energy management[29], climate control[12], flow problems[27]).

¿From the point of view of multi-agent interactions, auction-based trading is deceivingly simple. Trading within an auction house demands from buyers merely to decide on an appropriate price on which to bid, and from sellers, essentially only to choose a moment when to submit their goods. But those decisions—if rational—should profit from whatever information may be available in the market: participating traders, available goods and their expected re-sale value, historical experience on prices and participants' behaviour, etc. However, richness of information is not the only source of complexity in this domain. The actual conditions for deliberation are not only constantly changing and highly uncertain—new goods become available, buyers come and leave, prices keep on changing; no one really knows for sure what utility functions other agents have, nor what profits might be accrued—but on top of all that, deliberations are significantly time-bounded. Bidding times are constrained by the bidding protocol which in the case of DBP[5] auctions—like the traditional fish market[6]—proceeds at frenetic speeds.

Consequently, if a trading agent intends to behave aptly in this context, the agent's decision-making process may be quite elaborate. Clearly, the problem of choosing a successful bidding strategy by a trading agent in n-agents auction tournaments is clearly not deterministic and it will depend on many factors, in particular on the strategies themselves of the other competing agents. As long as the knowledge the agent will have about the other agents' strategies will be usually incomplete, our approach presented in this paper consists in looking at this problem as a decision-making problem under uncertainty.

As in any decision problem, the trading agent has to choose a decision, i.e. a bid, among a set of available alternatives, taking into account her preferences on the set of possible consequences in terms of maximising her benefit. In decision problems, given a (finite) set of situations Sit and a (finite) set of consequences X, a non-uncertain decision d is represented by a function $d : Sit \to X$. Then, in each situation, decisions can be easily ranked using, for instance, a real-valued utility function $u : X \to \Re$ modelling the preferences over consequences. However, uncertainty may be involved in many different aspects of the decision process, in particular, in a given situation, we may be uncertain on what the consequences of a decision are. Classical approaches to decision making under uncertainty assume that uncertainty is represented by probability distributions.

---

[5] *Downward bidding protocol*

[6] We will use the expression *fish market* to refer to the actual, real-world, human-based trading institution, and *FishMarket* to denote the artificial, formal, multi-agent counterpart. Hence, FM96.5 refers to a particular implementation of the *FishMarket* model of the fish market. Notice that we use the term *institution* in the sense proposed by North [19] as a "... *set of artificial constraints that articulate agent interactions*".

In such a case, if we are in a situation s_0 and we know the probability $P_{s_0,d}(x)$ of each possible consequence $x \in X$ of a decision d, then the global utility of the decision d is usually evaluated as the expected value of u with respect to $P_{s_0,d}$:

$$\mathcal{U}_{s_0}(d) = \Sigma_{x \in X} P_{s_0,d}(x)u(x).$$

This utility is used then to rank decisions (the greater the better). This kind of approach corresponds to the well-known Expected Utility Theory (EUT) [17], but it presents some problems and paradoxes, basically related to inferring the probabilities. Indeed, in our problem of trading agents the working assumption is that the knowledge the agent has about the other agents' strategies is reduced to a memory (or history) of previous successful biddings. In such a framework, we propose a kind of *case-based reasoning* to observe behaviour in previous similar situations. The uncertainty induced in these kind of processes is due to what extent we may consider two situations similar enough to presume a similar behaviour, and this kind of uncertainty is possibilistic rather than probabilistic. Recently, Dubois and Prade have proposed in [7] a qualitative decision theory which relies on the basic assumption that uncertainty about a decision problem is of *qualitative* nature and representable by *possibility distributions* over the set of consequences X. Given a qualitative[7] uncertainty scale V, a possibility distribution $\pi : X \to V$ provides a plausibility ordering on X in such a way that $\pi(x') \leq \pi(x)$ means that the consequence x is at least as plausible as x'. Based on such uncertainty representation, (qualitative) utility functions are defined and characterised by a set of axioms which can be regarded as a qualitative counterpart of Von Neumann and Morgenstern's axiomatics for the EUT.

In this work we build on this decision model to design bidding strategies for trading agents. After this introduction, Section 2 briefly describes the auction tournament environment. In Section 3, our theoretical decision model is described. Next section 4 is devoted to explain how this decision model can be applied to the design of bidding strategies while section 5 presents an heuristic-based approach for applying our model. Finally, we end up with some conclusions and an outline of our future work.

2 Auction-based Tournament Scenarios

In [23] we presented FM96.5, an electronic auction house based on the traditional *fish market* metaphor as an alternative approach to other proposals for electronic marketplace architectures(f.i. [25, 3]). In a highly mimetic way, the workings of FM96.5 involves the concurrency of several scenes governed by the market intermediaries identified in the fish market. Namely, seller agents register their goods with a seller admitter agent, and wait for receiving their earnings from a seller manager until the auctioneer has sold them in the auction room. Buyers, on the other hand, register with a buyer admitter, and bid in the auction room for goods which they pay through a credit line that is set up and updated with a

---

[7] In the sense that the ordering is the only that matters.

seller manager. The main scene is the auction itself, in which buyers bid for boxes of fish that are presented by an auctioneer who calls prices in descending order - the *downward bidding protocol*. Buyer and seller agents can trade goods as long as they comply with the *FishMarket institutional* conventions, incarnated in what we call an *interagent*[15], which constitutes the sole and exclusive means through which a trader agent —be it a software agent or a human trader— interacts with the market institution. An interagent gives a permanent identity to the trader and enforces an *interaction protocol* that establishes what illocutions can be uttered by whom and when.

In order to obtain an auction tournament environment, FM96.5 has been extended with some innovations that turn it into a multi-agent test-bed, as described in [21, 22][8]. This test-bed permits the definition, activation and evaluation of a wide variety of experimental trading scenarios (from simple toy scenarios to complex real-world scenarios) that we shall refer to as *tournaments*.

A tournament scenario will involve a collection of explicit parameters that characterize an artificial market. Such parameters define the bidding conditions (timing restrictions, increment/decrement steps, publicly available information, etc.), the way goods are identified and brought into the market, the resources buyers may have available, and the conventions under which buyers and sellers are going to be evaluated.

In rest of this section we sketch out our simplified[9] (formal) view of such tournament scenarios by introducing some of the elements composing them. We start by explicitly describing the dynamics of the *downward bidding protocol* governing the main activity within the *FishMarket*:

[**Step 1**] The auctioneer chooses a good out of a lot of goods that is sorted according to the order in which sellers deliver their goods to the sellers' admitter.

[**Step 2**] With a chosen good, the auctioneer opens a *bidding round* by quoting offers downward from the good's starting price, previously fixed by the sellers' admitter, as long as these price quotations are above a *reserve price* previously defined by the seller.

[**Step 3**] Several situations might arise during this round:

Bids: One (or several) buyer(s) submit his/their bids at the current price. If there is only one bid, the good is sold to the bidder. Otherwise, a collision comes about, the good is not sold, and the auctioneer restarts the round at a higher price.

No bids: No buyer submits a bid at the current price. If the reserve price has not been reached yet, the auctioneer quotes a new lower price, otherwise the auctioneer declares the good *withdrawn*[10] and closes the round.

[**Step 4**] The first three steps repeat until there are no more goods left.

---

[8] The sof tware package of this test-bed can be donwloaded from the FM project web page[30] and has been fully reported in [20].
[9] The interested reader may refer to [22] for a more thorough discussion.
[10] The good is returned to its owner.

Next, we identify the elements composing a *FishMarket* -like tournament scenario by introducing the notion of *Tournament descriptor*, which intends to encompass all the information characterizing tournament scenarios using the above downward bidding protocol. We define a **Tournament Descriptor** $\mathcal{T}$ as the 6-tuple

$$\mathcal{T} = \langle \Delta_{price}, \mathcal{B}, \mathcal{S}, Cr, \mu, E \rangle$$

where Δ_{price} is the decrement of price between two consecutive quotations uttered by the auctioneer; $\mathcal{B} = \{b_1, \ldots, b_n\}$ is a finite set of identifiers corresponding to all participating buyers, analogously $\mathcal{S}$ for the participating sellers; Cr is the initial endowment of each buyer at the beginning of each auction; $\mu \in \mathcal{M}$ is the tournament mode where $\mathcal{M} = \{$random, automatic, one auction, fish market, $\ldots \}$ is the set of tournament modes; and E is the buyer's evaluation function calculated as the cumulative benefits.

It is worth noticing that a number of tournament scenarios of varying degrees of realism and complexity can be generated by instantiating the definition above[11].

3 Possibilistic-based Decision Theory

In this section we describe the possibilistic-based decision making model that we shall subsequently employ for designing competitive bidding strategies for trading agents.

We start by introducing the basics of Dubois and Prade's possibilistic decision model[7] (with some simplifications), and then we follow with some extensions that we propose in order to show how this decision model generalizes other decision models such as, f.i., Gilboa and Schmeidler's CBDT[10].

3.1 Background

First of all we introduce some notation and definitions. $X = \{x_1, \ldots, x_p\}$ will denote a finite set of consequences, $(V, \leq)$ a linear scale of uncertainty, with $\inf(V) = 0, \sup(V) = 1$. $Pi(X)$ will denote the set of consistent possibility distributions on X over V, i.e. $Pi(X) = \{\pi : X \to V \mid \exists x \in X$ such that $\pi(x) = 1\}$. Finally, $(U, \leq)$ will denote a linear scale of preference (or utility), with $\sup(U) = 1$ and $\inf(U) = 0$, and $u : X \to U$ a utility function that assigns to each consequence x of X a preference level $u(x)$ of U. For the sake of simplicity here, we make the assumption that $U = V = [0, 1]$.

The working assumption of the decision model is that every decision $d \in D$ induces a possibility distribution $\pi : X \to V$ on the set X of consequences. Thus, ranking decisions amounts to ranking possibility distributions of $Pi(X)$. In such a framework, Dubois and Prade [7] propose the use of two kinds of qualitative utility functions to order possibility distributions. The basic underlying idea is

---

[11] [21] provide examples of several tournament instantiations.

based on the fact that a utility function $u : X \to U$ on the consequences can be regarded as specifying a fuzzy set of *preferred, good consequences*: the greater $u(x)$ is, the more preferred the consequence x is and the more x belongs to the (fuzzy) set of preferred consequences. On the other hand, a possibility distribution $\pi : X \to V$ specifies the fuzzy set of which consequences are plausible: the greater $\pi(x)$, the more plausible is the consequence x. Therefore, a conservative criterion is to look for those π's which, at some extent, make hardly plausible all the bad consequences, or in other words, all plausible consequences are good. On the contrary, an optimistic criterion that may be used to break ties is to look for those π's that, also to some extent, make plausible some of the good consequences.

For each utility function $u : X \to U$ the conservative and optimistic qualitative utilities used in the possibilistic decision model are respectively:

$$QU^-(\pi \mid u) = \min_{x \in X} \max(1 - \pi(x), u(x))$$
$$QU^+(\pi \mid u) = \max_{x \in X} \min(\pi(x), u(x)).$$

One can easily notice that $QU^-(\pi \mid u)$ and $QU^+(\pi \mid u)$ are nothing but the necessity and possibility degrees of the fuzzy set u w.r.t. the distribution π [1], or in other words, the Sugeno integrals of the utility function u with respect to the necessity and possibility measures induced by the distribution π. Moreover, when π denotes a crisp subset A (i.e. $\pi(x) = 1$ if $x \in A$, $\pi(x) = 0$ otherwise), $QU^-(\pi \mid u) = \min_{x \in A} u(x)$ and $QU^+(\pi \mid u) = \max_{x \in A} u(x)$, and hence, maximizing QU^- and QU^+ generalizes the well-known *maximin* and *maximax* decision criteria respectively. See [6] for an axiomatization of the preference relation induced by QU^-, QU^+, and other related utility functions.

3.2 Possible generalizations

It is well known in fuzzy set theory that the necessity and possibility measures account for a qualitative notion of fuzzy set inclusionship and intersection, respectively. Thus, in terms of fuzzy set operations, the decision criteria above using the QU^- and QU^+ functions can be read as the higher the degree of fuzzy set inclusionship of the π into u, the higher ranking of π according to the conservative criterion, while the higher the degree of fuzzy set intersection of π with u, the higher ranking of π according to the optimistic criterion.

Thus, besides those pure qualitative utilities, one can naturally think of introducing some other expressions of a more quantitative nature, but still accounting for a notion of inclusion and intersection. For instance, the most general way of defining the degree of intersection of π and u is:

$$dg(\pi \cap u) = \max_{x \in X}(\pi \cap u)(x),$$

where $(\pi \cap u)(x) = \pi(x) \otimes u(x)$, $\otimes$ being a t-norm[12] operation in $[0, 1]$. However, to define a degree of inclusion of π into u, there are at least two ways based on: (i)to what extent all elements of π are also elements of u; (ii) the proportion of elements of $\pi \cap u$ with respect to the elements of π. The former comes from a logical view while the latter comes from a conditioning view. They lead to the following expressions:

- $dg_l(\pi \subseteq u) = \min_{x \in X} \pi(x) \Rightarrow u(x)$,
  where $\Rightarrow$ is a many-valued implication[13] function,
- $dg_c(\pi \subseteq u) = \frac{\|\pi \cap u\|}{\|\pi\|}$,
  where $\| \ \|$ denotes fuzzy cardinality[14].

At this point, the following remarks are in order.

1. If both π and u define crisp subsets of consequences, then $dg_l(\pi \subseteq u)$ is either 1 or 0, while $dg_c(\pi \subseteq u)$ is nothing but the relative cardinality of π inside u, and for both, the degree is 1 only if $\pi \subseteq u$.
2. When $\otimes = \min$ and $\alpha \Rightarrow \beta = \max(1 - \alpha, \beta)$, we recover the qualitative utility functions: $dg_l(\pi \subseteq u) = QU^-(\pi \mid u)$ and $dg(\pi \cap u) = QU^+(\pi \mid u)$.
3. When $\otimes = product$, $dg_c(\pi \subseteq u)$ is nothing but the expected value $E(u)$ of the utility function u w.r.t. to the unnormalized probability distribution $P(x) = \pi(x)$, or in other words, the weighted average of the $u(x)$ values according to the weights $\pi(x)$. When π comes from a similarity function, then $dg_c(\pi \subseteq u)$ can be closely related to Gilboa and Schmeidler's CBDT.

Finally, based on the notions of degree of inclusion and intersection defined above, we can consider the utility functions $\mathcal{U}_*^-(\pi \mid u) = dg_*(\pi \subseteq u)$, $* = l, c$, and $\mathcal{U}^+(\pi \mid u) = dg(\pi \cap u)$.

4 Possibilistic-based Design of Bidding Strategies

An agent's bidding strategy must decide on an appropriate price on which to bid for each good being auctioned during each round composing the tournament. Due to the nature of the domain faced by the agent, we must demand that such bidding strategy balances the agent's short-term benefits with its long-term benefits in order to succeed in long-run tournaments.

In what follows we make use of the possibilistic-based decision-making model described above as the key element to produce a competitive bidding strategy.

---

[12] A t-norm $\otimes$ is a binary operation (usually continuous) in $[0, 1]$ which is non-decreasing, commutative, associative, and verifying $1 \otimes x = x$ and $0 \otimes x = 0$ for all $x \in [0, 1]$.

[13] An implication function $\Rightarrow$ is a binary operation in $[0, 1]$ which is non-increasing in the first variable, non-decreasing in the second variable, and verifying at least $1 \Rightarrow x = x$ and $x \Rightarrow 1 = 1$ for all $x \in [0, 1]$.

[14] If A denotes a fuzzy subset of X with membership function μ_A then $\|A\| = \Sigma_{x \in X} \mu_A(x)$

4.1 The Decision Problem

For each round composing a tournament scenario, the decision problem for a trading agent consists in selecting a bid from the whole set of possible bids—from the starting price down to the reserve price.

In order to apply the possibilistic decision model first we have to identify the variables involved in the decision problem of our interest.

We model market situations faced by our agent, denoted hereafter b_0, as vectors of features

$$s = (r, a, \tau, g, p_\alpha, p_{rsl}, \overline{\kappa}, \overline{E}, R)$$

characterizing round r of auction a such that τ is the type of the good g to be auctioned, p_α is its starting price, p_{rsl} is its resale price, $\overline{\kappa}$ is the vector of credits (κ_i is the credit of buyer b_i), $\overline{E}$ is the vector of scores (E_i is the score of buyer b_i), and R is the number of rounds left.

The decision set $\mathcal{D}$ will consist on the set of allowed bids our agent b_0 can submit. Given a new market situation s_0, we shall have $\mathcal{D} = \{bid(p) \mid p = p_\alpha - m.\Delta_{price}, m \in \mathbb{N}, p_{rsv} \leq p \leq \overline{\kappa}(b_0)\}$, where p_α and p_{rsv} are the starting and reserve prices in situation s_0, and $bid(p)$ means that the agent submits a bid at price p.

At each round, either the agent (b_0) wins, or buyer b_1 wins, ... , or buyer b_n wins by submitting bids at different prices. Therefore, the set X of outcomes (or consequences) is defined as the set $X = \{win(b_i, p) \mid i = 0, \ldots, n \; ; p \in [p_{rsv} + \Delta_{price}, p_\alpha]\}$, where $x = win(b_i, p)$ means that buyer b_i wins the round by submitting a bid at price p.

So, according to the decision model introduced in the previous subsection, given a current market situation s_0, it remains to assess, for each possible decision (bid) $d \in \mathcal{D}$, which are the possibility and utility values $\pi(x)$ and $u(x)$, for all $x \in X$, to be able to calculate a global utility for each d (using either QU^-, QU^+, or $\mathcal{U}$). This is done in the next subsections.

Hereafter we shall assume that the agent keeps a memory of cases M storing the history of (past and the current) tournaments, whose cases are of the form $c = (s, b, p_s)$, where b is the buyer who won the round characterized by s (as defined above) by submitting a bid at price p_s.

4.2 Generating possibility distributions from cases

In order to obtain a possibility degree for each consequence in X, we observe the behaviour of each agent in previous similar situations. Then, the uncertainty on the behaviour of each agent in front of a new market situation is estimated, as a possibility degree, in terms of the similarity between the current situation and those market situations where the agent exhibited that behaviour.

Given the current market situation s_0, for each possible bid $p_d \in \mathcal{D}$, our agent has to evaluate the possibility of each buyer (including himself) winning the round, i.e. the possibility of each consequence $x \in X$. Let $x = win(b_i, p_0)$ be a consequence and (s, b_i, p) a case in M. We shall assume as a working principle that "the *more similar* is (s_0, p_0) to (s, p), the *more possible* b_i will be the winner in s_0" (a similar principle has been recently considered in a framework of fuzzy case-based reasoning[4]). If $\tilde{s}$ denotes the fuzzy set of situations similar to s, the above principle can be given the following semantics:

$$\pi_{s_0}(win(b_i, p_0)) \geq \mu_{\tilde{s}}(s_0) \otimes \mu_{\tilde{p}}(p_0)$$

where $\mu_{\tilde{s}} : Sit \to [0, 1]$ denotes the membership function of the fuzzy set $\tilde{s}$ and $\mu_{\tilde{p}} : Prices \to [0, 1]$ denotes the membership function of the fuzzy set $\tilde{p}$. They are defined as $\mu_{\tilde{s}}(s') = \mathcal{S}(s, s')$ and $\mu_{\tilde{p}}(p') = \mathcal{P}(p, p')$, where $\mathcal{S}$ and $\mathcal{P}$ are fuzzy relations on the set of situations and on the set of prices respectively, accounting for a notion of proximity or similarity.

Therefore, we can estimate the possibility degrees for each $b_i \neq b_0$ as:

$$\pi_{s_0}(win(b_i, p_0)) = \max_{\{(s, b_i, p) \in M | p \leq p_0\}} \mu_{\tilde{s}}(s_0) \otimes \mu_{\tilde{p}}(p_0)$$

for all $win(b_i, p_0) \in X$. Observe that this defnition ensures that the possibility of winning is non-increasing with respect to the value of bids (i.e. the lower the bid, the lesser the possibility of winning).

¿From these possibilities we can construct an initial fuzzy set $Bid_{b_i}^0$ of the possible winning bids of each participating buyer $b_i \neq b_0$ by defining its membership function as

$$\mu_{Bid_{b_i}^0}(p) = \pi_{s_0}(win(b_i, p))$$

for all p such that $win(b_i, p) \in X$. However this fuzzy set may be further modified by means of a set of fuzzy rules which attempt at modelling the rational behaviour of buyers in particular situations that may not be sufficiently described by the cases in the memory. For instance, we consider the following set of fuzzy rules:

if $[\overline{\kappa}(b_i)$ is *high*] and $[R$ is *very_short*] and $[\overline{E}(b_i)$ is *low*]
then ΔBid_{b_i} is *very_positive*

if $[\overline{\kappa}(b_i)$ is *medium*] and $[R$ is *very_short*] and $[\overline{E}(b_i)$ is *low*]
then ΔBid_{b_i} is *slightly_positive*

expressing heuristic rules describing expected changes in the strategy of a buyer when only a few rounds are left (R is *very_short*), and he lags behind in the ranking ($\overline{E}(b_i)$ is *low*). In these situations, depending on the agents' current credit ($\overline{\kappa}(b_i)$), the fuzzy rules above model an increase in the agresiveness of the buyer, at different degrees, by yielding the expected increases (ΔBid_{b_i}) in the agent's bid. In general, by applying a set of fuzzy rules of that type in the standard way, we obtain for each buyer a fuzzy set ΔBid_{b_i} representing the expected variation of the observed bidding strategy of each buyer.

From the combination of the initial fuzzy set of possible bids $Bid_{b_i}^0$ with the fuzzy set of expected variations ΔBid_{b_i} we obtain the final fuzzy set of possible bids

$$Bid_{b_i}^\omega = Bid_{b_i}^0 \oplus \Delta Bid_{b_i}$$

where $\oplus$ denotes fuzzy addition, i.e.

$$\mu_{Bid_{b_i}^\omega}(p) = \max\{\min\{\mu_{Bid_{b_i}^0}(p_1), \mu_{\Delta Bid_{b_i}}(p_2)\} \mid p = p_1 + p_2\}.$$

Then, we make use of the fuzzy set Bid^ω to reassign possibilities to each consequence for each $b_i \neq b_0$

$$\pi_{s_0,p_d}(win(b_i,p)) = \begin{cases} \mu_{Bid^\omega(b_i)}(p), & \text{if } 0 < p < p_d \\ 0, & otherwise \end{cases}$$

Finally, to estimate the possibility of our agent winning with a bid at price p_d we look into the memory M for those cases such that the sale price was not greater than p_d. Let $M_{p_d} = \{(s,b_i,p) \in M \mid p < p_d, b_i \neq b_0\}$. Then

$$\pi_{s_0,p_d}(win(b_0,p)) = \begin{cases} \displaystyle\max_{(s,b_i,p')\in M_{p_d}} \mu_{Bid^\omega(b_i)}(p'), & \text{if } p = p_d \\ 0, & otherwise \end{cases}$$

These are the possibility values to be utilized when applying our decision model.

4.3 Assessing utilities

Given a new market situation s_0, for each consequence $x = win(b_i,p)$ our agent b_0 must assess the utility value $u(win(b_i,p))$ at the fact that buyer b_i wins the round by submitting a bid at price p. Several modelling options could be considered here. As a matter of example we propose here a particular utility function that aims at modelling an agent that prefers to wait and see when he is ahead, whereas he becomes more and more agressive when he lags behind in order to reach the first position in the tournament. It is based on the following scoring function:

$$f(b_i, s_0, p) = \begin{cases} k \cdot t, & \text{if } k \leq 0 \\ k \cdot t^{-1}, & \text{otherwise} \end{cases}$$

where $k = (\max_{j\neq i} \overline{E}(b_j)) - \overline{E}(b_i)$ and $t = (R-1)/(\max(\overline{\kappa}(b_i) - p, 1) \cdot (p_{rsl} - p))$, being p_{rsl} the resale price. We assume that $p_{rsl} - p \geq 0$, and $\overline{\kappa}(b_i) - p \geq 0$, i.e., buyers only take into consideration bids that can improve their score whenever they have enough credit to submit them. In the above definition of f, the factor $(max_{j\neq i}\overline{E}(b_j)) - \overline{E}(b_i)$ accounts for the position of buyer b_i with respect to the other buyers in the ranking of scores, the factor $p_{rsl} - p$ accounts for the benefit the agent would make if he wins the round, and the factor $\frac{R-1}{max(\overline{\kappa}(b_i)-p,1)}$ estimates the cost of winning the round. Then, based on the scoring function f, we propose the following utility function:

$$u(win(b_i,p)) = \begin{cases} r(f(b_0, s_0, p)), & \text{if } i = 0 \\ r(-f(b_i, s_0, p)), & \text{otherwise} \end{cases}$$

where r is a normalization linear scaling function which makes u to fall into [0,1].

To summarize, given a new market situation s_0, the decision process follows the following steps:

(i) for each decision $d = bid(p_d)$, where $p_d \in \mathcal{D}$,

    (a) for each consequence $x = win(b_i, p) \in X$ we calculate:
- the possibility $\pi_{s_0,d}(x)$
- the utility $u(x)$

    (b) the global utility assessed to each decision d will be calculated from either QU^-, QU^+, $\mathcal{U}^-$ or $\mathcal{U}^+$ by combining possibilities with utilities.

(ii) Our agent b_0 will choose one of the most preferred decision(one decision valued most by the global utility function).

5 An Heuristic Approach for the Development of Competitive Bidding Strategies

For each round, the resulting strategy performs a hybrid, two-fold decision making process that involves the usage of global(market-centered) probabilistic information in a first decision step, and individual(rival-centered) possibilistic information in a second, refining decision step.

The outright use of the possibilistic decision mechanism described above appears to be prohibitively expensive. Therefore, when facing the design of pragmatic bidding strategies we must attempt to propose flexible heuristic guidelines that prevent the agent from evaluating the whole set of alternative actions so that its deliberation process constrains to time and resource-boundedness. In what follows we propose a two-folded approach for decision making. In the first step a set of potential bids (as a subset of the whole set of possible bids) is selected according to the general trend of the market. Then, the second step consists in selecting the best bid for the agent according to the possibilistic decision model previously described.

We describe next how the first step is put into practice. Let s_0 be the current situation and M the available memory of cases. s_0, a first Assuming the principle that "*similar market situations* usually lead to *similar sale prices* of the good", the idea is to take advantge of the interpolation mechanism implicit in the fuzzy case-based reasoning model proposed in [5]. This amounts to consider, for each case[15] $(s, p) \in M$, a gradual fuzzy rule "*If Σ is $\tilde{s}$ then Υ is $\tilde{p}$*", where again $\tilde{s}$ and $\tilde{p}$ stand for the fuzzy set of situations similar to s and the fuzzy set of prices similar to p respectively; Σ and Υ are variables ranging over situations and prices resp. (**Caution:** the fuzzy set $\tilde{s}$ may be different from the fuzzy set with the same name appearing in subsection 4.2, since the criteria used to define how similar situations are may change from one purpose to another.) Such a fuzzy rule, together with the input situation s_0 gives the following fuzzy set *pbid* of prices (see [8]) for details about the semantics of fuzzy gradual rules):

$$\mu_{pbid}(p') = I(\mu_{\tilde{s}}(s_0), \mu_{\tilde{p}}(p')).$$

---

[15] Since we are only interested in the situation descriptor and the sale price we ommit in this section the buyer's identifier in the cases.

Here I is residuated many-valued implication[16], and assuming to have defined similarity functions $S^* : Sit \times Sit \rightarrow [0,1]$ and $T^* : prices \times prices \rightarrow [0,1]$, we may define $\mu_{\tilde{s}}(s_0) = S^*(s, s_0)$ and $\mu_{\tilde{p}}(p') = T^*(p, p')$. Considering all the cases in the memory M we come up with the following (fuzzy) set of potential bids:

$$\mu_{pbid}(p') = \min_{(s,p)\in M} I(S^*(s, s_0), T^*(p, p')).$$

Finally the set $\hat{B}_\alpha$ of candidate bids can be selected to be those having a membership degree to *pbid* above a certain value $\alpha > 0$, i.e. $\hat{B}_\alpha = \{p' \mid \mu_{pbid}(p') \geq \alpha\}$. It can be checked that $\hat{B}_\alpha = \cap_{(s,p)\in M} \{p' \mid T^*(p, p') \geq S^*(s, s_0) \otimes \alpha\}$, where $\otimes$ is the t-norm whose residuum is I.

Therefore, instead of considering the whole set of alternative bids, the proposed decision-making process will only evaluate those bids within $\hat{B}_\alpha$. The algorithm in figure 1 summarizes the process of selecting a bid out of $\hat{B}_\alpha$ using a utility function U.

6 Conclusions and Future Work

We have described a possibilistic-based decision method that attemps at modelling buyer agents' behaviour in electronic auction tournaments. Interestingly, competitions seem to be in vogue in the AI community as suggested by the many emerging initiatives. *Robocup*[13] is attempting to encourage both AI researchers and robotics researchers to make their systems play soccer, autonomous mobile robots try to show their skills in office navigation and in cleaning up the tennis court in the *AAAI Mobile Robot Competition*[14], and even automated theorem proving systems participate in competitions [24]. But surely our proposal is closer to the *Double auction* tournaments held by the Santa Fe Institute[2] where the contenders competed for developing optimized trading strategies. However, the main concern of our proposal consists in providing a method for performing multi-agent reasoning under uncertainty based on the modelling of the other agents' behaviour likewise [26], where the recursive modelling method [11] was used for constructing agents capable of predicting the other agents' behaviour in Double auction markets.

As to our future work, firstly this shall focus on the empirical evaluation of our proposal. Secondly, we will head towards the construction of actual agents capable of trading in actual auction markets under the rules of any bidding protocol.

---

[16] A residuated many-valued implication is a binary opereation in [0, 1] of the form $I(x, y) = \sup\{z \in [0,1] \mid x \otimes z \leq y\}$, where $\otimes$ is a t-norm, i.e., a binary, non-decreasing, associative and commutative operation in [0,1] such that $x \otimes 1 = x$ and $x \otimes 0 = 0$.

Function **Bid_Selection** $(M, \hat{B}_\alpha, s_0, U)$
  $\forall$ candidate bid $p_d \in \hat{B}_\alpha$
    $\forall$ buyer $\mathbf{b} \in \mathcal{B}$ such that $b \neq b_0$
      Retrieve all cases $c = (s, \mathbf{b}, p_s) \in M$
      $\forall$ price p
        Consequence $x := win(\mathbf{b}, p)$
        <u>if</u> $p < p_d$
          <u>then</u> $\pi(win(\mathbf{b}, p)) = 0$
          <u>else</u> $\pi(win(\mathbf{b}, p)) = \pi_{s_0, p_d}(win(\mathbf{b}, p))$
        $u(win(\mathbf{b}, p)) = r(-f(\mathbf{b}, s_0, p))$
      <u>end for</u>
    <u>end for</u>
    $b = b_0$
    Retrieve all cases $c = (s, b_0, p_s) \in M$
    $\forall$ price p
      Consequence $x := win(\mathbf{b_0}, p)$
      <u>if</u> $p \neq p_d$
        <u>then</u> $\pi(win(\mathbf{b_0}, p)) = 0$
        <u>else</u> $\pi(win(\mathbf{b_0}, p)) = \pi_{s_0, p_d}(win(\mathbf{b_0}, p))$
        $u(win(\mathbf{b_0}, p) = r(f(\mathbf{b_0}, s_0, p))$
    <u>end for</u>
    Calculate $U(bid(\mathbf{b_0}, p))$
  <u>end for</u>
  return $p = \arg\max\{U(bid(\mathbf{b_0}, p_d)) \mid p_d \in \hat{B}\}$
<u>end function</u>

Fig. 1. Bid Selection Procedure

Acknowledgements

This work has been partially supported by the Spanish CICYT project SMASH, TIC96-1038-C04001. Eduard Giménez and Juan A. Rodríguez-Aguilar enjoy the CIRIT doctoral scholarships 1998FI 0005 and FI-PG/96-8.490 respectively.

References

1. Zadeh L. A. Fuzzy sets as a basis for the theory of possibility. *Fuzzy Sets and Systems*, (1):3–28, 1978.
2. M. Andrews and R. Prager. *Genetic Programming for the Acquisition of Double Auction Market Strategies*, pages 355–368. The MIT Press, 1994.
3. A. Chavez and Pattie Maes. Kasbah: An agent marketplace for buying and selling goods. In *First International Conference on the Practical Application of Intelligent Agents and Multi-Agent Technology (PAAM'96)*, pages 75–90, 1996.
4. D. Dubois, F. Esteva, P. Garcia, L. Godo, R. Lopez de Mantaras, and H. Prade. Fuzzy modelling of case-based reasoning and decision. In Leake and Plaza, editors, *Proceedings 2nd. Int. Conf. on Case Based Reasoning (ICCBR'97)*, pages 599–611, 1997.

5. D. Dubois, F. Esteva, P. Garcia, and H. Prade. A logical approach to interpolation based on similarity relations. *Journal of Approximate Reasoning*, 17(1):1–36, 1997.

6. D. Dubois, Lluis Godo, Henri Prade, and Adriana Zapico. Making decision in a qualitative setting: from decision under uncertainty to case-based decision. In *Proceedings of the 6th.. Int. Conf. on Principles of Knowledge Representation and Reasoning(KR'98)*, 1998.

7. D. Dubois and H. Prade. Possibility theory as a basis for qualitative decision theory. In *Proceedings of the 14th International Joint Conference on Artificial Intelligence (IJCAI'95)*, pages 1924–1930, 1995.

8. D. Dubois and H. Prade. What are fuzzy rules and how to use them. *Fuzzy Sets and Systems*, 84:169–185, 1996.

9. Pere Garcia, Eduard Giménez, Lluís Godo, and Juan A. Rodríguez-Aguilar. Possibilistic-based design of bidding strategies in electronic auctions. In *The 13th biennial European Conference on Artificial Intelligence (ECAI-98)*, 1998.

10. I. Gilboa and D. Schmeidler. Case-based theory. *The Quarterly Journal of Economics*, 110:607–639, 1995.

11. Piotr Gmytrasiewicz and Edmund H. Durfee. A rigorous, operational formalization of recursive modeling. In *Proceedings of the First International Conference on Multi-Agent Systems*, pages 125–132, 1995.

12. B. A. Huberman and S. Clearwater. A multi-agent system for controlling builging environments. In *Proceedings of the First International Conference on Multi-Agent Systems (ICMAS-95)*, pages 171–176. AAAI Press, June 1995.

13. Hiroaki Kitano, Minoru Asada, Yasuo Kuniyoshi, Itsuki Noda, and Eiichi Osawa. Robocup: The robot world cup initiative. In *First International Conference on Autonomous Agents*, 1997.

14. David Kortenkamp, Illah Nourbakhsh, and David Hinkle. The 1996 AAAI Mobile Robot Competition and Exhibition. *AI Mag.*, 18(1):25–32, 1997.

15. Francisco J. Martín, Enric Plaza, and Juan Antonio Rodríguez-Aguilar. An infrastructure for agent-based systems: An interagent approach. *International Journal of Intelligent Systems*, 1998.

16. Noyda Matos, Carles Sierra, and Nick R. Jennings. Determining successful negotiation strategies: An evolutionary approach. In *Proceedings of the Third International Conference on Multi-Agent Systems (ICMAS-98)*, 1998.

17. J. Von Neumann and O. Morgenstern. *Theory of Games and Economic Behaviour*. Princeton Univ. Press, Princeton, NJ, 1944.

18. Pablo Noriega. *Agent-Mediated Auctions: The Fishmarket Metaphor*. PhD thesis, Universitat Autonoma de Barcelona, 1997. Also to appear in IIIA mongraphy series.

19. D. North. *Institutions, Institutional Change and Economics Perfomance*. Cambridge U. P., 1990.

20. Juan A. Rodríguez-Aguilar, Francisco J. Martín, Francisco J. Giménez, and David Gutiérrez. Fm0.9beta users guide. Technical report, Institut d'Investigació en Intel.ligència Artificial. Technical Report, IIIA-RR98-32, 1998.

21. Juan A. Rodríguez-Aguilar, Francisco J. Martín, Pablo Noriega, Pere Garcia, and Carles Sierra. Competitive scenarios for heterogeneous trading agents. In *Proceedings of the Second International Conference on Autonomous Agents (AGENTS'98)*, pages 293–300, 1998.

22. Juan A. Rodríguez-Aguilar, Francisco J. Martín, Pablo Noriega, Pere Garcia, and Carles Sierra. Towards a test-bed for trading agents in electronic auction markets. *AI Communications*, 11(1):5–19, 1998.

23. Juan A. Rodríguez-Aguilar, Pablo Noriega, Carles Sierra, and Julian Padget. Fm96.5 a java-based electronic auction house. In *Second International Conference on The Practical Application of Intelligent Agents and Multi-Agent Technology(PAAM'97)*, pages 207–224, 1997.
24. Christian B. Suttner and Geoff Sutcliffe. *ATP System Competition*, volume 1104 of *Lecture Notes in Artificial Intelligence*, pages 146–160. Springer Verlag, 1996.
25. M. Tsvetovatyy and M. Gini. Toward a virtual marketplace: Architectures and strategies. In *First International Conference on the Practical Application of Intelligent Agents and Multi-Agent Technology (PAAM'96)*, pages 597–613, 1996.
26. José M. Vidal and Edmund H. Durfee. Building agent models in economic societies of agents. In *Workshop on Agent Modelling (AAAI-96)*, 1996.
27. Michael P. Wellman. A market-oriented programming environment and its application to distributed multicommodity flow problems. *Journal of Artificial Intelligence Research*, (1):1–23, 1993.
28. Peter R. Wurman, , Michael P. Wellman, and William E. Walsh. The Michigan Internet AuctionBot: A Configurable Auction Server for Human and Software Agents. In *Second International Conference on Autonomous Agents (AGENTS'98)*, 1998.
29. Fredrik Ygge and Hans Akkermans. Making a case for multi-agent systems. In Magnus Boman and Walter Van de Velde, editors, *Advances in Case-Based Reasoning*, number 1237 in Lecture Notes in Artificial Intelligence, pages 156–176. Springer-Verlag, 1997.
30. The FishMarket Project. http://www.iiia.csic.es/Projects/fishmarket.

A π-calculus Model of a Spanish Fish Market
– Preliminary Report –

Julian Padget and Russell Bradford *

Department of Mathematical Sciences
University of Bath, BATH BA2 7AY, UK
{jap,rjb}@maths.bath.ac.uk

Abstract. This paper reports an educational exercise in using the π-calculus to model components of an electronic marketplace. Specifically, we are looking at the Spanish fish market, since we have participated in the construction of several simulations of this scenario over the past 18 months and now feel it is time to prepare a more precise description. Our objectives in doing this were (i) to gain familiarity with the π-calculus (ii) to find out whether the π-calculus might provide a suitable basis for defining the behaviour of components in an electronic marketplace. It is not our intention at this stage to establish the correctness of the components or the completeness of the model: these will be addressed later using existing tools and by developing new ones. In summary, this is an experience report.

1 The problem: an informal description

This analysis has arisen from joint work with the the Spanish government AI research institute (IIIA) at Bellaterra near Barcelona. Formerly, this laboratory was located at Blanes on the Costa Brava, north of Barcelona, and Blanes is the location of the actual fish market that has inspired this work on institutional modelling and agent specification.

In 1995 the business of formalizing the illocutions of the agents in an electronic fish market began using dynamic logic [13], along with the building of the first prototypes. In the summer of 1996, Bath and IIIA collaborated on the construction of three more prototypes, using various technologies to explore different aspects of the design space, culminating in FM96.5, which was described in detail in [17]. During this last phase, a new protocol was developed for downward bidding, which broke away from the naïve initial implementation where prospective buyers had to acknowledge every offer from the auctioneer—effectively enforcing a distributed lock-step in the thrall of the slowest connection. The new protocol, which we describe here, reduces communication by only requiring synchronization when a bid is made. The price for this protocol is that message delivery must be guaranteed and order must be preserved.

* This work has been partially supported by EPSRC grant GR/K27957 (http://www.maths.bath.ac.uk/~jap/Denton) and the CEC/HCM VIM project, contract CHRX-CT93-0401 (http://www.maths.bath.ac.uk/~jap/VIM)

UP FRONT PLAYERS	
the auctioneer	declares lots and prices, arbitrates on bids
the buyers' manager	admits buyers to the market
the sellers' manager	accepts lots from sellers

BACK STAGE	
the accountant	assists the buyers' manager by verifying credit-worthiness of a potential buyers; assists auctioneer, sellers' and buyers' manager by recording sales and updating credit records
the boss	initiates and terminates the market

SCENES	
buyers' admission	in which a buyer requests admission to the market and is either rejected or receives a NBI with which to participate in the auction.
sellers' admission	in which a seller requests admission to the market and deposits some fish for sale.
auction	in which the lots are sold to the highest bidder.
buyers' settlement	in which a buyer receives the lots for which he has successfully bid and is informed of his remaining credit.
sellers' settlement	in which a seller receives money corresponding to the fish deposited earlier.

Table 1. Players and scenes in the FishMarket

The Blanes fishermans' cooperative is like many thousands of other such institutions around the world: it exists to provide institutional guarantees to the buyers (a fair market price, quality of commodity) and the sellers (a fair market price although not perhaps as advantageous as under an English ascending price auction, a guaranteed market). There are many sociological and (micro-)economic aspects which could be explored from this point, but which would be inappropriate for this paper. For a synopsis, the interested reader is referred to [17]. The fair market price is established by a downward bidding open outcry auction—popularly known as a Dutch auction. Auctions have been the subject of microeconomic study for some years and it is accepted that the Dutch auction results in a price very close to the market valuation (that is, to the benefit of the fishermen).

The players and scenes comprising the fishmarket are summarized in Table 1 and this organization is largely reflected in Figure 1 except for the processes labelled NBI (for nomadic buyer interface) which we shall now explain. (Note: solid lines are used in Figure 1 for internal lines of communication and dashed denote external connections.) The term *open outcry* reasonably leads the reader to suppose that the buyer will shout "mine" (or something equivalent!) while the auctioneer calls out a decreasing sequence of numbers. In the Spanish fishmarket, at Blanes anyway, technology has interposed itself. While the auctioneer

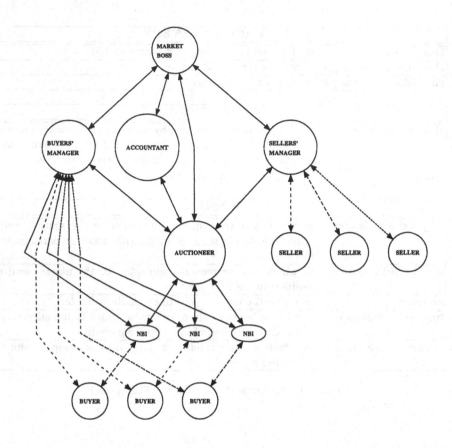

Fig. 1. Schematic of the agents and their communication channels in the FishMarket

calls out details of the lots, the decreasing sequence is displayed on a large electronic scoreboard overhead. And instead of shouting out, buyers are issued with electronic control boxes bearing a button which, when pressed, stops the descending count and identifies which box was responsible. It is this control box which inspired the introduction of the NBI, bringing numerous benefits with it. In particular, the auctioneer now need not be accessible to (electronic) buyers and so is not subject to interference from them. More importantly, the NBI serves as a mechanism capable of preventing manipulation of the auction by premature bidding, foot-dragging and spoofing, as will be seen later.

The task of the remainder of this paper is to report on our attempts to formalize the above in terms of the π-calculus.

2 A π-calculus model

The components of the market are presented largely in a top-down order, rather than the order in which we developed them: we began in the middle, focussing on the auction process and moved outward, adding detail as the overall structure became clearer. Here we begin with the market boss, moving on to the buyer's admitter, the auctioneer and the nomadic buyer interfaces. We do not include the sellers' manager or the accountant due to time and space limitations.

The progenitors of the area of process algebras are Hoare's Communicating Sequential Process (CSP) language [8] which found operational expression in the occam programming language and Milner's Calculus of Concurrent Systems (CCS), a forerunner of the π-calculus. The CSP family is designed for static checking, with application in embedded control systems and is simply unsuitable for the kind of dynamics that arise in multi-agent systems, so we do not consider it further. The CCS family has proven more fertile and related schemes are the Join Calculus [4] which is inspired by Berry's Chemical Abstract Machine (Cham) and the Ambient Calculus [1] amongst others.

Of these the Ambient Calculus looks promising for future investigation because the notion of ambient maps clearly to the scenes of multi-agent interaction (or the rooms of dungeon-style models), enabling agents to interact by entering a space (ambient), compared to the tediousness of hard-wired channel connections necessary in the π-calculus.

Why choose the π-calculus of all these? We have already stated what makes the CSP family unsuitable. Of the remaining schemes, the π-calculus is the most mature, although the evidence of all the variants suggests, there are inadequacies to be resolved. But to be more specific, of the many process calculi that now exist, the π-calculus most closely matches our requirements of a dynamically changing network of communicating processes. Or, more simply put, the FishMarket is a system of mobile processes, and the π-calculus is the most important calculus for the description of mobile processes, despite the deficiencies that we have encountered in the communications mechanism. Furthermore, we felt the need to discover for ourselves the extent to which the π-calculus is useful in "real life" problems. There have been many studies into the theory and semantics of the π-calculus, but very few examples of actual use. It may be, just as for the λ-calculus, the π-calculus is great for the theoretical understanding of computation, but in practice it is too low-level to be used as a serious tool.

Of the many variants of the π-calculus we chose, as a simple starting point, the basic synchronous form as found in [11], in particular we have found the non-deterministic choice (sum) operator essential, although its behaviour raises some interesting questions. To quote [11].

The summation form $\sum \pi_i.P_i$ represents a process able to take part in one—but only one—of several alternatives for communication. The choice is not made by the process; it can never commit to one alternative until it occurs, and this occurrence precludes the other alternatives.

When viewed as a mathematical description, e.g., for the purpose of determining bisimilarity, there is no problem. However, when viewed as a program to run, there is an element of time and therefore sequence involved. Consider the process $\bar{a}.P + \bar{b}.Q$. If a message arrives on a just before one arrives on b, do we expect to become P, or do we expect a non-deterministic choice of P or Q? Certainly, we *can* become P, but most people (and the quote above can be interpreted to support this), would say we *should* become P. If not then the π-calculus would be a difficult tool indeed, requiring many synchronisations to enforce this natural behaviour, and these synchronisations would generally have no counterpart in a "real" program.

In the following descriptions we have assumed that the natural interpretation is the case, i.e., choices are determined as and when messages arrive on channels.

Nevertheless, there is still a fundamental reason why the standard π-calculus is far from appropriate, as it stands, for modelling MAS: communication is synchronized. In the context of electronic marketplaces, if not for other MAS applications, this is an infeasible constraint, even with guaranteed quality of service provisions in forthcoming internet protocols. On the other hand, such a protocol may be employed at a lower communication layer, although it is not visible at the inter-agent illocution layer. Unfortunately, as we observe later, there is not an obvious way to hide this in specifying agent behaviour. However, we still believe this has been a useful exercise, since the experience and insights gained will carry over both to other process algebras and help us in exploring and extending the design space of process algebras in general. Therefore, please accept this as a flawed work which points the way to issues of greater potential.

2.1 Summary of π-calculus syntax and semantics

The main features of the π-calculus—and those necessary to read the remainder of this paper—are the means to read and write information over channels, the creation of channels, and parallel, alternative and sequential composition. Terms in the π-calculus are described as prefixes followed by terms, which is intentionally a recursive definition. Syntactic details are outlined below[1].

In order to keep this paper to a reasonable length, we cannot provide a full introduction to the π-calculus, limiting ourselves instead to this summary. For more information, the interested reader is referred to Pierce's excellent article [15] and subsequently to Milner [11] and the wider literature [12].

$x(y)$: reads an object from channel x and associates it with the name y. This operation blocks until the writer is ready to transmit. The scope of y is limited to the process definition in which y occurs. Channel names, on the other hand may be local (see ν below), parameters to process definitions (see below), or global.

---

[1] A word of warning: this description should not be taken as definitive, since there are numerous interpretations which vary slightly in details of syntax, and sometimes of semantics. It does however represent π-calculus adequately for the purposes of the discussion in this paper.

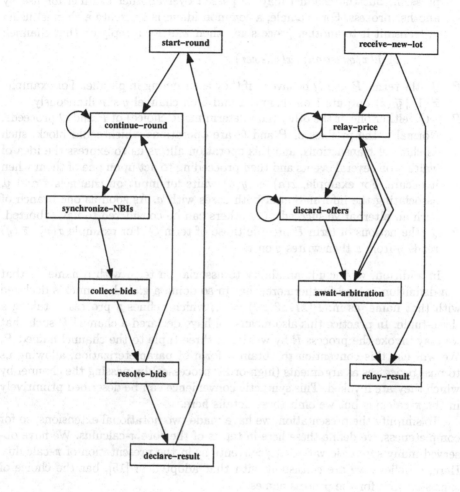

Fig. 2. State diagram of the auctioneer (left) and the nomadic buyer interface (right)

$\overline{x} \langle y \rangle$: writes the object named by y to the channel x. This operation blocks until the reader is ready to receive.

$\nu\, x\, ...$: creates a new channel named x. The scope of x is limited to the ν expression, but the channel may be passed over another channel for use by another process. For example, a common idiom is to create a channel using ν, transmit it to another process and then wait for a reply on that channel:

$$\nu\,(x)\,\overline{y}\,\langle x, question \rangle \,.\, x(answer)$$

$P \mid Q$: the terms P and Q behave as if they are running in parallel. For example, $\overline{x}\,\langle 1 \rangle \mid \overline{y}\,\langle 2 \rangle$ outputs 1 on channel x and 2 on channel y simultaneously.

$P + Q$: either one or the other (non-deterministic choice) of P and Q proceeds. Normally, the prefixes of P and Q are operations which could block, such as channel transactions, and this operation allows us to express the idea of waiting on several events and then proceeding to act upon one of them when it occurs. For example, $x(a) + y(a)$ waits for input on channels x and y, associating the information in both cases with a. As soon as one branch of such an alternative succeeds, the others can be considered to have aborted.

$P \,.\, Q$: the actions of term P precede those of term Q. For example $x(y) \,.\, \overline{z}\,\langle y \rangle$ reads y from x then writes y on z.

In addition, we include an ability to associate a term with a name — that is a definition — and furthermore, that in so doing a global channel is declared with that name, as in: $P(x1, x2, x3) = ...$, which defines a process P taking a three-tuple. In practice this also means we have declared a channel P such that we may invoke the process P by writing a three-tuple to the channel named P. We will use this convention to obtain a form of parameterization, allowing us to pass processes as arguments (high-order processes) by passing the channel by which they are invoked. This syntactic convenience can be described primitively in the π-calculus but we omit these details here.

To simplify the presentation, we have made two notational extensions, so for completeness, we define these here in terms of the core π-calculus. We have observed many syntactic variations/conventions in the presentation of π-calculus. Here, e believe we are consistent with that adopted in [15], bar the choice of sans-serif font for the process names.

scatter: we define the prefix $\overline{y_1 \ldots y_n}\,\langle x \rangle$ such that

$$\overline{y_1 \ldots y_n}\,\langle x \rangle \,.\, P \overset{\text{def}}{=}$$
$$\nu\,()$$
$$\overline{y_1}\,\langle x \rangle \,.\, \overline{w}\,\langle \rangle \mid \overline{y_2}\,\langle x \rangle \,.\, \overline{w}\,\langle \rangle \mid ... \mid \overline{y_n}\,\langle x \rangle \,.\, \overline{w}\,\langle \rangle \mid w() \,.\, ... \,.\, w() \,.\, P$$

where there are n occurrences of $w()$, which is to say the message x is output on all the channels $y_1 \ldots y_n$ in parallel (fork), following which, each sub-action outputs the null message on the private channel w. Subsequently, we await the receipt of n null messages on channel w (join), before proceeding to behave as P.

gather: while its counterpart is the prefix $y_1 \ldots y_n(x_1, \ldots, x_n)$, such that

$$y_1 \ldots y_n(x_1, \ldots, x_n) . P \stackrel{\text{def}}{=}$$
$$\nu \, (w_1, \ldots, w_n)$$
$$y_1(z_1) . \overline{w_1} \langle z_1 \rangle \mid \ldots \mid y_n(z_n) . \overline{w_n} \langle z_n \rangle \mid w_1(x_1) . \ldots . w_n(x_n) . P$$

which is to say, each sub-action reads a value z_i on channel y_i and then outputs it on the private channel w_i to be read into the corresponding x_i before behaving as P.

2.2 The Boss

The boss starts the market up by creating the various intermediaries with whom the buyers and sellers must communicate as well as the internal functionaries.

```
Boss() =
  ν (bm/boss, bm/auc, bm/acc, sm/boss, sm/acc, sm/auc, acc/boss, acc/auc, auc/boss)
    BM-Server(bm/boss, bm/acc, bm/auc)
    | SM-Server(sm/boss, sm/acc, sm/auc)
    | ACC-Server(acc/boss, bm/acc, sm/acc, acc/auc)
    | AU-Server(auc/boss, bm/auc, sm/auc, acc/auc)
    | Boss-Server(bm/boss, sm/boss, acc/boss, auc/boss)
```

The most obvious condition for signalling the the closing of the market is when all the lots have been sold. This also has the virtue that all the key players will be in well-defined states. However, the decision to close could, in principle, be taken at any time and this adds considerably to the complexity of its specification.

2.3 The Buyers' Manager

The Buyers' Manager (BM) accepts requests to participate in bidding from potential buyers. A buyer may not enter the market unless they have sufficient credit to make purchases and so a buyer may also make a deposit via the BM. If access is granted, the buyer then supplies a set of channels for communication with a nomadic buyer interface (NBI) and the BM also updates the auctioneer with the information about the new NBI. The BM also has responsibilities to the market boss, so should the boss signal the closing of the market, the BM must cease admitting new buyers.

The channel for further communication with between buyer and market is supplied by the buyer, thus the security of that channel is the responsibility of the buyer (or channel service provider). Or, looking at that from the buyer's point of view, he does not have to trust the security of a channel provided by the market - although the market must! This may also be important in a regulatory/legislative framework where agents are governed by the rules and laws of the agent's originating country, such as if the channel is required to support government monitoring. We are assuming services exist for the secure transfer of information about credit and for financial transactions. NBIs are rendered useless when a buyer leaves the market. The action of leaving the market is signalled via the NBI to the BM: in this way, the NBI can disable the bid function immediately, whereas if departure was signalled by communication with the BM and the NBI was subsequently disabled—by action of the BM—a bid could be made and accepted in between, leading to an inconsistent record or significant complexity in dealing with this special case, should it arise.

The Buyers' Manager is essentially a server: buyers make requests to enter the market passing a channel *buyer* for communication and an object *credit* which may be used to augment their credit. If the market is shutting as a result of a signal from the boss, then the buyer is sent the message **closed**. Otherwise, BM-Server forks, becoming BM-CheckCredit and BM-Server.

We do not go into the details of market shutdown, however we should emphasize that it is extremely tricky to specify correctly, with many chances for race conditions, and is considerably more difficult—by virtue of detail rather than techical challenge—than the more attractive bidding protocol aspect of the institution.

$$
\begin{aligned}
&\text{BM-Server}(bm/boss,\, bm/acc,\, bm/auc) = \\
&\quad bm/boss()\,.\,\text{BM-Shut}(bm/boss,\, bm/acc,\, bm/auc) \\
&\quad +\, enter(buyer,\, credit)\,.\,\text{BM-CheckCredit}(bm/acc,\, bm/auc,\, buyer,\, credit) \\
&\qquad\qquad\qquad\qquad\qquad\quad |\,\text{BM-Server}(bm/boss,\, bm/acc,\, bm/auc)
\end{aligned}
$$

If the market is shutting down, then BM-Shut will reply **closed** to the buyer using channel *buyer*. However, on the second signal from the boss, the BM terminates. There is a potential race condition here, in that the signal from the boss and a buyer request may both be present and non-determinism means that the buyer's request could be ignored, the server terminates and the buyer is left in limbo. A means to resolve this problem is discussed in section 3.

$$
\begin{aligned}
&\text{BM-Shut}(bm/boss,\, bm/acc,\, bm/auc) = \\
&\quad bm/boss()\, +\, enter(buyer,\, credit) \\
&\qquad .\,\overline{buyer}\,(\textbf{closed}) \\
&\qquad .\,\text{BM-Shut}(bm/boss,\, bm/acc,\, bm/auc)
\end{aligned}
$$

The decision to admit a buyer is based on whether he has deposited sufficient means of payment with the market. At the same time as the entry request is made, the buyer can also make a deposit with the market. The BM communicates with the accountant over the channel bm/acc passing a reply channel and the credit instrument offered by the buyer. The accountant simply responds **yes** or **no**. In the first case BM-CheckCredit becomes BM-CreateNewNBI; in the second it becomes BM-Goodbye.

```
BM-CheckCredit(bm/acc, bm/auc, buyer, credit) =
 ν ()
    _____
    bm/acc ⟨reply, credit⟩
    . reply(m)
      ⎡   [m = yes]
      ⎢   BM-CreateNewNBI(bm/auc, buyer)
    · ⎢ + [m = no]
      ⎣   BM-Goodbye(buyer)
```

The creation of a new NBI really comes down to the creation of the necessary
new channels: one each for *nbi/msg* and *nbi/offer* for the NBI links with the
auctioneer and one for the link between the NBI and the buyers' manager. Thus,
BM-CreateNewNBI becomes NBI and BM-leave. The communication channels
between the NBI and the buyer are supplied by the buyer in response to the **yes**
signalling admission to the market. The definition of BM-leave is not provided,
but serves to handle the settling up process with the buyer and delivery of the
lots bought.

```
BM-CreateNewNBI(bm/auc, bm/buyer) =
 ν (nbi/msg, nbi/offer, bm/nbi)
    _____
    bm/auc ⟨nbi/msg, nbi/offer⟩
    . bm/buyer ⟨yes⟩
    . bm/buyer(bid, offer, exit)
    . NBI(nbi/msg, nbi/offer, bid, offer, exit, bm/nbi) | BM-Leave(bm/nbi, bm/buyer)
```

If the buyer fails to satisfy the credit check, the message **no** is sent to the
prospective buyer and the process terminates.

```
BM-Goodbye(buyer) =
 _____
 buyer ⟨no⟩
```

2.4 The Auctioneer

```
AU-Server(auc/boss, auc/bm, auc/sm, auc/acc) =
  AU-StartRound(auc/boss, auc/bm, auc/sm, auc/acc, nil, 0, 0, {})
```

The auctioneer announces a new lot to the NBIs along with a starting price,
he then proceeds both to listen for bids and broadcast the new price until the
reserve price is reached, at which time, the lot is withdrawn (see Figure 2). The
auctioneer is started up by the market boss (see section 2.2), which passes the
channels provided by the boss and sets the initial values of the auctioneer state,
namely the lot (initially **nil**), the starting price (initially 0), reserve price (initially 0) and the set of *msg/offer* channel pairs (initially {}) for communicating
with the NBIs.

$$
\begin{aligned}
&\text{AU-StartRound}(auc/boss, auc/bm, auc/sm, auc/acc, lot, sp, rp, \{(msg_i, offer_i)\}) = \\
&\left\{
\begin{array}{l}
\textbf{if } |\{(msg_i, offer_i)\}| > 1 \\
\quad auc/bm(msg, offer) \\
\quad . \text{ AU-StartRound}(auc/boss, auc/bm, auc/sm, auc/acc, lot, sp, rp, \\
\qquad\qquad\qquad \{(msg_i, offer_i)\} \cup \{(msg, offer)\}) \\
\quad + \sum_{i=1} \quad \overline{msg_1 \ldots msg_n}(\textbf{bye}, msg, offer) \\
\qquad . \overline{msg}\,\langle\textbf{bye}\rangle \\
\qquad . \text{ AU-StartRound}(auc/boss, auc/bm, auc/sm, auc/acc, lot, sp, rp, \\
\qquad\qquad\qquad \{(msg_i, offer_i)\} \setminus \{(msg, offer)\}) \\
\quad + \overline{auc/sm}\,\langle\rangle \\
\qquad . \ auc/sm(lot, sp, rp) \\
\qquad . \overline{msg_1 \ldots msg_n}\,\langle lot\rangle \\
\qquad . \overline{offer_1 \ldots offer_n}\,\langle sp\rangle \\
\qquad . \text{ AU-ContinueRound}(auc/boss, auc/bm, auc/sm, auc/acc, sp, rp, \\
\qquad\qquad\qquad sp - 1, \{(msg_i, offer_i)\}) \\
\\
\textbf{otherwise} \\
\quad \overline{msg_1 \ldots msg_n}\,\langle\textbf{wait}\rangle \\
\quad . \ auc/bm(msg, offer) \\
\quad . \text{ AU-StartRound}(auc/boss, auc/bm, auc/sm, auc/acc, lot, sp, rp, \\
\qquad\qquad\qquad \{(msg_i, offer_i)\} \cup \{(msg, offer)\})
\end{array}
\right.
\end{aligned}
$$

AU-StartRound chooses between

1. admitting new buyers — in fact accepting the communication channels to their NBIs — using information received from the buyers' manager using channel auc/bm. As it stands, this definition does not guarantee to admit all waiting buyers before starting a new round. A partial remedy would be to compose AU-StartRound with the channel prioritiser described in section 3, but in the absence of a means to do the equivalent of a non-blocking read, something more sophisticated is required in the spirit of a solution to readers/writers with reader priority.
2. discarding connections to an NBIs given to a buyer who has decided to leave. The NBI sends the $msg/offer$ channel pair to the auctioneer, who removes it from the set of broadcast recipients and acknowledges the NBI so that it can safely terminate.
3. communicating with the sellers' admitter to obtain the next lot and the starting price using the channel auc/sm, this information is then broadcast over the channels $offer_1 \ldots offer_n$ to the NBIs. Subsequently, AU-StartRound becomes AU-ContinueRound passing the current price.

Note that an auction round does start unless there are at least two buyers.

If the current price of the lot reaches the reserve price, then a fake bid is entered and the NBI synchronization process is started in order to collect any bids that are in transit, or yet to be made, otherwise AU-ContinueRound chooses between

1. choosing between the NBIs, in effect, waiting for a buyer to bid via one of the channels $offer_i$ and then becoming AU-SynchronizeNBIs with the channel index i and the bid bid_i
2. broadcasting the current price to all the NBIs using the channels $offer_1 \ldots offer_n$ and then becoming AU-ContinueRound with the new (reduced) price.

It also has an exceptional duty to perform, namely when the Boss signals that the market must close. Although it might be desireable to recognize shutdown in other circumstances, to keep the model size down, we have here limited our handling of it to the top of the AU-ContinueRound loop, since that identifies one consistent place to stop.

$$
\begin{aligned}
&\text{AU-ContinueRound}(auc/boss, auc/bm, auc/sm, auc/acc, sp, rp, cp, \{(msg_i, \mathit{offer}_i)\}) = \\
&\left\{
\begin{array}{l}
\textbf{if } cp = rp \\
\text{AU-SynchronizeNBIs}(auc/boss, auc/bm, auc/sm, auc/acc, 0, -1, rp, \\
\qquad\qquad\qquad \{(msg_i, \mathit{offer}_i)\}) \\[2mm]
\textbf{otherwise} \\
auc/boss() \,.\, \text{AU-Shutdown}(auc/boss, auc/bm, auc/sm, auc/acc, \{(msg_i, \mathit{offer}_i)\}) \\
+ \sum_{i=1} \mathit{offer}_i(bid_i) \\
\qquad .\, \text{AU-SynchronizeNBIs}(auc/boss, auc/bm, auc/sm, auc/acc, i, bid_i, rp, \\
\qquad\qquad\qquad\qquad \{(msg_i, \mathit{offer}_i)\}) \\
+ \overline{\mathit{offer}_1 \ldots \mathit{offer}_n}\, \langle cp \rangle \\
\qquad .\, \text{AU-ContinueRound}(auc/boss, auc/bm, auc/sm, auc/acc, sp, rp, \\
\qquad\qquad\qquad cp - 1, \{(msg_i, \mathit{offer}_i)\})
\end{array}
\right.
\end{aligned}
$$

AU-SynchronizeNBIs executes when the first bid is received and issues a null message over the msg channel to each NBI. Subsequently, in parallel

1. it waits for an acknowledgement from each of the NBIs — in effect a global synchronization — after which a null message is output on channel $synch$ to enable AU-CollectBids to proceed.
2. it becomes AU-CollectBids with a singleton set containing the identity of the NBI whose bid was received first.

$$
\begin{aligned}
&\text{AU-SynchronizeNBIs}(auc/boss, auc/bm, auc/sm, auc/acc, i, bid, rp, \{(msg_i, \mathit{offer}_i)\}) = \\
&\overline{msg_1 \ldots msg_n}\, \langle \textbf{synchronize} \rangle \\
&.\, \nu\,() \\
&\quad \overline{msg_1 \ldots msg_n}\langle\textbf{synchronize}\rangle \,.\, \overline{synch}\,\langle\rangle \\
&\quad |\, \text{AU-CollectBids}(auc/boss, auc/bm, auc/sm, auc/acc, \{(msg_i, \mathit{offer}_i)\}, \\
&\qquad\qquad \{i\}, bid, rp, synch)
\end{aligned}
$$

AU-CollectBids chooses between

1. waiting for a null message on channel $synch$, which means it waits until all the NBIs have acknowledged the synchronization message, and then becomes AU-ResolveBids with the set of bidders B and the bid price bid
2. waiting for any other buyers to bid and dealing with the three cases of higher, equal and lower bids. A lower bid is ignored, and equal bid causes the identity of the NBI to be added to the set B and a higher bid replaces B with a new singleton set identifying the NBI and bid with the new bid price.

This is the heart of the distributed downward bidding protocol and in order for it to work, requires no-loss in-order delivery of messages. Thus the final synchronization message should only be processed *after* the final bid. Unfortunately, this cannot be guaranteed, since they could both be present on channels $synch$

and *offer$_i$*, although, in fact, the message on *synch* is only relayed after receipt of the last **synchronize** on *msg$_i$*. This potential race condition could be resolved by multiplexing, a solution for which we sketch in section 3.

$$
\begin{aligned}
&\text{AU-CollectBids}(auc/boss, auc/bm, auc/sm, auc/acc, \{(msg_i, offer_i)\}, B, bid, rp, synch) = \\
&\quad synch() \\
&\quad . \text{AU-ResolveBids}(auc/boss, auc/bm, auc/sm, auc/acc, \{(msg_i, offer_i)\}, B, bid, rp) \\
&\quad + \sum_{i=1} \ offer_i(bid_i) \\
&\qquad\qquad \Big[\ [bid_i > bid] \\
&\qquad\qquad\quad \text{AU-CollectBids}(auc/boss, auc/bm, auc/sm, auc/acc, \{(msg_i, offer_i)\}, \\
&\qquad\qquad\qquad\qquad\qquad \{i\}, bid_i, rp) \\
&\qquad\qquad + [bid_i = bid] \\
&\qquad\qquad\quad \text{AU-CollectBids}(auc/boss, auc/bm, auc/sm, auc/acc, \{(msg_i, offer_i)\}, \\
&\qquad\qquad\qquad\qquad\qquad B \cup \{i\}, bid, rp) \\
&\qquad\qquad + [bid_i < bid] \\
&\qquad\qquad\quad \text{AU-CollectBids}(auc/boss, auc/bm, auc/sm, auc/acc, \{(msg_i, offer_i)\}, B, \\
&\qquad\qquad\qquad\qquad\qquad bid, rp)
\end{aligned}
$$

If the winning bid is less than the reserve price, the lot is withdrawn and a new round starts. If B is a singleton set, then a single bid was received at price *bid* and the message **finish** is sent to all the NBIs to indicate the end of the bidding round and AU-ResolveBids becomes AU-DeclareResult. Otherwise, the NBIs are sent the message **repeat** to indicate that the bidding round is going to be repeated and AU-ResolveBids becomes AU-ContinueRound with the collision bid price increased by 25%.

$$
\begin{aligned}
&\text{AU-ResolveBids}(auc/boss, auc/bm, auc/sm, auc/acc, \{(msg_i, offer_i)\}, B, bid, rp) = \\
&\quad \Bigg\{ \ \textbf{if } bid < rp \\
&\qquad \overline{msg_1} \ldots \overline{msg_n} \ \langle \textbf{withdrawn} \rangle \\
&\qquad . \text{AU-StartRound}(auc/boss, auc/bm, auc/sm, auc/acc, \text{nil}, 0, 0, \\
&\qquad\qquad\qquad \{(msg_i, offer_i)\}) \\
&\quad \textbf{elseif } |B| = 1 \\
&\qquad \overline{msg_1} \ldots \overline{msg_n} \ \langle \textbf{finish} \rangle \\
&\qquad . \text{AU-DeclareResult}(auc/boss, auc/bm, auc/sm, auc/acc, \{(msg_i, offer_i)\}, B, bid) \\
&\quad \textbf{otherwise} \\
&\qquad \overline{msg_1} \ldots \overline{msg_n} \ \langle \textbf{repeat} \rangle \\
&\qquad . \text{AU-ContinueRound}(auc/boss, auc/bm, auc/sm, auc/acc, sp, rp, \\
&\qquad\qquad\qquad bid * 1.25, \{(msg_i, offer_i)\})
\end{aligned}
$$

To look at the preceding few definitions (AU-StartRound to AU-ResolveBids) from a different perspective, the whole bidding round process could be viewed as a super-step in bulk synchronous parallelism terminology, which terminates in response to a bid or on reaching the reserve price, but either way requires a global synchronization of the processes involved.

This phase should occasion some confusion to the reader familiar with the π-calculus. The reason is that in the standard π-calculus, as used here, all communications are synchronized, therefore there can be no notion of "message in transit" and the first bid to be received by the auctioneer, could reasonably be regarded as the winner, since there could not be any higher bid on its way. At this point, our solution is over-engineered because the protocol has been designed to function in an asynchronous context. However, we can finesse this criticism by handing-off work in the auctioneer to the NBIs: we observe that from the buyer's point of view, it is impossible to tell whether the descending price transmitted over the *offer* channel is relayed from the auctioneer or generated locally. Thus, the bidding round could be redefined so that the auctioneer simply issues a start command to the NBIs along with the starting price and reserve price and they then proceed, counting down and transmitting the price to the buyer. If/when the buyer bids, the NBI relays that to the auctioneer, which must now enter a bid resolution process of the like described above, since the first bid is now not necessarily the winner.

Finally, AU-DeclareResult sends the message **got** on channel msg_i to inform the ith NBI that its buyer's bid won, then the message **not** on every other msg channel. Subsequently, it becomes AU-StartRound.

$$
\begin{aligned}
&\text{AU-DeclareResult}(auc/boss, auc/bm, auc/sm, auc/acc, \{(msg_i, offer_i)\}, \{i\}, b) = \\
&\overline{msg_i} \langle \text{got} \rangle \\
&. \, \overline{msg_1} \ldots \overline{msg_{i-1}}, \overline{msg_{i+1}} \ldots \overline{msg_n} \langle \text{not} \rangle \\
&. \, \text{AU-StartRound}(auc/boss, auc/bm, auc/sm, auc/acc, \textbf{nil}, 0, 0, \\
&\qquad\qquad \{(msg_i, offer_i)\})
\end{aligned}
$$

2.5 The Nomadic Buyer Interface

The virtues of the nomadic buyer interface (NBI) are described elsewhere [17]: here it suffices to say that it provides the key to guaranteeing the integrity of the market as well as that of the buyer. The buyer connects to the NBI via the channels *bid*, *offer* and *exit*, while the NBI is linked to the auctioneer via two channels: *nbi/auc* for control messages and *auc/offer* for offer prices. As we have noted before, a single channel with multiplexing would suffice, but multiple channels where each is used for a single purpose, can make the exposition clearer.

We observe that, since communication is synchronous in the π-calculus, should the buyer not communicate with the NBI, the whole auction would deadlock. This could be rectified by the insertion of a buffer process in the NBI to handle buyer communications, but which we omit since this description, which was intended to be brief, is already overlong.

The NBI is created by the buyers' manager, receiving all the channels over which it will need to communicate. It receives the new lot description on channel *nbi/auc* and the starting offer price on channel *auc/offer*. This information is passed on to the buyer over channel *offer* and NBI becomes NBI-RelayPrice. It may be that there are too few buyers either initially, or at some stage, so the NBI must also deal with **wait** messages from the auctioneer, which it relays to the buyer (see Figure 2.

```
NBI(nbi/auc, auc/offer, bid, offer, exit, nbi/bm) =
   nbi/auc(wait)
   . offer ⟨wait⟩
   . NBI(nbi/auc, auc/offer, bid, offer, exit, nbi/bm)
 + nbi/auc(lot)
     . auc/offer(price)
     . offer ⟨lot, price⟩
     . NBI-RelayPrice(nbi/auc, auc/offer, bid, offer, exit, nbi/bm, price)
```

NBI-RelayPrice is effectively a loop, by means of which the current offer price
is relayed from the auctioneer to the buyer. However, at the same time three
other events may take place:

1. the buyer may signal a bid—pressing the button on the control box—by
   sending a null message to the NBI on channel *bid*; this is then relayed to the
   auctioneer over channel *nbi/auc* before becoming NBI-DiscardOffers.
2. another buyer may signal a bid, in which case, the auctioneer will send a
   synchronize message to all the NBIs over *nbi/auc*, which they must acknowledge, so NBI-RelayPrice becomes NBI-AwaitArbitration.
3. the buyer may signal his intention to leave the market using the *exit* channel,
   so this fact is communicated to the auctioneer and to the buyer's manager,
   however the NBI does not terminate until signalled by the auctioneer, in
   case it is needed to participate in a synchronization process for a bid in this
   round.

```
NBI-RelayPrice(nbi/auc, auc/offer, bid, offer, exit, nbi/bm, price) =
   auc/offer(new-price)
   . offer ⟨new-price⟩
   . NBI-RelayPrice(nbi/auc, auc/offer, bid, offer, exit, nbi/bm, new-price)
 + bid()
     . nbi/auc ⟨price⟩
     . NBI-DiscardOffers(nbi/auc, auc/offer, bid, offer, exit, nbi/bm, true)
 + nbi/auc(synchronize)
     . NBI-AwaitArbitration(nbi/auc, auc/offer, bid, offer, exit, nbi/bm, false)
 + exit()
     . nbi/bm ⟨bye⟩
     . nbi/auc ⟨bye⟩
     . nbi/auc(bye)
```

NBI-DiscardOffers chooses between

1. receiving and discarding subsequent lower offers that the auctioneer has
   broadcast between the buyer bidding and the auctioneer receiving the bid
   and beginning the synchronization process
2. receiving the synchronization message, indicating there are no lower offers
   to come, and becoming NBI-AwaitArbitration.

$$NBI\text{-}DiscardOffers(nbi/auc, auc/offer, bid, offer, exit, nbi/bm, flag) =$$
$$\overline{auc/offer}(price) \, . \, NBI\text{-}DiscardOffers(nbi/auc, auc/offer, bid, offer, exit, nbi/bm, flag)$$
$$+ \, nbi/auc() \, . \, NBI\text{-}AwaitArbitration(nbi/auc, auc/offer, bid, offer, exit, nbi/bm, flag)$$

NBI-AwaitArbitration first acknowledges the synchronization message from the auctioneer, then receives the result of the arbitration of the bids, which is passed on to the buyer, and then chooses between three cases:

1. the message is **finish** indicating the lot was awarded, then the process become NBI-RelayResult.
2. the message is **repeat** indicating the lot was not awarded and that the round is restarting, so a new starting price is received and NBI-AwaitArbitration becomes NBI-RelayPrice.
3. the message is **withdrawn** indicating that no bids were received above the reserve price, so the lot is withdrawn and a new round will begin with a new lot.

$$NBI\text{-}AwaitArbitration(nbi/auc, auc/offer, bid, offer, exit, nbi/bm, flag) =$$

$$\overline{nbi/auc} \, \langle \textbf{synchronize} \rangle$$
$$. \, nbi/auc(result)$$
$$. \, \overline{offer} \, \langle result \rangle$$
$$\left[\begin{array}{l} [result = \textbf{finish}] \\ NBI\text{-}RelayResult(nbi/auc, auc/offer, bid, offer, exit, nbi/bm, flag) \\ + [result = \textbf{repeat}] \\ \quad auc/offer(price) \\ \quad . \, \overline{offer} \, \langle price \rangle \\ \quad . \, NBI\text{-}RelayPrice(nbi/auc, auc/offer, bid, offer, exit, nbi/bm, price) \\ + [result = \textbf{withdrawn}] \\ \quad \overline{offer} \, \langle \textbf{withdrawn} \rangle \\ \quad . \, NBI(nbi/auc, auc/offer, bid, offer, exit, nbi/bm) \end{array} \right.$$

If the buyer using this NBI was one of those who made a bid—indicated by the parameter *flag* being **true**—the buyer is relayed the message (**got** or **not**) from the auctioneer saying whether the bid was successful, NBI-RelayResult then becomes NBI. Otherwise, the message from the auctioneer is discarded and NBI-RelayResult becomes NBI.

$$NBI\text{-}RelayResult(nbi/auc, auc/offer, bid, offer, exit, nbi/bm, flag) =$$
$$\left\{ \begin{array}{ll} nbi/auc(result) & \text{if } flag = \textbf{true} \\ . \, \overline{offer} \, \langle result \rangle & \\ . \, NBI(nbi/auc, auc/offer, bid, offer, exit, nbi/bm) & \\ \\ nbi/auc(result) & \textbf{otherwise} \\ . \, NBI(nbi/auc, auc/offer, bid, offer, exit, nbi/bm) & \end{array} \right.$$

2.6 Missing aspects and components

Unfortunately, despite the length of this already, there are still many missing components. The obvious omissions are the remainder of market boss, the sellers' admitter, the rest of the buyers' admitter and the accountant. As of each of these is added, it is likely that further complexity may be added to the existing components—modularity seems elusive, as yet, in π-calculus system descriptions. However, in considering the expected behaviour of the missing items, we cannot see, in principle, their action or structure being significantly different from the idioms we have developed so far, and specifically, the buyers' manager provides a suitable rôle model.

3 Lessons

We undertook this task for two reasons: (i) because a formal model of the Fish-Market was long overdue and (ii) because we wanted to see how effective the π-calculus would be in helping us to model a prototypical multi-agent system. The second point makes it sound like we may be seeking to criticise the π-calculus: that is not so. We are relatively naïve users who have sought to use it to solve our particular problem. We may have used it unwisely and we may have even been mistaken in choosing to use it for the task we have. So with those caveats in mind, we can now make some more general remarks about the process and the formalism.

3.1 Idioms

We have discovered (or perhaps re-discovered) several useful idioms while writing this description of the FishMarket. Here we describe a few of them.

The idea of passing channels to other processes to use for a reply we have found quite convenient. This style, also found in many other places (e.g., [15]) is quite natural, and can be likened to passing a reply continuation in actor semantics. It also has the benefit of sitting comfortably in the client-server paradigm that we have adopted. This construction can be see as a specific case of a more general pattern of processes as parameters, in the sense that rather than seeing the continuation as a return point, it is really "what to do next". Thus a convention could be established, akin to the continuation-passing style:

$$A(k_1) = \nu k_2 (B(k_2) \mid k_2() . C(k_1))$$
$$B(k_1) = \ldots \overline{k_1}\langle\rangle$$

that is, the first parameter is the continuation channel, which is signalled as the process's last action, thus invoking the continuation.

It is tempting (when approached from a practical computer science view of the world, where everything has a cost) to reuse channels as much as possible. However, from a descriptive point of view, this is a disaster. Using them for more than one purpose rapidly causes confusion, as one needs to multiplex and de-multiplex messages according to meaning, and this multiplies the complexity of description way beyond what is saved from economising on channels.

Unfortunately, using many channels forces you into employing memorable naming conventions, again making definitions harder to sketch, since they get much longer plus you have to pass them around as arguments to processes to provide a form of modularity. We discuss modularity further, below.

There are places in our description that require synchronisation of sets of processes, e.g., at the end of a bidding round. We have solved this by waiting on a process that broadcasts to the processes that need to synchronise, and itself waits for all of them to reply. It would be nice if we could capture this idea in a simnple abstraction: after all, this is very much like the superstep concept of BSP ([18]).

3.2 Modularity

As with all expressive computational languages there is a question of namespaces and modularity. In fact, as names are channels in the π-calculus, the wanton use of names has security aspects: to have a name is to have a capability to talk to a process, and thus potentially to subvert the FishMarket. In view of this we have been careful to ensure that internal channels to the FishMarket (the solid lines in Figure 1) are private; also buyers and sellers provide their own channels to talk with the admitters and NBIs. To allow global channels would be a recipe for trouble: for reasons of both unintended and intended (but malicious) name capture.

The downside of this is the ungainly way we have to pass many channels as parameters to each process description. Though this is a syntactic difficulty, it would be nice if some more convenient way of restricting the namespace could be used. In consequence, we are currently examining the Ambient calculus [1].

Shared channels overcomes the non-determinism problem, but messages have to be tagged to identify sender. Furthermore, dedicated channels are required for the reply and so the appropriate one must be selected from a set (pre-allocated) which is further complication. A more in-the-spirit solution would have the sender transmit a reply channel as we have done for the buyers arriving at the buyers' manager.

A pattern for modularisation is to define all process behaviours using channels passed as parameters and then composing them all use the parallel construct and passing newly created channels for communications. We can see this in the definition of the market in section 2.2.

Although our chosen scenario is not particulary complicated among electronic trading platforms, and although we have omitted many aspects that should be present in a complete modelling, we have found that one is very easily swamped with detail in using the π-calculus. It is true that the π-calculus is relatively low-level and as a foundational calculi of distributed systems, this is to be expected. Nevertheless, we were not prepared for the wealth of detail it became necessary to manage in the form of the multiplicity of states required for each agent, the number of channels, and beyond that, the even larger number of channel names, all of which made it hard to keep one's attention on the global picture. Clearly, some abstractions are needed to make it easier to focus on the actions of agents.

3.3 Proactive vs. reactive models

In several places in the system, we initially used non-determinism to express the notion that an agent would either follow its agenda (proactive) or deal with communications from another agent. However, we shortly realized this was unsatisfactory, since non-determinism means there is no guarantee that one of the branches will ever be executed, consequently important messages could be ignored for ever—or at least a long time. Crucial examples of this were the BM telling the auctioneer about new buyers—quality of service requires all waiting buyers to be admitted at the beginning of a round—the boss signalling the closing of the market—again quality of service demands immediate response—and the NBI receiving the buyer exit signal—once again quality of service requires this should be acknowledged immediately. Thus we conclude that non-determinism is only applicable in those places where true concurrency exists, for example in the action of the NBIs (see NBI-RelayPrice) and the collection of bids (see AU-CollectBids).

The unfortunate consequence is that we must use explicitly sequenced communication, in effect, polling, in order to ensure that market control communications are processed properly. This confirms us in our view that a more actor-like model offers a more attractive framework for the formalization of the kinds of agents seen in this particular problem.

With this in mind, one can conceive of an abstraction expressed in the π-calculus:

$$agent(\{(m_i, P_i)\}) =$$
$$in(m, s, a_1 \ldots a_n) \cdot \begin{cases} P(in, s, a_1 \ldots a_n) & \text{if } (m, P) \in \{(m_i, P_i)\} \\ \mid agent(\{(m_i, P_i)\}) & \\ agent(\{(m_i, P_i)\}) \text{ otherwise} \end{cases}$$

such that an agent is parameterized by a set of pairs of messages and processes and that it repeatedly reads in a message m from sender s with arguments $a_1 \ldots a_n$ and having found the corresponding process, invokes it with a channel back to itself, the sender and the arguments to run in parallel with itself. For simplicity here, unrecognized messages are ignored.

A lower cost solution—although not so general—is to compose the agent with a buffer process which merges two input streams, but gives priority to one of them. This can be defined briefly as follows:

$$B = a(x) \cdot \bar{c}\langle x \rangle \cdot B + b(y) \cdot B1(y)$$
$$B1(y) = a(x) \cdot \bar{c}\langle x \rangle \cdot B1(y) + \bar{c}\langle y \rangle \cdot B$$

However, this only increases the probability that an a message will be able to overtake a b message: we are still at the mercy of non-determinism in $B1$.

We observe that the development of the individual agents was relatively stratightforward, since each had their own set of tasks to perform. However, as soon as unexpected interactions had to be addressed as well, this wove a significant additional thread of complexity through each agent's processes, leading to a re-think of the specification of the original behaviour and also to significant doubt as to the validity of the result. The problem is that the specification is trying to serve two purposes: describing the normal and the abnormal behaviour of the agent. It becomes like trying to verify a tightly written fragment of assembly code by eye, when one would prefer to keep these aspects separate—in the specification—and then amalgamate them automatically. This appears to have much in common with the "Aspect Oriented Programming" project [9].

4 Related work

Most papers about the π-calculus focus on variants of the language and proofs of their correctness. We have not yet found any papers discussing its use driven by a need to build a model in a multi-agent application domain. On the other hand, there is a detailed modelling of the same FishMarket [13], against which to contrast this model. Noriega and Sierra use Concurrent Descriptive Dyanmic Logic (CDDL) to define a Belief-Desire-Intent (BDI) model of the FishMarket. It is our belief, given our understanding of the CDDL description, and discussions with the authors, that it and the π-calculus approach are complementary. The CDDL model defines aspects of the market at several levels: the agents themselves, the set of illocutions (names plus signatures) and a logical declarative specification of agent behaviour. From our experience so far, we see the π-calculus model as being more operational (although still declarative in the functional programming sense) and focussing on the specification of the behaviour of the agents in terms of sending and receiving messages. Indeed, the whole ethos of π-calculus is process-centred and as we noted above in the section "Lessons", the means to construct abstractions is not particularly straightforward or well-defined. It is also curious, despite the pivotal rôle of communication, how awkward it is to use channels—see our dilemma above regarding single-use channels versus multiple-use with tagged data—to lift them from the level of sockets to that of illocutions. Although this all sounds relatively negative, the process has been rewarding and it also does have its place in multi-agent systems specification: it is precisely because the π-calculus forces details to be spelt out in terms that have an unambiguous implementation, that we arrive at a more rigorous description from an operational perspective. Indeed, in order to carry this experiment to its logical conclusion, we have recently developed another FishMarket simulation working entirely from this specification and using a programmer who had neither worked on the problem before nor seen the π-calculus before. We are pleased to report that only minor bugs (of a syntactic nature) have been found in the description, although it is still intended to put this model through a π-calculus simulator/checker.

The last remark brings us to the other aspect of related work: π-calculus analysis and animation systems. We believe two are of note: the Pict system [16] and Executable Pi Calculus (EPI) [7]. The main drawback of Pict are the restrictions it places on sums, which is a common pattern of behaviour in this specification: see the auctioneer, for example. Nevertheless, we will carry out some experiments with Pict in the near future to determine its limits more precisely. EPI has only recently been made generally available and again we will be experimenting with this shortly.

The message to take away from this experiment is that although the π-calculus does have its drawbacks, further investigation is needed into its use in developing MAS. In particular, we would observe that a model must be careful not to take advantage the synchronous nature of the π-calculus and either to use an asynchronous variant or not use inherently asynchronous protocols within a synchronous framework. Here, we are particularly mindful of the interaction between auctioneer and NBIs, but feel this is an instance of a more general lesson.

5 Links to other papers in this volume

We pointed out in the introduction that the work presented here stems from earlier collaboration with IIIA on the development of the Spanish FishMarket scenario. Consequently, the paper on bidding strategies [5] offers a means to define decision procedures that could communicate with the auction architecture we have specified here via the nomadic buyer interfaces.

The associated workshop on Deception, Fraud and Trust in Agent Societies at Autonomous Agents '98 very clearly established that the single greatest perceived obstacle to electronic commerce is lack of trust. While some seek to provide confidence through the support of well-known institutions (banks etc.), the approach we are exploring here is to create trust by have a verifiable marketplace. That may still need an independent certification authority, but may also offer the opportunity for electronic commerce to develop outside the control of existing trusted parties. Thus, as a first foray in this direction, we have attempted to specify a marketplace using not only a formal system, but also a potentially executable system, which offers the opportunity for proving properties of the virtual institution, such as fairness, correctness of initial conditions, termination of bidding rounds, correctness of bid resolution and information privacy. Of course, such an approach is not limited to Spanish FishMarkets and could — and should — be experimented with in other more complex trading domains, such as that outlined in [6] which handles cross-border documentation issues.

The focus of this paper has been how and when the entities within a virtual institution coordinate but says nothing — apart from the explicit passing of data tuples — about what agents communicate, which is unsatisfactory in the desperately low-level at which this is treated. Again, this is a topic where material from other workers in the field can be plugged in, such as the simple contract language presented in [3] or more generally using KQML [10] or FIPA ACL [14].

Such communication languages are necessary for the building of realistic trading systems, but would over-complicate a description such as that given here. On the other hand, a formalization of their interpretation to the marketplace would be necessary in a fully specified system, if the goal of trader trust is to be achieved.

The specification mechanism outlined here is very low level, because the π-calculus is itself low level. Programming systems like Pict [16] and EPI [7] aim to build on the π-calculus in the way that functional programming has built on the foundation of λ-calculus, making many useful, but inessential in terms of theory, extensions to the model to enable higher level descriptions. The ZEUS system [2] works at a higher level still in that it provides a graphical user interface for constructing agent systems, generating code to combine components from pre-existing libraries. Given the complexities of building such distributed systems and the tediousness of work with a purely text-based representation, plus a very distinct need for a component-oriented, constructive approach in order to control those complexities, as well as making automatic verification tractable, such agent system generators seem to offer a very positive way forward.

6 Acknowledgements

Thanks are due to Gabriele Dionisi (Università degli Studi Milano) for developing a FishMarket model from this specification and the European Commission for funding his stay in Bath through the VIM project in the framework of the HCM programme. Andreas Kind developed and maintained the supporting (Eu)Lisp development environment. We also acknowledge the ever-constructive discussions of the Denton project teams at Bath and Southampton and observations from the Declarative Systems Seminar, also at the University of Southampton.

References

1. Luca Cardelli and Andrew Gordon. Mobile ambients.
   http://www.cl.cam.ac.uk/users/adg/Research/Ambit/index.html.
2. Jaron C. Collis and Lyndon C. Lee. Building electronic marketplaces with the zeus agent toolkit. In Carles Sierra and Pablo Noriega, editors, *Agent Mediated Electronic Trading*, volume 1571 of *LNAI*. Springer Verlag, 1999.
3. Joakim Eriksson, Niclas Finne, and Sverker Janson. Sics marketspace — an agent-based market infrastructure. In Carles Sierra and Pablo Noriega, editors, *Agent Mediated Electronic Trading*, volume 1571 of *LNAI*. Springer Verlag, 1999.
4. Cédric Fournet, Georges Gonthier, Jean-Jacques Lévy, Luc Maranget, and Didier Rémy. A calculus of mobile agents. In *7th International Conference on Concurrency Theory (CONCUR'96)*, pages 406–421, Pisa, Italy, August 26-29 1996. Springer-Verlag. LNCS 1119.
5. Pere Garcia, Eduard Gimenez, Lluis Godo, and Juan A. Rodriguez-Aguilar. Possibilistic-based design of bidding strategies in electronic auctions. In Carles Sierra and Pablo Noriega, editors, *Agent Mediated Electronic Trading*, volume 1571 of *LNAI*. Springer Verlag, 1999.

6. Steven Y. Goldsmith, Laurence R. Phillips, and Shannon V. Spires. A multi-agent system for coordinating international shipping. In Carles Sierra and Pablo Noriega, editors, *Agent Mediated Electronic Trading*, volume 1571 of *LNAI*. Springer Verlag, 1999.

7. Peter Henderson. Executable pi calculus (epi). http://diana.ecs.soton.ac.uk/ ph/e-pi.htm.

8. C. A. R. Hoare. *Communcating Sequential Processes*. Prentice Hall, 1985.

9. G. Kiczales, J. Lamping, A Mendhekar, C. Maeda, C Lopes, J-M. Longtier, and J. Irwin. Aspect-oriented programming. available via http://www.parc.xerox.com/spl/projects/aop/.

10. Yannis Labrou and Tim Finin. A proposal for a new kqml specification. http://www.csee.umbc.edu/~jklabrou/publications/tr9703.ps, 1997. Also available as a UMBC technical report.

11. Robin Milner. The Polyadic π-Calculus: a Tutorial. Preprint of Proceedings International Summer School on Logic and Algebra of Specification, 1991.

12. Uwe Nestmann. Calculi for mobile processes. available through http://www.cs.auc.dk/mobility/.

13. P. Noriega and C. Sierra. Towards Layered Dialogical Agents. In *Third International Workshop on Agent Theories, Architectures, and Languages, ATAL-96*, 1996.

14. FIPA ACL. Foundation of Intelligent Physical Agents. Agent communication language. http://drogo.cselt.stet.it/fipa/spec/fipa97.htm, 1997.

15. Benjamin C. Pierce. Foundational calculi for programming languages. In Allen B. Tucker, editor, *Handbook of Computer Science and Engineering*, chapter 139. CRC Press, 1996.

16. Benjamin C Pierce and David N Turner. Pict: A Programming Language Based on the Pi-Calculus. Technical Report 476, Indiana University, March 1997.

17. J.A. Rodríguez, P. Noriega, C. Sierra, and J.A. Padget. FM96.5 A Java-based Electronic Auction House. In *Second International Conference on The Practical Application of Intelligent Agents and Multi-Agent Technology: PAAM'97*, 1997.

18. L G Valiant. A Bridging Model for Parallel Computation. *Communications of the ACM*, 33(8):103–111, August 1990.

Information Integration
for Electronic Commerce*

Chiara Ghidini[1] and Luciano Serafini[2]

[1] DISA – University of Trento, Via Inama 5, 38100 Trento, Italy
ghidini@cs.unitn.it
[2] ITC–IRST, 38050 Povo, Trento, Italy
serafini@itc.it

Abstract. In agent-mediated electronic commerce, agents need to exchange information with other agents and to integrate the information obtained from other agents in their own information. Integration is a very complex task as: information is *distributed* among different agents; each agent *autonomously* represents and manages a piece of information; information might be *partial*, as agent cannot wait to have complete information before acting; finally information is *redundant*, as the same information might be represented by two different agents. The goal of this paper is to provide a formal semantics for information integration able to cope with distributed, autonomous, partial, and redundant information. In the paper we introduce two examples from an electronic commerce scenario which emphasize critical problems in the integration of information, we define a semantics for information integration, and we test its adequacy by formalizing the examples.

1 Introduction

In agent-mediated electronic trading each agent is associated with a system for the management of the information. This information constitutes agents *goals*, *plans*, and *beliefs* about the state of the market. An agent plans and performs actions, such as negotiation, evaluation of different offers, contract stipulation, etc., on the basis of the information available in its system. In many cases however, an agent doesn't have enough information for pursuing its goals and, in order to properly plan its actions, it needs to collect suitable extra information from other agents. In defining a system for the management of the agent's information, we have therefore to consider at least two aspects. The first concerns the internal structure of such a system. This includes how beliefs, goals, plans, etc., are represented and how to reason about them. The second aspect concerns how

* The work with Fausto Giunchiglia about contexts has provided many of the intuitions and motivations underlying the work described in this paper. We thank the Mechanized Reasoning Group at DISA (University of Trento), ITC–IRST (Trento) This work is part of the MRG project *Distributed Representations and Systems* (http://www.cs.unitn.it/~mrg/distributed-intelligence/).

the information, obtained by communicating with the other agents, is integrated in the agent's information.

In this paper we address the problem of the integration of information that different agents have. We don't consider the representational aspects of belief, goals, etc[1]. For this reason we introduce a simplifying hypothesis on the structure of the information system of each agent: we suppose that agents represent information by a relational database.

Focusing on the problem of exchanging and integrating information, a set of agents can be abstracted to a set of databases able to communicate via some agent communication mechanism. These databases are *distributed, partial, autonomous,* and *redundant*. Distribution means that databases of different agents are different systems, each of them containing a specific piece of information. Autonomy means that the database of each agent is autonomous regarding the design, the execution, and the communication with the other agents. Therefore different databases may adopt different conceptual schemata (including domain, relations, naming conventions, . . .), and certain operations are performed locally, without interactions with the other agents. Redundancy means that the same piece of information may be represented, possibly from different perspectives, in the databases of different agents. Redundancy not only means that information is duplicated, but also that the information of two databases might be related. Redundancy is what makes communication possible. Indeed communication (as intended in this paper) allows information to be duplicated from an agent to another. This is possible only if this information is representable in the database of both agents, and therefore only if the databases of the agents are redundant.

Distribution, partiality, autonomy, and redundancy generate many problems in integrating the information contained in different databases. Several approaches have been proposed in the past. An incomplete list is [4, 13, 14, 11]. However they all fail to represent all these issues in a uniform way. The goal of this paper is to provide a formal semantics for information integration able to cope with these problems. This is a key point to understand, specify, and verify the behavior of a multi-agent system for electronic commerce.

The semantics for information integration proposed in this paper, called *Local Model Semantics* (LMS hereafter), is an extension to first order languages of the semantics of contexts proposed in [9]. It is based on the intuition that the database of an agent can be though as a partial view (thought as a context) on a common world.

The paper is structured as follows. In Section 2 we introduce motivating examples. In Section 3 we review the basic concepts of semantics of databases. In Section 4 we introduce the concept of integration information schema and in Section 5 we define LMS for information integration. Section 6 defines logical consequence for information integration. In Section 7 we formalize the examples

---

[1] We have addressed representational issues, such as multi agent beliefs, in some previous paper (see for instance [10, 8, 5]). These approaches are homogeneous with the formalism presented in this paper and can be easily integrated in it.

via LMS. Then we compare LMS with the most relevant formalisms for information integration (Section 8) and we make some concluding remarks (Section 9).

2 Motivating Examples

Two common examples of information integration occurring in electronic commerce are constituted by information exchange and information gathering. Information exchange between two agents is the basis for electronic commerce interaction protocols, such as *contract-net*. In information gathering, so called mediator agents or broker agents [17, 12, 15] collect information from a number of information providers and integrate it in a unique database.

Example 1 (Cooperation via information exchange). Let I be a company which produces and sells assessments for Italian cars, and E be a company which does the same for European sport cars. The assessment process is the same for both companies and consists of 10 tests (e.g. for comfort, brakes, consume, ...). For each test a car is assigned a rating from 1 to 10. I assigns a final score from A to F computed as follows: a car is assigned an A if its total evaluation after the 10 tests is less than $\frac{100}{6}$, a B if it is between $\frac{100}{6}$ and $2 * \frac{100}{6}$, and so on. E instead assigns a final score from 0 to 10 obtained by dividing the total valuation by 10 and rounding to the nearest half point. Figure 1 compares the two scales. Suppose that, in assessing to *car1*, I assigns *car1* a total evaluation of 80 after the

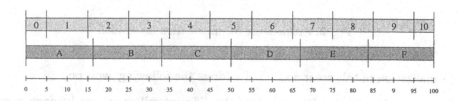

Fig. 1. Comparison of the different scales

first 9 tests, but for some reason the tenth test cannot be done. Since I doesn't want to loose the data of the previous 9 tests, a partial information is included in the assessment database of I and *car1* will be assigned a partial evaluation which is either E or F. I and E decide to collaborate by exchanging the data about common products (i.e. Italian sports cars). However they are not completely cooperative. Indeed I decides to communicate only complete information (i.e. no information about partial tests are communicated) and E decides not to communicate the assessments of a specific sport car, say *Ferrari F40*, because it is to critical. A formal model of this example must address the following aspects:

Semantic heterogeneity: The two scales 0–10 and A–F constitute an heterogeneous measure of the same aspects;

Different domains: The domain of European sport cars is different from that of Italian cars;

Domain overlapping: European sport cars and Italian cars overlap on Italian sport cars;

Partiality: The incomplete assessment of *car1* generates partial information;

Autonomy of communication: Each company decides to communicate only a specific subset of the data.

Example 2 (Information gathering). Let m be a mediator of an electronic market place for fruits composed of three fruits sellers: 1, 2, and 3. m collects information about fruit prices from 1, 2, and 3 and integrates it in a unique homogeneous database. Customers that need information about fruit prices, instead of connecting each seller, can submit a single query to the mediator. Figure 2 gives a graphical representation of the structure of this example. Circles represent databases and arrows represent information flow between databases. A

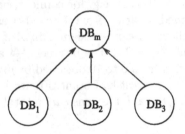

Fig. 2. Architecture for information integration

formalization of this scenario should address the following aspects:

Semantic heterogeneity: Prices of the different sellers are not homogeneous. Suppose for instance that prices of database 1 don't include taxes, while prices of database 2 and 3 do.

Different domains: The sellers provide different subsets of fruits and therefore the domains of their databases are different.

Heterogeneity on common domains: The domain of fruits can be represented at different level of details by different sellers. We suppose, for instance, that the database 1 contains prices for red apples and yellow apples, while database 2 and 3 don't make this distinction and provide a single price just for apples.

Directionality of the communication: The information about prices goes from the sellers' databases to the mediator, but no information runs in the opposite direction.

Modularity: A new fruit seller might join the market place. This happens in a transparent way w.r.t the database of the old sellers; i.e. the databases of the old sellers are not affected by this change.

3 Technical Preliminaries

The basic building blocks for the formalization of information integration are the models of the information of each single agent. Since agents represent information via a relational database, a formal model of information integration is build on top of the formal models of the relational databases of the agents.

To this purpose we exploit well established results in this field. We follow [1] in the notation and terminology. We assume that a countably infinite set **att** of *attributes* is fixed. Let **dom** be a countable set of individual symbols, called *domain*. For any $A \in$ **att** the *domain of* A is a non empty subset $dom(A)$ of **dom**. Domains of attributes are mutually disjoint. The set of *relational symbols* is a countable set **R** of symbols disjoint from **att** and **dom**, such that for any $R \in$ **R**, the *sort of* R is a finite sequence of elements of **att**.

Given **att**, **dom**, and **R**, L denotes the *relational language* over **att**, **dom**, and **R**, i.e. the sorted first order language with sort **att**, constant symbols **dom**, relational symbols **R**, and no function symbols. A *database schema* is a pair $S = \langle \mathbf{R}, \Sigma \rangle$, where Σ is a set of closed formulae of L, called *integrity constraints*.

A database schema S is essentially a theory in the language L. A database on the schema S is formalized as an interpretation of L satisfying S. A *complete database* db on a schema S is a first order interpretation of L in the domain **dom**, which maps each $R \in$ **R** of sort $\langle A_1, \ldots, A_n \rangle$, into a finite subset of $dom(A_1) \times, \ldots, \times dom(A_n)$, each $d \in$ **dom** in itself, and such that db classically satisfies Σ (in symbols db $\models \Sigma$). A complete database contains complete information about the elements of the domain, namely for each tuple of elements of the domain and each relation, either such a tuple belongs to the relation or not. In many applications, however, it is important to consider databases with partial information, namely databases in which it is possible to specify disjunctive facts or existential facts. A *partial database* DB on a schema S is a set of complete databases on the schema S. Intuitively a partial (incomplete) database is represented extensionally as the set of all its possible completions. For instance, the partial database in which "John has a car" is the set of interpretations which state that John has a specific car, for any car in the domain of the database. In the following we let the specification "partial" implicit.

An important feature of a database is its query language as we suppose that each database communicates with the others via query answering. For the purpose of this paper we consider *first order queries* (see [1], chapter 5), i.e., queries defined by first order open formulae. A formula ϕ with free variables in $\{x_1, \ldots, x_n\}$ is denoted by $\phi(x_1, \ldots, x_n)$. For each tuple $d_1, \ldots, d_n$ of elements of **dom**, if the expression obtained by replacing each x_i with d_i in ϕ is a formula of L, then it is denoted by $\phi(d_1, \ldots, d_n)$. In the other case $\phi(d_1, \ldots, d_n)$ is undefined.

4 Information Integration Schema

The formalization of information integration is done in two steps. In the first step (described in this section) we define an *information integration schema* which describes the structure of the database of each single agent and how the information of different agents is integrated. in the second step (described in next section) we define an *information integration state* as a formal model of an information integration schema.

Let I be a (at most) countable set of indexes, each of which denotes an agent (or equivalently its database). The first component of an information integration schema is a family $\{S_i\}_{i \in I}$ (hereafter $\{S_i\}$) of database schemata. S_i represents the schema of the database of agent i.

The second component of an information integration schema represents how the databases of the different agents are integrated. Due to the fact that information is distributed, we cannot assume that a common data structure shared by two agents exists. Therefore two agents can communicate only via query answering. Heterogeneity implies that, if an agent j wants to get the information in i-th database about the set of individuals which satisfy the property ψ, it j must perform the following operations: (1) rewriting the query ψ in the language of i (e.g. ϕ), (2) map back the answer of i (which is a set of objects in the domain of i) into a set of objects in its own domain. Figure 3 gives a graphical example of the query-answering between two heterogeneous databases where the properties ψ and ϕ are instantiated in $circle(x)$ and $square(x)$, respectively. The

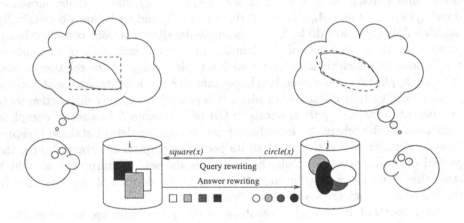

Fig. 3. Example of query and result rewriting

specification of query rewriting schemata is obtained introducing the definition of *view constraints*; the specification of result rewriting schemata is obtained introducing the definition of *domain constraints*.

Definition 1 (View Constraint). *Let S_i and S_j be two database schemata. A view constraint from S_i to S_j is an expression* $i : \phi(x_1, \ldots, x_n) \rightarrow j : \psi(x_1, \ldots, x_n)$, where $\phi(x_1, \ldots, x_n)$ and $\psi(x_1, \ldots, x_n)$ are formulae (or equivalently queries) of the language of S_i and S_j, respectively[2].

Intuitively the view constraint $i : \phi(x_1, \ldots, x_n) \to j : \psi(x_1, \ldots, x_n)$ means that the agent j can ask the agent i the sub-query $\phi(x_1, \ldots, x_n)$ in order to answer the query $\psi(x_1, \ldots, x_n)$. Sets of view constraints from S_i to S_j are denoted by VC_{ij}.

Definition 2 (Domain Constraint). Let S_i and S_j be two database schemata. A domain constraint from S_i to S_j is an expression of the form $\mathsf{T}_{j:B}^{i:A}$ or $\mathsf{S}_{j:B}^{i:A}$ where A and B are formulae with one free variable of S_i and S_j respectively.

Intuitively $\mathsf{T}_{j:B}^{i:A}$ captures the fact that from the point of view of j, for any object of $\mathbf{dom}_i$ which is in the answer set of the query A there is a corresponding object in $\mathbf{dom}_j$ which is in the answer set of the query B. Conversely $\mathsf{S}_{j:B}^{i:A}$ captures the fact that from the point of view of j, for any object d of $\mathbf{dom}_j$ which is in the answer set of B in S_j, there is an object in $\mathbf{dom}_i$ which corresponds to d and which is in the answer set of A. Sets of domain constraints from S_i to S_j are denoted by DC_{ij}.

An interschema constraint IC_{ij} from S_i to S_j is a pair $IC_{ij} = \langle DC_{ij}, VC_{ij} \rangle$.

Definition 3 (Information Integration Schema). An Information Integration Schema on I is a pair $IIS = \langle \{S_i\}, \{IC_{ij}\} \rangle$ where, for each $i, j \in I$ with $i \neq j$, S_i is a database schema and IC_{ij} is an interschema constraint from S_i to S_j.

5 Semantics for Information Integration

The collection of the states of the agents' databases at a given instant point is called information integration state. An information integration schema describes a class information integration states, i.e. those which satisfy the interschema constraints. In this section we provide the formal notion of information integration state, and we define when an information integration state satisfies the constraints of an information integration schema. An *information integration state* is defined by formalizing the database of each agent as a context and by taking the perspective described in [9] for the semantics of contexts and of contextual reasoning. The formal semantics associated to each database i represents the description of the current state of the real world from i-th partial point of view. Therefore the formal semantics of the information integration schema $\langle \{S_i\}, \{IC_{ij}\} \rangle$ contains a set $\{DB_i\}$ of databases, each DB_i being a partial database on the schema S_i.

According to this perspective, databases may have distinct domains. Namely there is no global domain there is rather a set of domains, each associated to an agent (database). In order to propagate information about related objects

---

[2] We define view constraints as pairs of formulae with the same set of free variables for the sake of simplicity. View constraints can be easily generalized by dropping this requirement.

we introduce a family of relations between objects of the different databases' domains. This relation is called *domain relation*. A domain relation from $\mathbf{dom}_i$ to $\mathbf{dom}_j$ represents the capability of agent j to map the objects of $\mathbf{dom}_i$ in its domain (i.e. $\mathbf{dom}_j$). Formally, let $\mathbf{dom}_i$ be the domain of DB_i. A domain relation r_{ij} from $\mathbf{dom}_i$ to $\mathbf{dom}_j$ is a subset of $\mathbf{dom}_i \times \mathbf{dom}_j$. A pair $\langle d, d' \rangle$ being in r_{ij} means that, from the point of view of j, d in $\mathbf{dom}_i$ is the representation of d' in $\mathbf{dom}_j$. A domain relation for Example 1, restricted to the domains of rating values, is

$$r_{\mathrm{EI}} = \left\{ \begin{array}{l} \langle 0, A \rangle, \ \langle 1, A \rangle, \ \langle 2, B \rangle, \ \langle 3, B \rangle, \ \langle 3, C \rangle, \ \langle 4, C \rangle, \\ \langle 5, D \rangle, \ \langle 6, D \rangle, \ \langle 7, E \rangle, \ \langle 8, F \rangle, \ \langle 9, F \rangle, \ \langle 10, F \rangle \end{array} \right\}$$

A formal semantics for information integration is composed of a set of databases (as defined in Section 3) and set of domain relations from the schema of a component to that of the others. Domain constraints imply that only certain domain relations are accepted. Analogously view constraints imply that only certain combinations of databases are admitted.

Definition 4 (Satisfiability of Domain Constraint). *Let S_i and S_j be two database schemata. The domain relation r_{ij} satisfies the domain constraint $T_{j:B}^{i:A}$ if for any $d \in \mathbf{dom}_i$ such that $\mathrm{DB}_i \models A(d)$ there is a d' such that $\langle d, d' \rangle \in r_{ij}$ and $\mathrm{DB}_j \models B(d')$. Analogously r_{ij} satisfies the domain constraint $S_{j:B}^{i:A}$ iff for any $d \in \mathbf{dom}_j$ such that $\mathrm{DB}_j \models B(d)$, there is a d' such that $\langle d', d \rangle \in r_{ij}$ and $\mathrm{DB}_i \models A(d)$*

Definition 5 (Satisfiability of View Constraint). *Let DB_i and DB_j be two databases on S_i and S_j, and r_{ij} be a domain relation. The tuple $\langle \mathrm{DB}_i, \mathrm{DB}_j, r_{ij} \rangle$ satisfies the view constraint $i : \phi(x_1, \ldots, x_n) \to j : \psi(x_1, \ldots, x_n)$ if for any $\langle d_k, d'_k \rangle \in r_{ij}$ $(1 \leq k \leq n)$, $\mathrm{DB}_i \models \phi(d_1, \ldots, d_n)$ implies that $\mathrm{DB}_j \models \psi(d'_1, \ldots, d'_n)$.*

An intuitive interpretation of satisfiability of a view constraint can be given in terms of relations between the results of queries to the databases. A domain relation r_{ij} can be interpreted as a mapping from relations in i into relations in j. Formally if $X \subseteq \mathbf{dom}_i^n$ is a relation in DB_i then $r_{ij}(X)$ is defined as

$$\{\langle d'_1, \ldots, d'_n \rangle \in \mathbf{dom}_j^n \mid \langle d_1, \ldots, d_n \rangle \in X \text{ and for all } 1 \leq k \leq n \ \langle d, d'_k \rangle \in r_{ij}\}$$

According to this fact, $\langle \mathrm{DB}_i, \mathrm{DB}_j, r_{ij} \rangle$ satisfies $i : \phi(x_1, \ldots, x_n) \to j : \psi(x_1, \ldots, x_n)$ if and only if $r_{ij}(X) \subseteq Y$, being X and Y the result of the query $\phi(x_1, \ldots, x_n)$ to DB_i, and the result of query $\psi(x_1, \ldots, x_n)$ to DB_j respectively.

Definition 6 (Information Integration State). *Let $\{S_i\}$ be a set of database schemata. Let $\{\mathrm{DB}_i\}$ be a set of databases, each DB_i being a database on S_i, and $\{r_{ij}\}$ be a family of domain relations. An information integration state on the information integration schema $\langle \{S_i\}, \{IC_{ij}\} \rangle$ is a pair $iis = \langle \{\mathrm{DB}_i\}, \{r_{ij}\} \rangle$ such that for all $i, j \in I$, $i \neq j$, $\langle \mathrm{DB}_i, \mathrm{DB}_j, r_{ij} \rangle$ satisfies IC_{ij}.*

6 Logical Consequence

Interschema constraints, like integrity constraints in single databases (see [1], Chapter 8), imply that certain facts in a database are consequences of other facts in, possibly distinct, databases. The formal characterization of such a relation is crucial as it allows to formally check inconsistencies in the databases and to understand how information propagates through databases independently from the specific information state. In this section we formalize this relation by the notion of *logical consequence*. Logical consequence is a relation between formulae of the relational languages of the databases. To define logical consequence we introduce some extra notation. A *labeled formula* is a pair $i : \phi$. It denotes the formula ϕ and the fact that ϕ is a formula of the database schema S_i. If no ambiguity arises, labeled formulae are called formulae. Given a set of labeled formulae Γ, Γ_j denotes the set of formulae $\{\gamma \mid j : \gamma \in \Gamma\}$. From now on we say that ϕ is a *i-formula* to specify that ϕ is a formula of the schema S_i.

We extend the set of variables of each S_i to a set of *extended variables*. For each $j \in I$, each variable x of sort A in S_i, and each attribute B in S_j, $x^{j:B\rightarrow}$ and $x^{\rightarrow j:B}$ are variables of sort A. Notationally we write e to mean an extended variable. Intuitively a variable x of sort A (without indexes) occurring in $i : \phi$ is a placeholder for a generic element of $dom_i(A)$; the extended variable $x^{j:B\rightarrow}$ of sort A occurring in $i : \phi$ is a placeholder for an element of $dom_i(A)$ which is an image, via r_{ji}, of the element of $dom_j(B)$ denoted by x; analogously $x^{\rightarrow j:B}$ occurring in $i : \phi$ is a placeholder for an element of $dom_i(A)$ which is a pre-image, via r_{ij}, of the element of $dom_j(B)$ denoted by x.

Given an information integration state *iis* on an information integration schema IIS, an *assignment* is a total function a which maps a pair $\langle e, i \rangle$ into an element of $dom_i(A)$. a is an *admissible assignment* if for any variable x of sort A and any variable $x^{i:A\rightarrow}$ and $x^{\rightarrow i:A}$ of sort B

1. if $T_{j:B}^{i:A} \in DC_{ij}$, then $\langle a(x, i), a(x^{i:A\rightarrow}, j) \rangle \in r_{ij}$
2. if $S_{j:A}^{i:B} \in DC_{ji}$, then $\langle a(x^{\rightarrow i:A}, j), a(x, i) \rangle \in r_{ji}$.

Definition 7 (Satisfiability). *Let iis* $= \langle \{DB_i\}, \{r_{ij}\} \rangle$ *be an information integration state. A i-formula* ϕ *is satisfied in* $db \in DB_i$ *by an assignment* a, *in symbols* $db \models \phi[a]$, *according to the definition of satisfiability in first order logic. A i-formula* ϕ *is satisfied in* DB_i *by an assignment* a, *in symbols* $DB_i \models \phi[a]$, *if for any* $db \in DB_i$, $db \models \phi[a]$. $i : \phi$ *is satisfied in iis by an assignment* a, *in symbols iis* $\models i : \phi[a]$, *if* $DB_i \models \phi[a]$.

Notationally, for any set of i-formulae Γ, $DB_i \models \Gamma[a]$ means that $DB_i \models \gamma[a]$ for any $\gamma \in \Gamma$. Let DB_i be a database on S_i and a an assignment for any set of i-formulae Γ, ϕ. $\Gamma[a] \models_{DB_i} \phi[a]$ if and only if for all $db_i \in DB_i$, $db_i \models \Gamma[a]$ implies that $db_i \models \phi[a]$.

Definition 8 (Logical Consequence). *Let IIS be an information integration schema and* Γ *be a set of formulae. A formula* $i : \phi$ *is a logical consequence of* Γ, *in symbols* $\Gamma \models_{IIS} i : \phi$, *if for any information integration state* $\langle \{DB_i\}, \{r_{ij}\} \rangle$

on IIS and for any admissible assignment a, if for all $j \neq i$, $DB_j \models \Gamma_j[a]$, then $\Gamma_i[a] \models_{DB_i} \phi[a]$.

7 Modeling the Examples

Example 3 (Formalization of example 1). In the scenario of example 1 there are two agents I and E containing two databases with local schemata S_I and S_E respectively.

Local Schemata S_I and S_E contain two attributes *value* (for evaluation values) and *car* (for cars). $dom_I(value) = \{A, \ldots, F\}$ and $dom_E(value) = \{1, \ldots, 10\}$. $dom_I(car)$ is the set of Italian cars, and $dom_E(car)$ is the set of European sport cars.

S_I and S_E contain a binary predicate $eval(x, y)$ of sort $\langle car, value \rangle$ meaning that the result of the assessment of car x is y. S_I contains a unary predicate *sport-car(x)* of sort *car.* meaning that x is a sport car; S_E contains a unary predicate *it-car(x)* of sort *car*, meaning that x is an Italian car.

Interschema Constraints We remind that domain constraints from i to j represent the capability of j to map in its domain the answers of queries submitted to i. In our example, the complete cooperation of I in answering the queries submitted by E, corresponds to the fact that any sport car in $\mathbf{dom_I}$ is translated in an Italian car in $\mathbf{dom_E}$ and, vice versa, for any Italian car c in $\mathbf{dom_E}$ there is a sport car in $\mathbf{dom_I}$ which is mapped into c. This is represented by the domain constraints:

$$T^{I:sport-car(x)}_{E:it-car(x)} \qquad S^{I:sport-car(x)}_{E:it-car(x)} \tag{1}$$

The domain constraint from E to I must take into account that E is not completely cooperative as it refuses to give information about the car Ferrari *F40*. This means that, when E answers to a query submitted by I any Italian car in $\mathbf{dom_E}$ with the exception of *F40*, can be translated into a sport car in $\mathbf{dom_I}$ and vice versa. This is represented by the domain constraints:

$$T^{E:it-car(x)\wedge x\neq F40}_{I:sport-car(x)} \qquad S^{E:it-car(x)\wedge x\neq F40}_{I:sport-car(x)} \tag{2}$$

Both companies are completely cooperative w.r.t the domains of the attribute *value*. I.e. I is able to translate any evaluation A–F of the domain of E in 1–10, and vice versa. This is represented by the following domain constraints:

$$T^{I:value}_{E:value} \qquad S^{I:value}_{E:value} \qquad T^{E:value}_{I:value} \qquad S^{E:value}_{I:value} \tag{3}$$

Let's consider view constraints. Both companies agree on cars names. E.g., the intended meaning of "car2" in the database of both companies is a unique car whose name is car2. This is represented by the view constraints:

$$I : x = c \rightarrow E : x = c \qquad E : x = c \rightarrow I : x = c \tag{4}$$

for any car name c which is in the language of I and E. Evaluation transformation is formalized by two sets of view constraints that reflect the comparison between the two different scales in Figure 1:

$$
\begin{array}{ll}
\mathsf{I}:x=A \to \mathsf{E}:x=0 \vee x=1 \vee x=2 & \mathsf{E}:x=0 \to \mathsf{I}:x=A \\
\mathsf{I}:x=B \to \mathsf{E}:x=2 \vee x=3 & \mathsf{E}:x=1 \to \mathsf{I}:x=A \\
\quad\vdots & \quad\vdots \\
\mathsf{I}:x=F \to \mathsf{E}:x=8 \vee x=9 \vee x=10 & \mathsf{E}:x=10 \to \mathsf{I}:x=F
\end{array}
\tag{5}
$$

Finally, the intended meaning of the predicate $eval(x,y)$ in both databases coincides. This is formalized by the view constraints:

$$
\mathsf{I}:eval(x,y) \to \mathsf{E}:eval(x,y) \qquad \mathsf{E}:eval(x,y) \to \mathsf{I}:eval(x,y) \tag{6}
$$

The information integration schema IIS_v for this example is composed by S_I, S_E, and the domain constraints and view constraints defined above. An example of information integration state iis on the schema IIS_v is:

DB$_\mathsf{I}$	DB$_\mathsf{E}$	r_IE	r_EI

DB$_\mathsf{I}$ — db$_1$

eval	
car	value
car1	E
car2	F
car3	C

db$_2$

eval	
car	value
car1	F
car2	F
car3	C

DB$_\mathsf{E}$ — db$_3$

eval	
car	value
car2	4
car3	5
Porche 960	7
F40	10

r_IE:
$\langle A,0 \rangle$
$\langle A,1 \rangle$
$\langle C,5 \rangle$
$\langle E,8 \rangle$
$\vdots$
$\langle car1,car1 \rangle$
$\langle car2,car2 \rangle$
$\vdots$
$\langle F40,F40 \rangle$

r_EI:
$\langle 0,A \rangle$
$\langle 1,A \rangle$
$\langle 5,C \rangle$
$\langle 7,E \rangle$
$\vdots$
$\langle car1,car1 \rangle$
$\langle car2,car2 \rangle$
$\vdots$

Let us now address the aspects pointed out in Example 1.

Semantic heterogeneity: View constraints (5) allow to relate the (heterogeneous) values 0–10 and A–F. From the definition of satisfiability of a view constraint, (5) influence the definition of the domain relations r_IE and r_EI. Let us analyze by mean of an example how the two databases exchange data about cars. In the information integration state iis depicted above $DB_\mathsf{E} \models eval(car3,5)$. By view constraint (6), and by $\langle 5,C \rangle \in r_\mathsf{EI}$ it follows that $DB_\mathsf{I} \models eval(car3,C)$. Another information integration state on the same schema is obtainable from iis by replacing $\langle 5,C \rangle$ with $\langle 5,D \rangle$ in r_EI (this is still a domain relation which satisfies view constraints (5)). Again view constraint (6) forces $DB_\mathsf{I} \models eval(car3,D)$. However in order to satisfy view constraint (5) and domain constraint $T^{E:value}_{I:value}$ either $\langle 5,C \rangle \in r_\mathsf{EI}$ or $\langle 5,D \rangle \in r_\mathsf{EI}$. This implies that, for any information integration state on the schema IIS_v, $DB_\mathsf{E} \models eval(car3,5)$ implies $DB_\mathsf{I} \models eval(car3,C) \vee eval(car3,D)$. The above observations are summarized by the following properties of the logical consequence of IIS_v.

$$
\mathsf{E}:eval(car3,5) \not\models_{IIS_v} \mathsf{I}:eval(car3,C) \tag{7}
$$

$$\mathsf{E}: eval(car3,5) \not\models_{IIS_v} \mathsf{I}: eval(car3,D) \qquad (8)$$

$$\mathsf{E}: eval(car3,5) \models_{IIS_v} \mathsf{I}: eval(car3,C) \vee eval(car3,D) \qquad (9)$$

Notice that the properties of $\models_{IIS_v}$ shown above formalize that semantic heterogeneity between the two scales prevents to find a one to one translation between rates. In particular the fact that neither $\mathsf{I}: eval(car3,C)$ nor $\mathsf{I}: eval(car3,D)$ are logical consequences of $\mathsf{E}: eval(car3,5)$ (equations (7) and (8)) formalizes that we cannot translate the rate 5 to a unique value (C or D) because of the fact that 5 might be obtained rounding off a valuation between 4.5 and 5, or by rounding off a valuation between 5 and 5.5. However equation (9) enable us to infer the partial information that car3's final score in the second scale is either C or D from the fact that car3's final score in the first scale is 5.

Different domains: The domains of I and E contain different objects. For instance the domain of E contains the car *Porche 960* which is not an Italian car and it is not contained in the domain of I.

Domain overlapping: The overlapping on Italian sport cars is formalized by domain constraints (1) and (2)

Partiality: The incomplete assessment of *car1* is represented in *iis* by the fact that $DB_I \models eval(car1,E) \vee eval(car1,F)$ but neither $DB_I \models eval(car1,E)$ nor $DB_I \models eval(car1,F)$.

Autonomy of communication: I doesn't communicate to E partial information about evaluation. For instance, the partial evaluation on *car1* in I does not entail any evaluation (even partial) in E;

$$\mathsf{I}: eval(car1,E) \vee eval(car1,F) \not\models_{IIS_v} \mathsf{E}: \exists x.eval(car1,x)$$

despite the fact that each of the disjuncts in I entails an eval statement in E.

$$\mathsf{I}: eval(car1,E) \models_{IIS_v} \mathsf{E}: eval(car1,7) \vee eval(car1,8) \qquad (10)$$

$$\mathsf{I}: eval(car1,F) \models_{IIS_v} \mathsf{E}: eval(car1,9) \vee eval(car1,10) \qquad (11)$$

The fact that E doesn't communicate to I any data about $F40$, corresponds to the property that for any evaluation X in 1–10.

$$\mathsf{E}: eval(F40,X) \not\models_{IIS_v} \mathsf{I}: \exists x.eval(F40,x) \qquad (12)$$

The above property is the consequence of the fact that the domain relation r_{EI} might not associate any element to $F40$ (see domain constraint (2)). Non cooperativeness of E does not prevent I to be cooperative. Indeed I communicates information about $F40$ to E and the following property holds for any evaluation X in A–F.

$$\mathsf{I}: eval(F40,X) \models_{IIS_v} \mathsf{E}: \exists x.eval(F40,x) \qquad (13)$$

The proof is similar to that of equation (9) and is obtained from the fact that domain constraint 1) forces the pair $\langle F40, F40 \rangle$ to be in r_{IE}.

Example 4 (Formalization of example 2).   The information integration schema for this example is composed of four databases, one for each fruit seller, and a one for the mediator agent. Let S_i ($i = 1, 2, 3$) be the local schema of the sellers and S_m be the local schema for the mediator.

Local Schemata Each S_i ($i = 1, 2, 3$) and S_m contain the attribute *fruit-name*, with domain a set of names (of fruits), and the attribute *price*, with domain the set of money amounts expressed in dollars. S_i ($i \in I$) and S_m contain a predicate *has-price*(x, y) of sort $\langle fruit\text{-}name, price \rangle$ meaning that x costs y.

Interschema Constraints Let us consider domain constraints. Since the mediator retrieves information concerning the prices of *all* the available fruits, for any object in a domain of a seller, there exists a corresponding object in the domain of the mediator. This is formalized by the following domain constraints:

$$T_{m:A}^{i:A} \qquad \text{for any } i = 1, 2, 3 \text{ and for any } A = fruit\text{-}name, price \qquad (14)$$

Let us now consider view constraints. Constants in each seller preserve the same meaning in the mediator with the exception of *red-apple* and *yellow-apple* in the database of the first seller which correspond just to *apple* in the mediator (that is the mediator is not interested in maintaining the distinction between different kinds of apples). This is formalized by the view constraints

$$i : x = c \rightarrow m : x = c \qquad (15)$$

for any $i = 1, 2, 3$ and any constant c in S_i different from the constants *red-apple* and *yellow-apple* in S_1.

The fact that *red-apple* and *yellow-apple* in S_1 is rewritten as *apple* in S_m is represented by the view constraint:

$$1 : x = red\text{-}apple \rightarrow m : x = apple \qquad (16)$$
$$1 : x = yellow\text{-}apple \rightarrow m : x = apple \qquad (17)$$

The first seller, provides fruit prices without including taxes, since the mediator considers prices with tax, the prices of the first seller must be increased by the tax rate. (say 0.07). This is represented by the view constraint:

$$1 : has\text{-}price(x, y) \rightarrow m : \exists y' has\text{-}price(x, y') \wedge y' = y + (0.07 * y) \qquad (18)$$

The second and third seller, adopts prices with taxes and no transformation is necessary. The view constraint from 2 and 3 to m is therefore the following:

$$2 : has\text{-}price(x, y) \rightarrow m : has\text{-}price(x, y) \qquad (19)$$
$$3 : has\text{-}price(x, y) \rightarrow m : has\text{-}price(x, y) \qquad (20)$$

The information integration schema for example 2 is $S_m = \langle \{S_i\}, \{IC_{ij}\} \rangle$, where IC_{mi} is empty for any $i = 1, 2, 3$ and IC_{im} contains the interschema constraints (15)–(20).

An example of information integration state on the federated database schema IIS_m contains the databases DB_1, DB_2, DB_3, DB_m depicted below and the domain relations r_{im} $(i = 1, 2, 3)$ defined as identity relations except for the pairs ⟨*red-apple, apple*⟩ and ⟨*yellow-apple, apple*⟩ in r_{1m}; all the other domain relation are empties.

DB_m

db₄

has-price	
fruit-name	*price*
apple	0.856$
apple	1.284$
apple	1$
apricot	0.8$
banana	0.7$
banana	3$
mellon	2$
pineapple	0.5$
water-mellon	3.4$

DB_1

db₁

has-price	
fruit-name	*price*
red-apple	0.8$
yellow-apple	1.2$

DB_2

db₂

has-price	
fruit-name	*price*
apple	1$
apricot	0.8$
banana	0.7$
pineapple	0.5$

DB_3

db₃

has-price	
fruit-name	*price*
banana	3$
mellon	2$
water-mellon	3.4$

Let us now address the issues pointed out in Example 2.

Semantic heterogeneity: The first issue concerns the resolution of the heterogeneity on the prices of the different sellers. View constraints (18)–(20) specify how eliminate this heterogeneity.

Different domains: Different databases have different domains. E.g. the second database contains *apricot* which is not contained in the domain of the first database.

Heterogeneity on common domains: The domain of fruits is described at different levels of detail in the different databases. This heterogeneity is removed in importing information into the mediator via view constraints. Notice that view constraints (16) and (17) force the domain relation r_{1m} to map both red apples and yellow apples in apples and to solve the heterogeneity between the domain of DB_1 and that of the mediator.

Directionality of the communication: The fact that all the interschema constraints are from $i \in \{1, 2, 3\}$ to m implies that no information runs in the opposite direction. This corresponds to the following property: for any formula ϕ in the language of m, and for any formula ψ of the language of a seller (say i)

$$\text{if} \quad \not\models_{IIS_m} i : \psi \quad \text{then} \quad m : \phi \not\models_{IIS_m} i : \psi$$

This must be read: if a fact ψ is not in the database of seller i, then it cannot be imported as the result of submitting any query ϕ to the mediator.

Modularity: Suppose that a new seller (say 4) joins the market. Let S_4 be the schema of its database. The new information integration schema is obtained by adding the local schema S_4 and a set of interschema constraints IC_{4m} which formalizes how the mediator imports information from 4. Notice that neither the mediator schema nor the information sources schemata and the interschema constraints between them are modified. Modularity is therefore guaranteed. Notice that autonomy is also preserved. Indeed due to directionality of communication is easy to prove that the information sources 1, 2, and 3 are not modified by the addition of new sellers.

8 Related Work

The main advantages of LMS w.r.t the approaches proposed in the past derives from the fact that LMS is not based on a unique model of the world but on a combination partial models each of which represents the point of view of an agent i on the world. Most of the other approaches are instead based on a complete description of the world, and the semantics of the databases are built by filtering the information of such a description. However a description of the real world is hardly to be available, especially in the case of a set of autonomous agents which are supposed to operate in an open environment. In most of the cases, indeed, the database of each agent has its own semantics which corresponds to a partial description of the real world.

A significant attempt to develop a logic based formal semantics for heterogeneous information integration is the idea of *cooperative information system* (CIS) described in [4]. A CIS is quite similar to an information integration state. It is composed of a set of database schemata and a set of so called interschema assertions. Database schemata represent the individual information sources and are theories in description logics [3]. Interschema assertions formalize relations between different database schemata. CISs formalize a certain degree of autonomy, each database having its own language, domain, and schema. Furthermore CISs formalize a certain degree of redundancy by means of interschema assertions, which capture four different kinds of semantic interdependencies between concepts and relations in different databases. A first difference between CIS and LMS concerns the domains. A model for a CIS is defined over a global domain which is the union of the domains of the databases. This implies that a constant c in different databases is interpreted in the same object c in the CIS. As a consequence in CIS one cannot represent various forms of redundancy between objects belonging to different database domains, e.g. the fact that a database domain is an abstraction of another database domain. A second difference concerns partiality. CIS models complete databases and cannot express partiality. Totality affects directionality. Indeed in CIS every interschema constraints from S_1 to S_2 entails the converse interschema assertion in the opposite direction. This prevents CIS to completely represent directionality in the communication between databases.

Subrahmanian [14] uses annotated logic [2] to integrate a set of deductive databases in an unique amalgamated database called amalgam. The amalgam, in addition to the disjoint union of the databases, contains a supervisory database. The supervisory database is a set of clauses (called amalgamated clauses) which resolve conflicts due to inconsistent facts and compose uncertain information of different database sources. [14] investigates the relation between the models of the amalgam and the models of its components. Subrahmanian takes a more general approach then ourselves as he considers formulas with complex sets of truth values and time intervals. However the intuition behind amalgamated clauses (contained in the supervisory database) is very close to that of a generalization of view constraints described in [6]. From our perspective adopting a global amalgamated database is the reason of the main drawback of Subrahmanian's approach. Indeed global amalgamated database prevents one to associate distinct deductive mechanism to each database in the system. Furthermore amalgamated database doesn't support local inconsistency. I.e. the inconsistency of a local database forces the inconsistency of the whole amalgamated database. Differently, our approach allows an integration information state in which the i-th database is inconsistent while the other are consistent.

Vermeer et al. [16] exploit the semantic information provided by the integrity constraints of the single databases to achieve interoperability among them. The spirit of this approach is similar to ours, although they mainly address a different problem. In [16] different databases are integrated in an unique integrated view. The consistency of such an integrated view is checked by using integrity constraints of component databases. Vermeer et al. argue that semantic relations are expressed by relationships between objects (cf. domain relations) and relations between classes are the result of object relationships (cf. definition of satisfiability of domain/view constraints w.r.t. a domain relation).

9 Conclusions

In this paper we have provided a formal semantics, called Local Models Semantics (LMS), for the integration of information of different agents. We have provided two examples from the electronic commerce scenario which involve many of the challenging aspects of information integration. We have defined LMS introducing the key concepts of domain constraint and view constraint which formalize how the information of different agents is integrated. Then we have argued that LMS is an adequate formalism for information integration in electronic commerce by formalizing the examples presented in the paper. Finally we have compared LMS with the main formalisms in the area of information integration. In [7] we have defined a sound and complete calculus based on ML systems [10] which allows to reason about LMS.

References

1. S. Abitebul, R. Hull, and V. Vianu. *Foundation of Databases*. Addison-Wesley, 1995.
2. H.A. Blair and V.S. Subrahmanian. Paraconsistent Logic Programming. *Theoretical Computer Science*, 68:35–51, 1987.
3. A. Borgida. Description Logics in Data Management. *IEEE Transactions on Knowledge and Data Engineering*, October 1995.
4. T. Catarci and M. Lenzerini. Representing and using interschema knowledge in cooperative information systems. *International Journal of Intelligent and Cooperative Information Systems*, 2(4):375–398, 1993.
5. A. Cimatti and L. Serafini. Multi-Agent Reasoning with Belief Contexts II: Elaboration Tolerance. In *Proc. 1st Int. Conference on Multi-Agent Systems (ICMAS-95)*, pages 57–64, 1996. Also IRST-Technical Report 9412-09, IRST, Trento, Italy. *Commonsense-96*, Third Symposium on Logical Formalizations of Commonsense Reasoning, Stanford University, 1996.
6. C. Ghidini and L. Serafini. Foundation of Federated Databases, I: A Model Theoretic Perspective. Technical Report 9709-02, IRST, Trento, Italy, 1997.
7. C. Ghidini and L. Serafini. Distributed First Order Logics. In *Proceedings of the Second International Workshop on Frontiers of Combining Systems (FroCoS'98)*, Amsterdam, Holland, October, 2–4 1998. To appear.
8. F. Giunchiglia. Contextual reasoning. *Epistemologia, special issue on I Linguaggi e le Macchine*, XVI:345–364, 1993. Short version in Proceedings IJCAI'93 Workshop on Using Knowledge in its Context, Chambery, France, 1993, pp. 39–49. Also IRST-Technical Report 9211-20, IRST, Trento, Italy.
9. F. Giunchiglia and C. Ghidini. Local Models Semantics, or Contextual Reasoning = Locality + Compatibility. In *Proceedings of the Sixth International Conference on Principles of Knowledge Representation and Reasoning (KR'98)*, pages 282–289. Morgan Kaufmann, 1998. Also IRST-Technical Report 9701-07, IRST, Trento, Italy.
10. F. Giunchiglia and L. Serafini. Multilanguage hierarchical logics (or: how we can do without modal logics). *Artificial Intelligence*, 65:29–70, 1994. Also IRST-Technical Report 9110-07, IRST, Trento, Italy.
11. R.V. Guha. Microtheories and contexts in cyc. Technical Report ACT-CYC-129-90, MCC, Austin, Texas, 1990.
12. A.Y. Levy, A. Rajaraman, and J.J. Ordille. Querying Heterogeneous Information Sources Using Source Descriptions. In *Proceedings of the 22nd VLDB Conference*, Bombay, India, 1996.
13. J. Mylopoulos and R. Motschnig-Pitrik. Partitioning Information Bases with Contexts. In *Third International Conference on Cooperative Information Systems*, Vienna, 1995.
14. V.S. Subrahmanian. Amalgamating Knowledge Bases. *ACM Trans. Database Syst.*, 19(2):291–331, 1994.

15. V.S. Subrahmanian, S. Adah, A. Brink, R. Emery, J.J. Lu, A. Rajput, T.J. Rogers, R. Ross, and C. Ward. HERMES: A Heterogeneous Reasoning and Mediator System, 1997. Submitted for Publication. HTML version available at http://www.cs.umd.edu/projects/hermes/overview/paper/index.html.

16. M.W.W. Vermeer and P.M.G. Apers. The Role of Integrity Constraints in Database Interoperation. In *Proceedings of the 22nd VLDB Conference*, Mumbai(Bombay), India, 1996.

17. G. Wiederhold. Mediators in the architecture of future information systems. *IEEE Computer*, 25(3):38–49, 1992.

Author Index

Springer
and the
environment

At Springer we firmly believe that an international science publisher has a special obligation to the environment, and our corporate policies consistently reflect this conviction.
We also expect our business partners – paper mills, printers, packaging manufacturers, etc. – to commit themselves to using materials and production processes that do not harm the environment. The paper in this book is made from low- or no-chlorine pulp and is acid free, in conformance with international standards for paper permanency.

Lecture Notes in Artificial Intelligence (LNAI)

Lecture Notes in Computer Science